AN INTRODUCTION
ACCOUNTS

An Introduction to Book-Keeping and Accounts

Second Edition

KEN CLARKE
Principal, Havering Technical College

FRED CROOK
Lecturer in Business Studies, Brooklands Technical College

HOLT, RINEHART AND WINSTON
LONDON • NEW YORK • SYDNEY • TORONTO

Holt, Rinehart and Winston Ltd: 1 St Anne's Road,
Eastbourne, East Sussex BN21 3UN

British Library Cataloguing in Publication Data

Clarke, Ken
    An introduction to book-keeping and accounts.
    — 2nd ed. — (Holt business texts)
    1. Book-keeping
    I. Title   II. Crook, Frederick
    657'.2   HF5635

ISBN 0–03–910597–0

Typeset in Great Britain by Multiplex medway ltd, Maidstone.
Printed in Great Britain by Biddles of Guildford Ltd.

Last digit is print no: 9 8 7 6 5 4 3 2 1

Contents

Preface to first edition

The aim of this book is to help students who are taking the Book-keeping and Accounts Option Module on the Business Education Council General Award courses. It is hoped that the text will also be useful to students who are following other first level Book-keeping and Accounts courses.

KEN CLARKE AND FRED CROOK
LONDON 1981

Preface to second edition

This book has been thoroughly revised and additional material introduced. The aim of the book is to help you through your accounts and book-keeping course. The text covers all the main topics and areas of work required for CPVE, BTEC, RSA, LCCI and other first level courses.

Students should use this work to assist them in their understanding and practice of topics covered throughout their course. It is essential, however, that you thoroughly practise the skills to which you have been introduced; make sure that you attempt all of the assignments at the end of each chapter before progressing to the next. In this way you will gain most from your course of study and be better prepared for your accounts and book-keeping examinations.

The tax tables are reproduced with the permission of the Controller of Her Majesty's Stationery Office.

KEN CLARKE AND FRED CROOK
LONDON

Note to Lecturers

A booklet of assignments which can be used in conjunction with this text is available free on request from the publishers.

1. Introduction: the purpose of book-keeping

1.1 The Purpose of Book-Keeping

Most people realize how sensible it is to have some record of their personal finances. Not only is it useful to know the position now, but it is very helpful to have some idea of your financial position in the future, i.e. will you be able to afford a present for a friend in four or five months' time, or can you afford to pay for a holiday next year? Without some record of the money transactions an individual makes, it becomes very difficult to answer even these questions with any degree of certainty. Obviously, the records that are required for a trader or businessman will be more complicated than those of an individual. Moreover, many other people or bodies will be interested in a trader's financial records, e.g. those bodies which may lend money, such as banks or finance houses; or the Government with regard to taxes owed. There is, therefore, a need to keep an accurate record of all the various transactions that take place. The process of recording these transactions is known as book-keeping. There are a number of rules and skills to be learned in book-keeping to ensure that records are kept accurately and can be easily understood and used in the business. On the other hand, accounting involves more than just the recording of transactions. Accounting calls for a greater understanding of the various transactions and an ability to analyse and interpret the information that has been collected. Thus, it can be seen that book-keeping and accounts are 'tools' of management. Their purpose is to measure, in money terms, the way in which the business has been run. This constant measuring process enables the management to guide the organization towards its objectives. To some extent the examination of the way in which book-keeping and accounting enable managers to guide the organization is the study of book-keeping and accounts itself. However, we can gain an insight into the process first by identifying what the objectives of an organization may be and then explaining what information we would expect our book-keeping system to give us to enable us to move towards this objective.

1.2 Measurement of Profit

If asked what is the purpose of a business some people would reply 'to make money' and others 'to make a profit'. It is important at this stage to realize that these two answers are different. Profit and money are quite different things and it is possible to make profit and at the same time find that our balance of cash has been reduced. For example, suppose that you buy a car for £50 cash and you sell this car for £75 to a friend who promises to pay you at the end of the month. In this situation the car has been sold for a profit of £25 and yet you have £50 less cash! The reverse situation may occur where you buy goods on credit and sell for cash; here the increase in cash will be greater than the profit.

Generally, the purpose of business is not merely to make a profit but to maximize profits. We should note nevertheless that some businesses or organizations may have different objectives. For example, a firm in the short run may wish to maximize their share of the market and in such a case may sacrifice some profit. Some organizations such as clubs, charities, public utilities may aim at making neither a profit nor a loss or may even content themselves with minimizing their losses. However, in all of the above cases our accounting system will need to be capable of showing what profit or loss is made so that the organization can tell how successful it has been in achieving its objectives and take action accordingly. We may, however, for the sake of simplicity at this stage call profit that which 'is left from sales after all the costs involved in making the sale have been accounted for'.

1.3   Measurement of Cash Balance

We have established in Section 1.2 above the difference between cash and profit and we can see the concern with profit level as an objective, but we will be in error if we conclude that providing that our level of profit is as planned, we will be satisfied with the performance of the organization. We should not disregard the importance of cash to the organization as a shortage may cause some difficulty in continuing trading activity. For instance, if we are unable to renew our stocks our level of sales may fall.

1.4   Measurement of Debts

If we sell goods to our customers on credit, i.e. they take the goods and pay later, our system must be capable of keeping a record of what customers owe us and what they pay. If our system does not record this information, we would not be able to remind our customers that they should pay us, and if they forget to pay this would reduce our profit. We may wish to place some upper limit on the amount which our customer owes us. Similarly, if we buy goods on credit, we need to be able to tell how much we owe our suppliers so that we pay them within a reasonable length of time and that we pay them the correct amount.

1.5   Analysis of Profit

If our system tells us our profit level, it may be necessary to analyse how the profit has reached this level. Such an analysis may enable us to correct any error in our planning. As we have already stated profit is what remains after we have sold the goods and accounted for the cost of the goods and expenses in selling these goods.

Example. If we buy goods which cost us £150 and sell these same goods for £200 we have a profit of £50. This is our *gross profit*. If, however, in selling these goods we incur expenses such as advertising £5, postage and packing materials £2, our profit of £50 is reduced by total expenses of £7 to £43. This is our *net profit*. Such an analysis of profit may be set out as follows:

Sales	£200
Less Cost of Sales	150
Gross Profit	50

Less Advertising £5	
Postage and Packing £2	
	7
Net Profit	43

This analysis of profit is shown diagrammatically in Fig. 1.1.

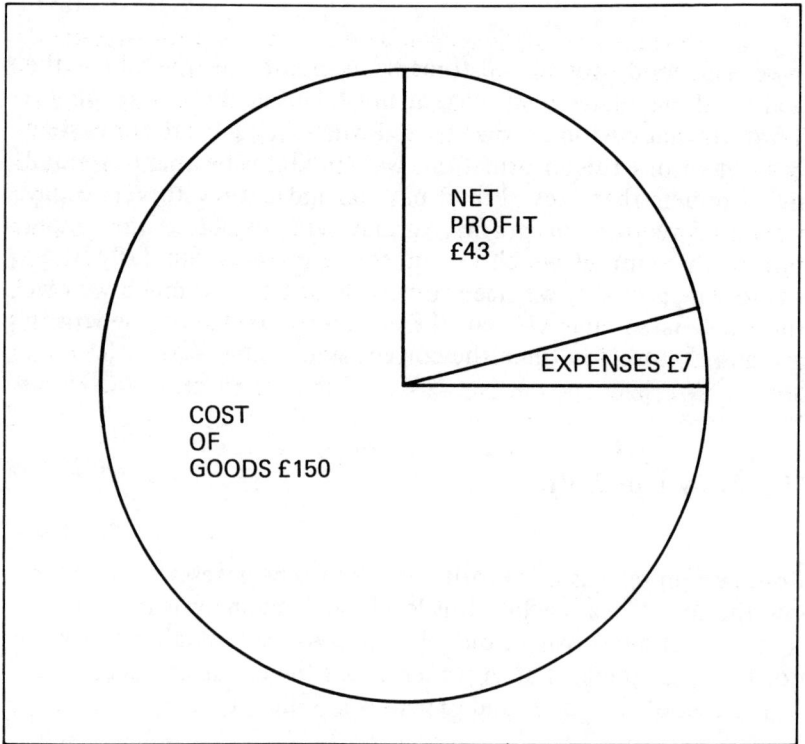

Figure 1.1 *Distribution of sales revenue of £200*

If we are not satisfied with this level of profit, we may examine our analysis to see if we can in future:

1. Increase our sales revenue.
2. Reduce our cost of sales.
3. Reduce expenditure on:

   (a)   Advertising.
   (b)   Postage and packing.

In order to draw up such an analysis, our records must be capable of recording sales, cost of sales, and each class of item of expense.

1.6   Measurement of the Worth of the Business

We have seen how an organization may at any one time own goods, cash, and be owed payment from its credit customers — all of which are representative of the normal flow of its trading activity. These items which the organization owns are called *current assets*, current because of their fluid nature. In addition, many organizations own goods of a more permanent nature such as motor vehicles, premises, machinery, etc., which it uses to process the flow of current assets. These permanent assets are called *fixed assets*. The net worth of the firm is the total of these items which the firm owns (value of all current assets plus value of fixed assets) less the total value of outstanding debts of the firm to its credit suppliers, called *current liabilities*. Our system must, therefore, be capable of recording the value of each class of fixed asset if we are to measure the net worth of the business.

1.7   Measurement of Capital

As we have discovered in Section 1.2 above, there is a distinction between money and profit and there exists the same distinction between money and capital. Many people regard their capital as being the total amount of money which they own, but let us consider again the example of the car in Section 1.2. This assumes that we begin with £50 cash which we may record as our capital.

We then exchange this £50 for an asset – the car – which is also worth £50 – our wealth, our total value of assets remains the same; we are merely holding our asset in a different form. When we sell the car for £75 on credit we find that we have exchanged our asset – the car (stock) – for another asset – the debt (debtors) worth £75. Our capital has increased by the amount of profit on the car. Our rate of return on our starting capital of £50 is 50%. In the above example had we sold the car at a loss, the capital would be reduced. Not only do changes in capital give us a measure of how profitable our business is, but we can calculate in percentage terms how good our rate of return on our investment is.

We can say then that capital is not merely held in cash but in a variety of forms and a variety of mixes. In fact, the capital of a business can be regarded as the net worth of the business, see Section 1.6 above, i.e.

Fixed assets + Current assets – Current liabilities = Capital

Since capital represents the value of our investment in the business, a measurement of capital from our system can also be regarded as essential.

1.8   Obtaining Information from Book-Keeping

The way in which our book-keeping system gives us the information above is the subject of the chapters which follow. An overall understanding of the book-keeping process is not essential in the early stages of practical book-keeping, since the understanding of the relationship between the various accounting records will evolve as you practise book-keeping techniques. However, you are advised to read Chapter 21 before proceeding to Chapter 2 as this will help you to understand what your ledger entries mean.

1.9   Summary

Some of the important points that our records will reveal are summarized in Fig. 1.2.

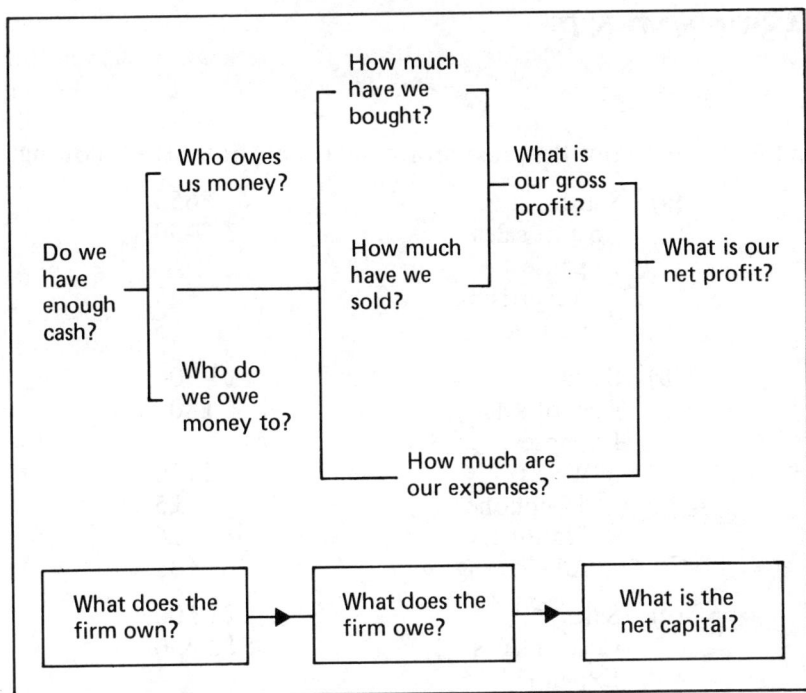

Figure 1.2 *Some of the important questions that our accounting records will answer*

ASSIGNMENTS

A1.1   Find out the gross profit and net profit for the following:

(a)	Sales	£650
	Cost of sales	£490
	Expenses:	
	Advertising	£25
	Postage	£5
(b)	Sales	£1 500
	Cost of sales	£800
	Expenses:	
	Wages	£150
	Telephone	£5
	Stationery	£6
	Advertising	£35
(c)	Sales	£3 500
	Cost of sales	£2 430
	Expenses:	
	Wages	£185
	Delivery expenses	£35
	Postage	£50
	Stationery	£35
	Advertising	£30

A1.2   A firm has the following assets:

Stock	£3 000
Premises	£10 000
Motor Vans	£5 000
Cash	£1 500
Machinery	£1 000
Furniture	£500

(a)   Which of these assets are:
   (i)   Current assets?
   (ii) Fixed assets?
(b)   If the firm owes £1750 to its suppliers what is the net worth of the business?
(c)   What is the firm's capital?

2. Ledger entries

2.1 Making Ledger Entries

The system of book-keeping most widely used is called the *double-entry system*. As its name suggests this means that each transaction is entered into the ledger twice. The aim of this double entering is to record each transaction from both points of view; an aim which is considered in more detail in Chapter 3.

We will for the main part concern ourselves with making double entries for each transaction but for the purpose of this chapter, so that we can get used to making entries in the ledger, we will limit ourselves to making single entries in the cash account.

The traditional ledger paper that we use is shown below. You will notice that the page is divided down the centre with spaces for date, particulars, folio numbers (Fol. No.) and cash (£.p.) on each side. The left-hand side of the page is called the *debit side* and the right-hand side is the *credit side*. Note that the left-hand side of the page is the debit side and the right-hand side the credit side throughout the ledger no matter what the account.

DEBIT SIDE					CREDIT SIDE				
Date	Particulars	Fol. No.	£	p	Date	Particulars	Fol. No.	£	p

2.2 Entries in the Cash Account

The cash account in the ledger is used to record cash (notes and coins) received by the firm and cash (notes and coins) paid by the firm. Of course, in practice many of these transactions will be carried out through the firm's bank account and will involve cheques rather than notes and coins. However, the operation of the bank account and the procedure for dealing with cheques are the subject of a later chapter. Each time a transaction occurs which involves the inflow or outflow of cash we will record three details:

1. The date that the transaction occurred.
2. A *brief* description of the transaction. One-word descriptions are usually sufficient, e.g. sales, purchases, telephone, wages.
3. The amount of cash involved. Note: the folio number column (Fol. No.) relates to the cross-referencing of double entries. Since we are not concerned at this time with double entries there is no need to concern ourselves with the folio numbers.)

For the purpose of the cash account any cash which the business receives will be recorded in the debit side (left-hand side) of the cash account, and any cash which the business pays will be recorded in the credit side (right-hand side).

Example. Suppose that during January 19–1 the following cash transactions took place:

Jan 1   Cash sales £80.00
Jan 2   Cash sales £70.00
Jan 3   Bought goods for resale £50.00
Jan 7   Paid wages £30.00
Jan 10   Cash sales £95.00
Jan 18   Cash sales £35.00
Jan 19   Bought goods for resale £30.00
Jan 30   Bought stationery £40.00

These transactions would appear in the cash account as shown below:

CASH RECEIVED   CASH PAID OUT

Jan 1	Sales		80	—	Jan 3	Purchases		50	—
Jan 2	Sales		70	—	Jan 7	Wages		30	—
Jan 10	Sales		95	—	Jan 19	Purchases		30	—
Jan 18	Sales		35	—	Jan 30	Stationery		40	—

Notes to entries

Debits.

⎧ Jan 1 ⎫   Goods are sold for cash and therefore £80 will be
⎨ Jan 2 ⎬   received into the business. The description used when
⎪ Jan 10 ⎪   goods are sold in the normal course of business is
⎩ Jan 18 ⎭   'sales'.

Credits.

Jan 3   Goods are bought by the business and therefore cash is
         paid out. *Where goods are being bought for resale the
         description is 'purchases'.* It can be important therefore
         to find out the nature of the business so that we know
         when to describe a transaction as 'purchases'; if a car
         dealer buys a car this is 'purchases', if a florist buys

flowers this is 'purchases'. Any item which is *not bought for resale is not purchases* and therefore must be described in some other way.

Jan 7 The firm pays out to the workers their wages.

Jan 30 The firm buys stationery which we assume is going to be used by the firm itself and we therefore describe the transaction not as purchases but as stationery.

General. You will notice that each transaction is entered in the appropriate side on the next line, in other words, there is no need to miss lines when entering transactions. Figures are written neatly in columns, units above units, tens above tens.

The description is short, one word if possible. There is no need to write in the credit side 'paid wages'; the fact that the entry is in the credit side of the cash account shows that cash has been paid out.

2.3 Balancing the Cash Account

In order to find out how much cash the firm now holds in the example above, we carry out an operation known as *balancing* or *ruling off* the account — in this case we balance the cash account. The method which follows should be applied when we balance any account in the ledger.

Calculations

Step 1. Add up the debit side (cash received total £280.00).

Step 2. Add up the credit side (cash paid out total £150.00).

Step 3. Since the debit side (cash received £280) is greater than the credit side (cash paid £150) by £130 (£280-£150), we know that the amount of cash that we should have on hand, the balance, is £130.

Ledger entries

Step 4. Enter the balance in the *light side*, i.e. the side with the smallest total.

Step 5. Rule off the account with a space for the total *on the same line on both sides.*

Step 6. Re-add and enter the total in both sides, double underlining the totals. Include the balance in the total. Both totals should now be the same.

Step 7. Carry down the balance to the opposite side ready to continue making entries for additional transactions.

Since the debit side is greater than the credit side in this case we describe the balance as a debit balance of £130.00.

CASH RECEIVED					CASH PAID OUT				
Jan 1	Sales		80	–	Jan 3	Purchases		50	–
Jan 2	Sales		70	–	Jan 7	Wages		30	–
Jan 10	Sales		95	–	Jan 19	Purchases		30	–
Jan 18	Sales		35	–	Jan 30	Stationery		40	–
					Jan 30	Balance	c/d	130	–
			280	–				280	–
Feb 1	Balance	b/d	130	–					

Brought down

Double ruling on the same line

Re-added totals equal – therefore balance correct

Carried down

Where the account is balanced at the end of the day, date the balance carried forward on the next day

The cash account has a 'debit balance' of £130, i.e. cash in hand at the start of business on 1 Feb

ASSIGNMENTS

A2.1   Copy the cash account shown below into your ledger and balance and rule off. Carry down the balance for the next period.

June 1	Balance	b/d	12	80	June 4	Purchases		5	60
June 3	Sales		48	25	June 10	Purchases		4	00
June 12	Sales		63	28	June 11	Wages		10	00
June 25	Sales		104	36	June 12	Electricity		4	00
					June 13	Telephone		8	00
					June 25	Travelling		2	00
					June 30	Purchases		5	40

Continue the cash account that you have drawn up for a further period by entering the following transactions and then balancing the account again.

July 1   Sold goods for cash £23.30
July 5   Bought goods for resale paid cash £9.20
July 14   Paid for travelling expenses £3.52
July 17   Sold goods for cash £35.90
July 18   Paid wages £10.00
July 20   Bought stationery £7.28
July 25   Bought goods for resale paid cash £4.50
July 31   Sold goods for cash £39.20

A2.2   Open a cash account in your ledger and enter the following transactions which relate to the business of A. Swindle, a second-hand car dealer. You should balance and rule off the account at the end of each month (28 Feb and 31 March).

Feb 1   Sold motor car for cash £350.00
Feb 4   Bought car paid cash £130.00
Feb 7   Bought stationery £3.20

Feb 10   Bought car paid cash £120.00
Feb 12   Sold car for cash £390.00
Feb 15   Paid insurance premium £8.00
Feb 18   Bought car for cash £90.00
Feb 25   Sold car for cash £350.00
Feb 28   Paid wages to salesman £50.00

March 4   Sold car for cash £150.00
March 7   Bought car for cash £85.00
March 10   Paid electricity bill £8.20
March 16   Sold car for cash £230.00
March 25   Bought stationery £5.20
March 28   Paid cleaner £3.50
March 31   Sold car for cash £400.00

A2.3   While refilling his fountain pen B. Shifty made a blot
on his cash account which obscured the entry for
Aug 15. The account appears below: you are required
to calculate the amount of the entry.

CASH ACCOUNT

Aug 1	Balance		143	98	Aug 5	Purchases			33	80
Aug 4	Sales		83	92	Aug 6	Purchases			14	28
Aug 16	Sales		102	31	Aug 7	Stationery			3	90
Aug 25	Sales		123	98	Aug 6	Electricity			8	00
					Aug 15	Purchases				
					Aug 20	Wages			10	00
					Aug 29	Purchases			16	20
					Aug 30	Balance	c/d		354	75
			454	19					454	19
Sept 1	Balance	b/d	354	75						

3. Double entries

Chapter 1 ended with a summary of the important questions which we hope that our records will answer and in Chapter 2 we have gone some of the way to answering one of these – 'Do we have enough cash?'. In this chapter we will go some of the way towards answering three more of these questions – 'How much have we sold? How much have we bought? What are our expenses?'

3.1 Duality Concept

In a business each time that a transaction occurs it will have two effects. This dual effect is known as the *duality concept* and we will examine the dual effects of each of the five sample trans-actions shown below:

Jan 1   Bought goods for resale for cash £10.00
Jan 2   Sold goods for cash £30.00
Jan 3   Bought stationery for use in the firm £5.00
Jan 4   Sold goods for cash £15.00
Jan 5   Paid wages to employee £12.00

Both effects of each of the transactions above are illustrated in Fig. 3.1. Study these effects carefully before proceeding.

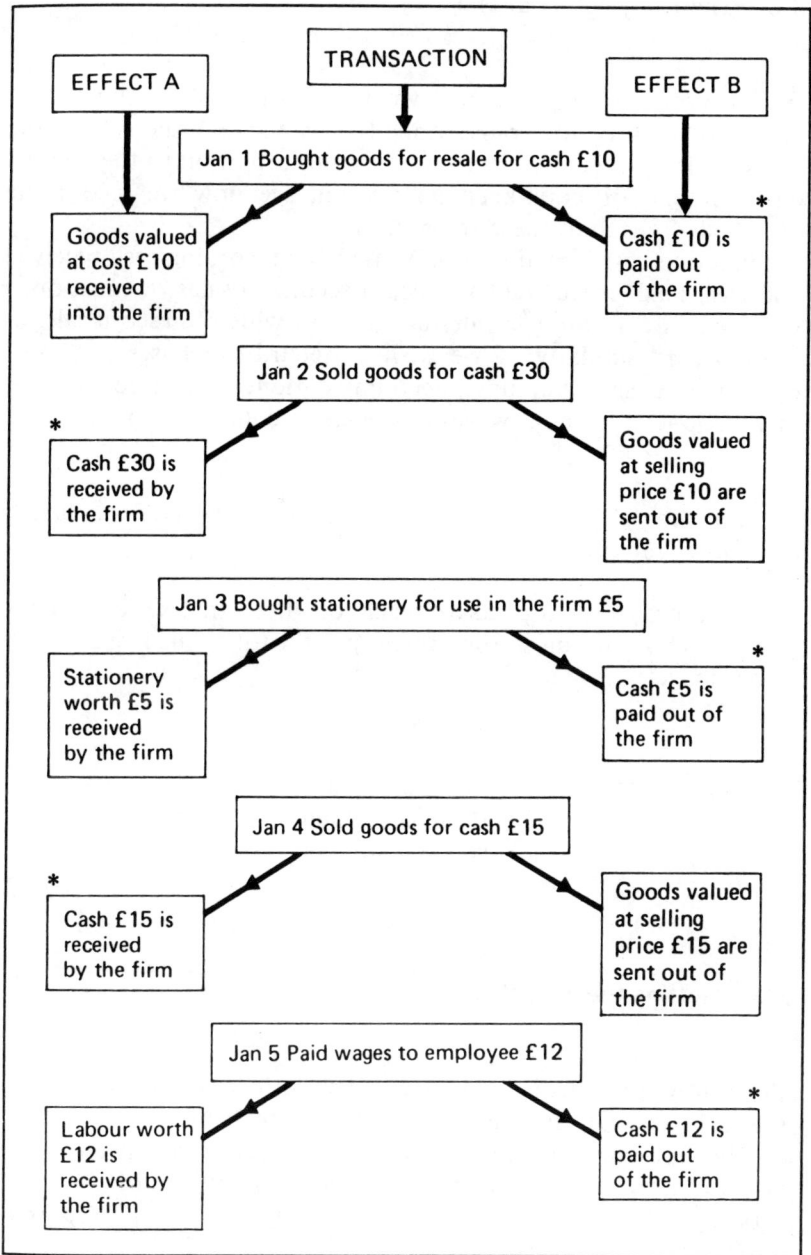

Figure 3.1 *Diagrammatic representation of the effects of each transaction*

3.2   The Ledger Accounts

We have seen in Chapter 2 how we deal in our books with the cash effects of each of the transactions (i.e. in Fig. 3.1 the side of the transaction marked *). If we now turn our attention to the double-entry system of book-keeping, we will see how we record the other side of each of these transactions.

Since the cash account is only used for recording cash received and cash paid, if we want to keep a record of sales we must open up a separate account, a sales account, in which to record sales as they occur. Similarly, if we wish to record purchases, we must open up a separate purchases account, stationery must be recorded in a stationery account, wages in a wages account and so on.

In fact each different class of transaction must have a separate account in the ledger.

To record both aspects of each of these transactions in the example above we must, therefore, open the following five accounts in our ledger:

> Cash account
> Sales account
> Purchases account
> Stationery account
> Wages account

3.3   Getting the Side Right

Refer now to the diagram of the dual effects of transactions in Fig. 3.1. You will notice that all of the effects of the transactions on the left-hand side of the page (Effect A) represent an *inflow* into the firm of goods, cash and labour. The effects of the transactions on the right-hand side of the page (Effect B) represent *outflows*.

All effects which refer to an *inflow* are recorded on the *debit side* (left) of the ledger in the appropriate account. All effects which refer to an *outflow* are recorded on the *credit side* (right) of the ledger in the appropriate account.

DEBIT IN   CREDIT OUT

The book-keeping entries to record the five transactions can be summarized as shown in Fig. 3.2 overleaf.

The book-keeping entries themselves will appear in the ledger as follows:

Date	Particulars	Fol No.	£	p	Date	Particulars	Fol No.	£	p
			CASH ACCOUNT						
Jan 2	Sales		30	—	Jan 1	Purchases		10	—
Jan 4	Sales		15	—	Jan 3	Stationery		5	—
					Jan 5	Wages		12	—
			PURCHASES ACCOUNT						
Jan 1	Cash		10	—					
			SALES ACCOUNT						
					Jan 2	Cash		30	—
					Jan 4	Cash		15	—
			STATIONERY ACCOUNT						
Jan 3	Cash		5	—					
			WAGES ACCOUNT						
Jan 5	Cash		12	—					

3.4   Notes to the Ledger Entries

1. Each transaction is now double entered in the ledger with a debit in one account and a credit in the other.
2. The date of every entry is the date that the transaction occurred.
3. The short one-word description now describes the name of the account where the other one of the two entries appears:

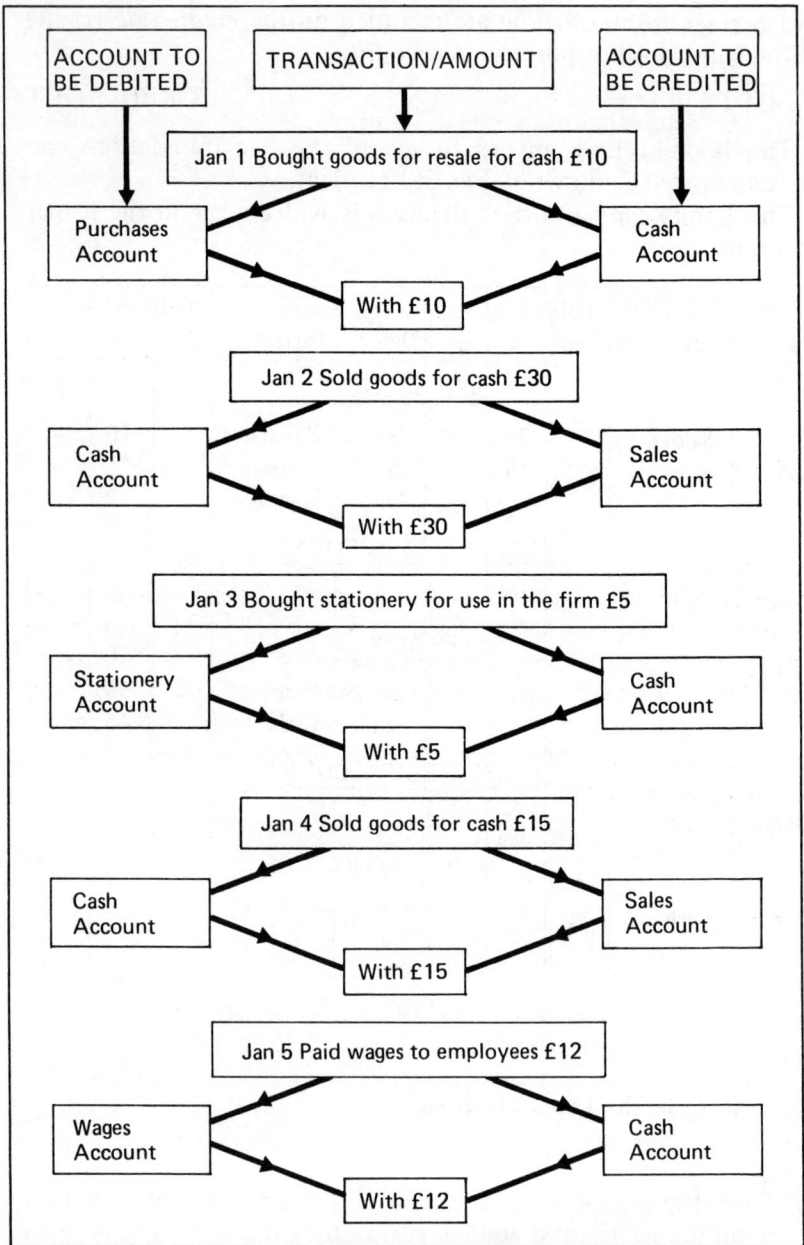

Figure 3.2   *Summary of the book-keeping entries to record the five transactions. Note: one debit and one credit each time*

for example, if we look at the entry for the cash sale which occurred on Jan 2 in the cash account, the particulars read 'Sales' and in the sales account the particulars read 'Cash'. This means that our short description now also gives us a cross-reference for the double entry.

4. Both transactions for sales, Jan 2 and Jan 4, are entered in the same accounts — there is therefore no need for a separate sales account. You are advised to return to the list of transactions on page 16, and looking at each one in turn, find both entries in the ledger and make sure that you understand why every entry has occurred where it has.

3.5 Folio Numbers

In practice each account in the ledger will appear on a separate page but for the purposes of book-keeping theory where we are using only a few sample entries to explain and learn the principles, this would mean wasting large quantities of paper. It is far better to rule off pages of ledger to divide them into separate accounts. Remember to leave sufficient room to make all the entries necessary in each account. Number each account as you open it so that in the above example the account numbers would be:

Cash account	(1)
Purchases account	(2)
Sales account	(3)
Stationery account	(4)
Wages account	(5)

In practice these account numbers would be page numbers. Now when you enter into your ledger account in the particulars column the name of the account where the other entry appears write the page number of the double entry in the folio numbers column as well. The previous example with folio numbers therefore will appear:

Date	Particulars	Fol No.	£	p	Date	Particulars	Fol No.	£	p
					CASH ACCOUNT (1)				
Jan 2	Sales	3	30	–	Jan 1	Purchases	2	10	–
Jan 4	Sales	3	15	–	Jan 3	Stationery	4	5	–
					Jan 5	Wages	5	12	–
				PURCHASES ACCOUNT (2)					
Jan 1	Cash	1	10	–					
				SALES ACCOUNT (3)					
					Jan 2	Cash	1	30	–
					Jan 4	Cash	1	15	–
				STATIONERY ACCOUNT (4)					
Jan 3	Cash	1	5	–					
				WAGES ACCOUNT (5)					
Jan 5	Cash	1	12	–					

3.6 Working from the Cash Account

For the sake of simplicity all of the early examples and assignments involve cash transactions only and therefore in every case
one of the ledger entries will be in the cash account. This means
that providing that you get the side right in the cash account
(debit side – money in, credit side – money out) you only have to
make the double entry in the opposite side in the other account,
i.e. if you have cash sales £10 then cash is received, the cash
account must be debited therefore the sales account must be
credited. If you have bought stationery, £15, then cash is paid
out, the cash account must be credited therefore the stationery
account must be debited. This method of working out on which
side entries should be placed will be very useful later on even when
the transaction does not involve cash.

Because all the transactions that you will be dealing with for a while involve cash it would be possible for you to make all the cash account entries at one time, and then subsequently complete the double entries. You are strongly advised *not* to do this. Complete both entries at the same time. This does mean that you will have to judge how much room to leave for each account in your ledger, but it also means that you will avoid omitting entries and that you will get practice in the correct procedure.

ASSIGNMENTS

A3.1 Draw up in your notebook the table shown below and for each transaction listed below write in the name of the account to be debited and the name of the account to be credited.

(a) Cash sales £50.00
(b) Stationery purchased for use in the business £30.00 cash
(c) Goods £25.00 bought for resale
(d) Wages paid to an employee £15.00
(e) The payment of a telephone bill £25.00
(f) The payment of a gas bill £35.00
(g) Goods sold for cash £45.00
(h) A refund received from the electric company, £5, which was an overpayment for an electricity bill
(i) A refund to a cash customer for goods which he returned as faulty

Q	ACCOUNT TO BE DEBITED	ACCOUNT TO BE CREDITED
(a)		
(b)		
(c)		
(d)		
(e)		
(f)		
(g)		
(h)		
(i)		

A3.2   (a)   Open up ledger accounts as you require and make
                    double entries for the transactions listed below:

        June 1 Sold goods for cash £33.90
        June 4 Bought goods paid cash £12.90
        June 5 Paid wages £15.00
        June 6 Sold goods for cash £33.28
        June 7 Sold goods for cash £28.90
        June 8 Paid wages £15.00
        June 9 Bought goods paid cash £4.90
        June 10 Sold goods paid cash £23.40

      (b)   Balance cash account.

A.3.3   (a)   Open up the ledger accounts which you require
                    and make double entries for the transactions
                    listed below:

        Feb 1   Sold goods for cash £75.28
        Feb 2   Bought goods for resale: paid cash £22.98
        Feb 4   Sold goods for cash £35.98
        Feb 5   Bought stationery £23.98 cash
        Feb 9   Paid wages £33.90 cash
        Feb 9   Sold goods for cash £83.20
        Feb 10   Paid electricity bill £12.90 cash
        Feb 11   Paid rent £14.20 cash
        Feb 12   Bought goods for resale £10.30 cash
        Feb 13   Sold goods for cash £130.90
        Feb 14   Sold goods for cash £120.90

      (b)   Balance your cash account and bring down the
                    balance to Feb 15.

A3.4   Open up the ledger accounts which you require and
             make double entries for the transactions listed below:

        Aug 1   Sold goods for cash £55.00
        Aug 2   Bought goods for resale: paid cash £35.00
        Aug 3   Sold goods for cash £75.00
        Aug 4   Bought stationery cash £7.00

Aug 5	Paid wages cash £20.00
Aug 6	Sold goods for cash £70.00
Aug 8	Paid electricity bill cash £10.00
Aug 9	Bought goods for resale: paid cash £35.00
Aug 10	Paid haulage charges cash £5.00
Aug 11	Paid wages cash £20.00
Aug 12	Sold goods for cash £80.00
Aug 13	Bought stationery cash £8.00
Aug 16	Sold goods for cash £50.00
Aug 17	Bought postage stamps cash £5.00
Aug 18	Paid rates cash £30.00
Aug 19	Paid wages £20.00
Aug 21	Sold goods for cash £80.00

4. Capital and drawings

4.1 Entity Concept

We have seen that one of the purposes of keeping financial records of a business is to measure how successful the business is in terms of profit or loss. We must therefore be very careful to ensure that the financial records of the business are kept separate from the personal financial transactions that the owner of the business may make. We must for the purposes of book-keeping keep the owner and his business quite separate. This separation of the owner's business transactions from his personal transactions is carried out by assuming that the business is a separate entity – as if it was a different person from the owner. This division for the sole trader is an artificial one and, legally, if the business fails the owner would be liable to meet the debts of the firm from his personal wealth (in the case of limited companies this separation is a real one at law). However, the idea of a separate business entity gives us a solution to the problem of separating out the business transactions from the personal transactions of the owner, enabling us to record how successful or otherwise the business has been.

4.2 The Owner's Capital

Suppose that on 1 Jan B. Good starts business with £100 capital in cash. From B. Good's point of view the fact that he has decided to risk £100 in a business venture does not alter the fact that he still thinks of it as his own £100. He is quite correct in thinking this and to record this transaction in his business ledger he must make the entry which appears below.

CASH		CAPITAL	
Jan 1 Capital 100			Jan 1 Cash 100

It can be seen from the above entries that £100 cash has been received into the business in the form of *capital*. To record the credit entry we open a *capital account*. This capital account is B. Good's personal account with his firm. The credit entry of £100 represents the £100 that he has lent to his firm. If the business is successful, B. Good will eventually be able to take back out of the firm £100 plus profits if he wishes. To illustrate this point we will now examine how the ledger would appear if on 2 January B. Good were to change his mind about starting up in business and withdrew his capital. £100 would move back out of the business (credit cash £100) and the business's debt to B. Good would be reduced by £100 repaid (debit capital £100) – result no cash, no capital.

CASH		CAPITAL	
Jan 1 Capital 100	Jan 2 Capital 100	Jan 2 Cash 100	Jan 1 Cash 100

Whenever the owner of the business uses some of the business's cash for personal transactions the ledger entry must record this transaction as a withdrawal of some of the capital from the firm.

4.3   The Drawings Account

It is not usual for a businessman to vary his capital from day to day and entries in the capital account should be a fairly rare occurrence. At the same time it is recognized that the owner of the business may frequently require to withdraw cash from the business for his personal use in anticipation of his business making a profit. Rather than make many entries in the capital account to record these withdrawals a separate ledger account is set up in the ledger called a *drawings account*. Each time that the owner withdraws cash from the business (makes drawings) the cash account will be credited and the drawings account will be debited with the amount withdrawn. At the end of the financial period the balance of the drawings account is transferred to the capital account to reveal what is left as capital account balance. Later we will see how profits are also transferred to the capital account. This is summarized in Fig. 4.1.

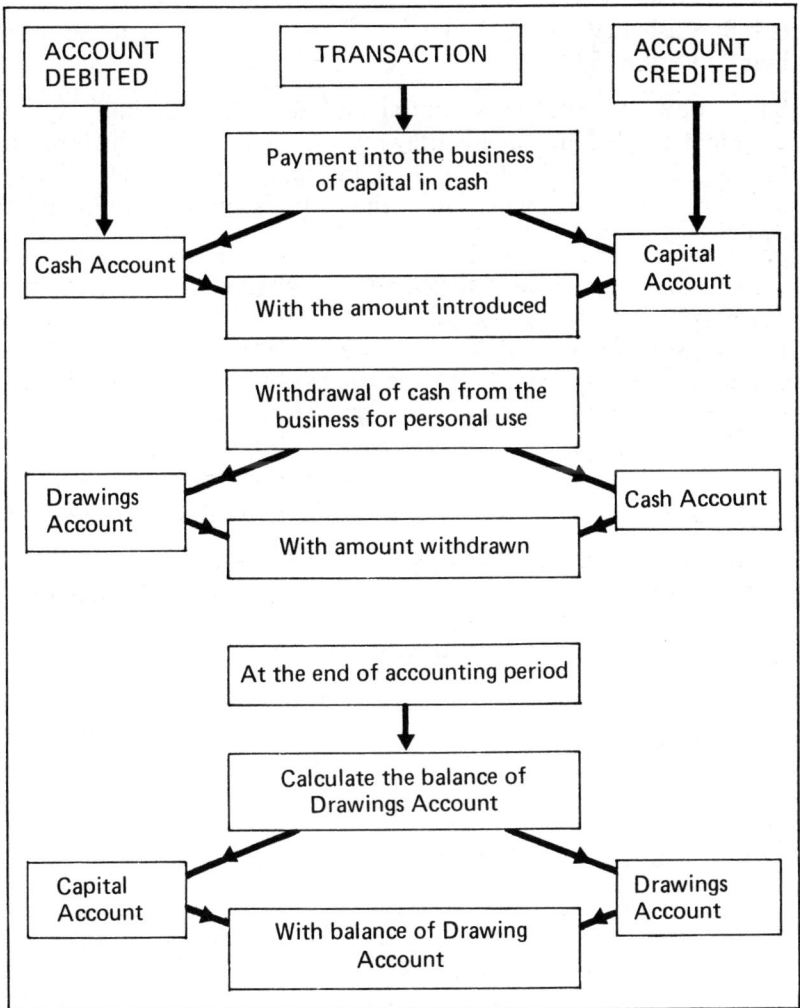

Figure 4.1 *Summary of entries to the drawings account*

Example. On 1 January A. Spender started business with capital in cash £1000. During the following two months in addition to his normal business transactions he withdrew from cash for his personal use the following amounts:

Jan 7 Cash £30.00
Jan 15 Cash £45.00
Jan 18 Cash £14.00
Jan 27 Cash £34.00
Feb 8 Cash £29.00
Feb 27 Cash £15.00

Show how A. Spender's capital and drawings accounts would appear if the balance of his drawings account were transferred to his capital account at the end of February. Show also the cash account extract showing how these transactions would affect cash.

CASH ACCOUNT (EXTRACT)

Jan 1	Capital	1000	–	Jan 7	Drawings	30	–
				Jan 15	Drawings	45	–
				Jan 18	Drawings	14	–
				Jan 27	Drawings	34	–
				Feb 8	Drawings	29	–
				Feb 27	Drawings	15	–

CAPITAL ACCOUNT

| Feb 28 | Drawings | 167 | – | Jan 1 | Cash | 1000 | – |

DRAWINGS ACCOUNT

Jan 7	Cash	30	–	Feb 28	Capital Account	167	–
Jan 15	Cash	45	–				
Jan 18	Cash	14	–				
Jan 27	Cash	34	–				
Feb 8	Cash	29	–				
Feb 27	Cash	15	–				
		167	–			167	–

Notes to ledger entries

1. Notice how the double entry on 28 February (drawings account and capital account) leaves a nil balance in the drawings account. The balance of drawings has been transferred to capital.
2. Notice that the new balance on 28 February of capital is £833, i.e. £1000 − £167, and that it is a credit balance. If the capital account were now balanced it would appear as follows:

CAPITAL ACCOUNT

Feb 28	Drawings	167	—	Jan 1	Cash	1000	—
Feb 28	Balance	833	—				
		1000	—			1000	—
				March 1	Balance	833	—

4.4 Capital and Drawings not in Cash

The word 'capital' is capable of being interpreted in a variety of ways. To the lay person it may mean the amount of cash owned and to the economist it may mean tools and machines. However, when an accountant refers to capital he is referring to the amount that the business owes to the proprietor or owner.

We have considered the situation where the owner 'lends' cash to the business. However, many businesses start with little or no cash and the owner of the business may lend to the business other items of value such as stock of goods or premises. Consider the following examples.

Example A. A. Richman decides to start business on 1 January. He is fortunate that he owns a shop, a quantity of goods which he can sell, and £50 in cash. He therefore decides that the shop that he owns will become the business premises and the stock will be sold through the business. If the business premises are worth £10 000 and the stock £1000 what is his capital?

Solution. Instead of paying into the business just cash as his capital, he is paying into the business:

Premises	£10 000
Stock	£1 000
Cash	£50
TOTAL	£11 050

His capital is therefore £11 050. The ledger entries recording these transactions may appear as follows:

CASH

| Jan 1 | Capital | 50 | — |

PREMISES

| Jan 1 | Capital | 10 000 | — |

STOCK

| Jan 1 | Capital | 1 000 | — |

CAPITAL

				Jan 1	Cash	50	—
				Jan 1	Premises	10 000	—
Jan 1	Balance	11 050	—	Jan 1	Stock	1 000	—
		11 050	—			11 050	—
				Jan 1	Balance	11 050	—

Example B. I. Makamint starts business with capital in cash £11 050 on 1 January. On the same day he buys, out of the cash he has lent to the business, premises £10 000 and a quantity of stock £1000. What is his capital?

Solution. I. Makamint's and A. Richman's positions as far as capital is concerned are identical and although at the start of the day A. Richman's capital is represented by cash, premises and stock, whereas I. Makamint's capital is all represented in cash, by the end of the day both businesses are identical as can be shown by the ledger entries in I. Makamint's ledger shown below:

CASH (1)

Jan 1	Capital		11 050	–	Jan 1	Premises	③ 10 000	–
					Jan 1	Purchases	④ 1 000	–
					Jan 1	Balance	50	–
			11 050	–			11 050	–
Jan 1	Balance		50	–				

CAPITAL (2)

					Jan 1	Cash	1	11 050	–

PREMISES (3)

Jan 1	Cash	1	10 000	–

PURCHASES (4)

Jan 1	Cash	1	1 000	–

Notes to ledger entries

1. A comparison of both ledgers reveals the same balances on all accounts.
2. Notice that they both hold goods valued at £1000 but Richman refers to this item as stock and Makamint as purchases. For our present purposes it is sufficient to understand that both these items represent the quantity of goods available for sale. A full explanation of the term 'stock' is given in a later chapter.

The ledger entries are summarized in Fig. 4.2 overleaf.

4.5 Drawings other than in Cash

In the same way that the proprietor may introduce capital into the firm in some form other than cash, he may also withdraw capital from the firm in some form other than cash. For example, the owner may take from the firm goods for his personal use. The principle of debiting a drawings account should be followed whether the drawings be in cash, goods, or some other form and the credit entry must appear in the account of the item being withdrawn. See Fig. 4.3.

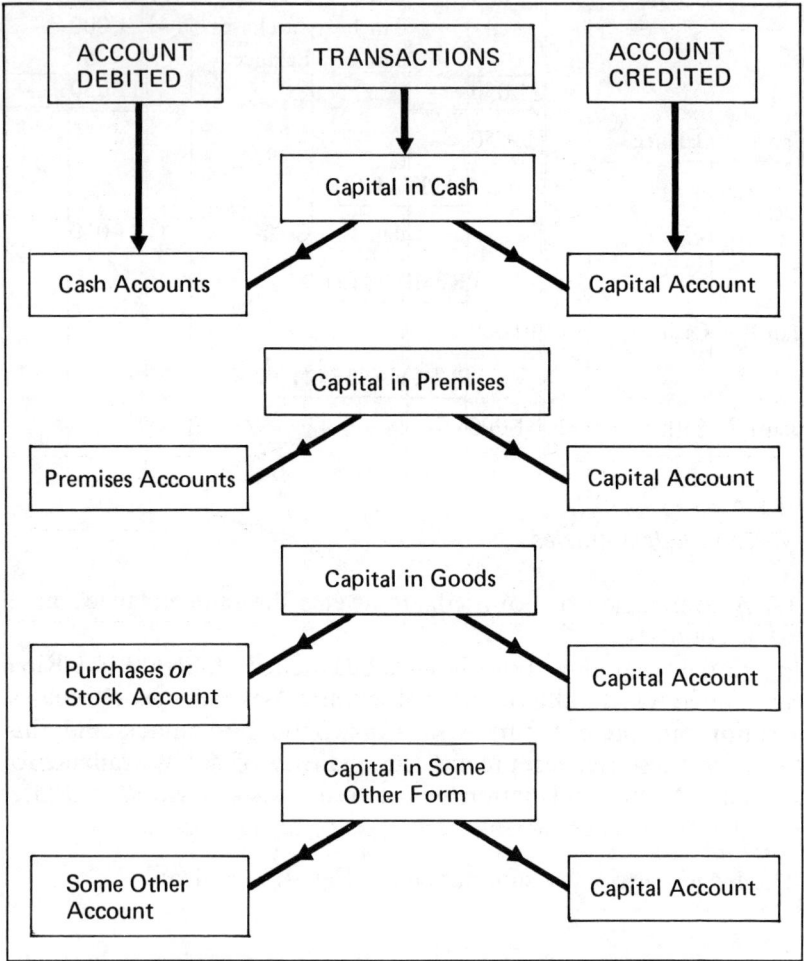

Figure 4.2 *Summary of ledger entries*

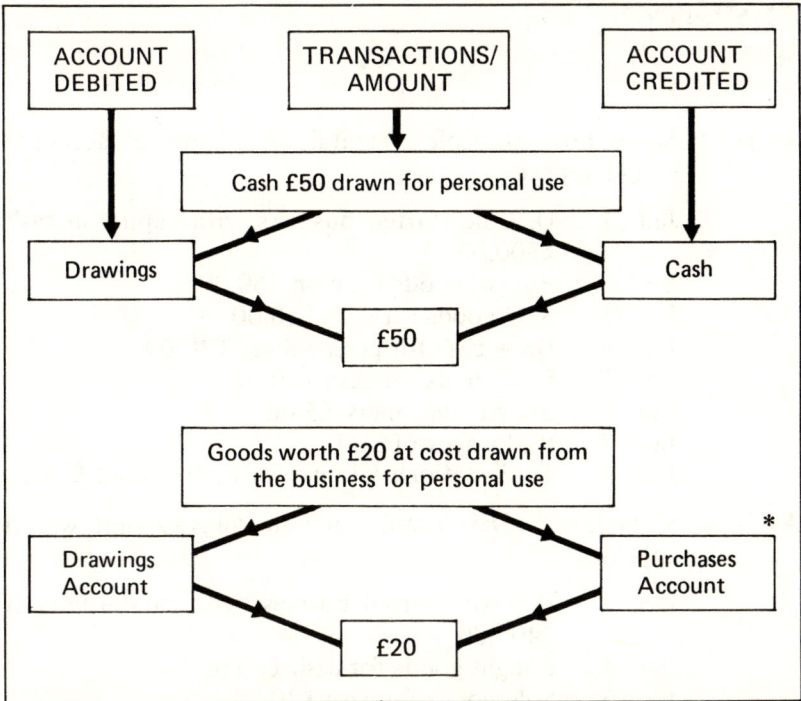

Figure 4.3 *Debiting a drawings account for drawings other than cash.* To be quite accurate a separate account 'goods drawn account' should be opened to record the credit entry for this item, and the balance should be transferred to the purchases account at the end of the financial period. However, unless drawn goods are significant this step can be ignored*

ASSIGNMENTS

A4.1   Show how D. Cole's capital and drawings accounts would appear:

Jan 1		D. Cole started business with capital in cash £300.00
Jan 2		Bought goods for cash £60.00
Jan 3		Sold goods for cash £40.00
Jan 4		Drew cash for personal use £30.00
Jan 5		Sold goods for cash £70.00
Jan 6		Bought stationery £5.00
Jan 7		Paid wages £10.00
Jan 8		Took stationery home for personal use £3.00

A4.2   Show how D. Dave's capital and drawings accounts would appear:

Jan 1		D. Dave started business with capital in cash £400.00
Jan 4		Bought goods for cash £80.00
Jan 5		Sold goods for cash £30.00
Jan 7		Paid wages £15.00
Jan 8		Sold goods for cash £90.00
Jan 9		Bought stationery £6.00
Jan 10		Drew cash for personal use £25.00
Jan 11		Bought goods paid cash £20.00
Jan 12		Sold goods for cash £90.00
Jan 13		Had a win on the horses £350.00 which he paid in as additional capital.
Jan 14		Sold goods for cash £120.00
Jan 15		Bought cash register paid cash £30.00
Jan 16		Paid wages £15.00
Jan 17		Bought goods paid cash £10.00
Jan 18		Transferred ownership of his private motor car to the business. The car is valued at £500.00

5. The trial balance

5.1 The Purpose of the Trial Balance

A *trial balance* is merely a list of accounts in a ledger with the amounts of their various balances. It is produced to check the accuracy of the book-keeping. It can be produced at any time but the accuracy of the ledger should always be checked before the preparation of the trading and profit and loss accounts described in the next section. Any errors which are left in the ledger when the trading and profit and loss accounts are produced will result in inaccurate and misleading financial statements and in addition the errors themselves will be compounded.

The trial balance is not part of the ledger and does not, therefore, require double entries. *It is a summary of the ledger.*

5.2 Producing a Trial Balance

The double-entry system of book-keeping that we have been using involves making similar entries in both the debit side and the credit side of the ledger. This means that, providing that all the double entries are carried out correctly, the total of all the entries on the debit side of the ledger should be the same as the total of all the credit entries in the ledger. This is one way in which we may make a check on the accuracy of the ledger. The trial balance involves a similar process to totalling both sides of the ledger except that each account is taken in turn and the balance of each account is calculated and listed on journal paper, a sample of which is shown below:

Date	Particulars	Fol No.	£	p	£	p

The name of the account is listed in the Particulars column; if the account has a debit balance the amount of the balance is listed in the left-hand cash column, if the account has a credit balance the amount of the balance is listed in the right-hand cash column. For the trial balance there is no need to enter the date and unless the trial balance is a lengthy one, there is little purpose in entering the folio numbers.

Finally, the left-hand cash column and the right-hand cash column are totalled separately. Both these totals should be the same. If they are not then there may be an error in our ledger entries.

Examine the ledger entries which appear opposite.

Looking at each account in turn you will notice that:

Cash account has a debit balance of	£202
Capital account has a credit balance of	£100
Purchases account has a debit balance of	£40
Sales account has a credit balance of	£165
Postage account has a debit balance of	£3
Rent account has a debit balance of	£20

Date	Particulars	Fol No.	£	p	Date	Particulars	Fol No.	£	p
			CASH ACCOUNT (1)						
Jan 1	Capital	2	100	–	Jan 2	Purchases	3	20	–
Jan 3	Sales	4	35	–	Jan 5	Postage	5	1	–
Jan 4	Sales	4	40	–	Jan 6	Purchases	3	20	–
Jan 8	Sales	4	35	–	Jan 7	Rent	6	10	–
Jan 9	Sales	4	20	–	Jan 10	Postage	5	2	–
Jan 12	Sales	4	35	–	Jan 11	Rent	6	10	–
					Jan 12	Balance		202	–
			265	–				265	–
Jan 13	Balance		202	–					
			CAPITAL ACCOUNT (2)						
					Jan 1	Cash		100	–
			PURCHASES ACCOUNT (3)						
Jan 2	Cash	1	20	–					
Jan 6	Cash	1	20	–					
			SALES ACCOUNT (4)						
					Jan 3	Cash	1	35	–
					Jan 4	Cash	1	40	–
					Jan 8	Cash	1	35	–
					Jan 9	Cash	1	20	–
					Jan 12	Cash	1	35	–
			POSTAGE ACCOUNT (5)						
Jan 5	Cash	1	1	–					
Jan 10	Cash	1	2	–					
			RENT ACCOUNT (6)						
Jan 7	Cash		10	–					
Jan 11	Cash		10	–					

These accounts and their amounts are listed as follows:

		Dr		Cr	
Cash		202	–		
Capital				100	–
Purchases		40	–		
Sales				165	–
Postage		3	–		
Rent		20	–		
		265	–	265	–

Debit balances and credit
balances are equal.

The total of the debits and the total of the credits are equal. This gives us evidence that our book-keeping entries are correct but it does not prove beyond doubt that the ledger is error free. Some errors which will be discussed later will not be revealed by a trial balance.

5.3 Errors Disclosed by the Trial Balance

If the trial balance fails to agree, that is to say that the two totals are different, it means that there has been an error either in the compilation of the trial balance or in the ledger entries. Every effort should be made to find the source of the error and the following procedure should be adopted:

1. Check the addition of the trial balance itself to ensure that it is not an addition error.
2. Check that the correct amounts have been entered as the balances of the ledger accounts and make sure that the balances have been entered in the correct side of the trial balance.
3. One of the most common sources of errors in the ledger is the omission of one of the double entries. Therefore, calculate

the 'difference' in the trial balance (take one total from the other) and if there is a transaction of this value make sure that both ledger entries have been made.

4. Another common fault is to enter a transaction into the ledger twice on the same side — either two debits or two credits instead of one credit and one debit. In such a case the effect will be a doubling of the error. To eliminate this kind of error as a possible source, halve the difference of the trial balance and check that transactions of this value have been entered correctly.

5. Check the calculations of the balances of the ledger accounts.

6. Check all double entries.

If the trial balance is 'out' by a round number, say £1, £100 or £00.01, the source of the error is more than likely to be a calculation error, therefore check all calculations first.

ASSIGNMENTS

A5.1 Enter the following transactions in the ledger of A. Johnson and extract a trial balance on 7 January 19–1.

Jan 1   A. Johnson started business as a second-hand piano dealer with capital in the form of cash £100.00 and two pianos at cost £20.00 and £25.00 respectively

Jan 2   Bought three second-hand pianos for cash £20.00 each

Jan 3   Paid haulage expenses £10.00

Jan 4   Sold two pianos for cash £45.00 each

Jan 5   Paid for advertising £3.00

Jan 6   Paid assistant's wages £15.00

Jan 6   Sold two pianos for cash £50.00 each

Jan 7   Sold remaining piano for £60.00

Jan 7   Drew cash for personal use £20.00

Jan 7   Paid advertising expenses £2.00

Jan 7   Paid haulage expenses £15.00

A5.2 A. Patel started business as a piano dealer with £200 in cash on 12 September 19–1. He has no knowledge of book-keeping and is at a loss as to how to keep the financial records of his business. He has up to now just kept a day-to-day diary of the transactions that have occurred. His diary appears as follows:

Sept 12   Bought 3 pianos today 1 at £12 2 at £34 each
Bought cash register for £23
Paid for advert in local paper £3

Sept 13   Bought 4 pianos at £16 each today and 10×9p postage stamps
Sold 2 pianos for £83 each
MEET ABDUL FOR LUNCH

Sept 14	WIFE'S BIRTHDAY TODAY Sold 2 pianos for £45 each Bought adding machine £6
Sept 15	Sold 2 pianos at £12 each Bought 1 piano for £3
Sept 16	Paid haulage firm for moving pianos £43
Sept 17	Sold piano for £92

He explains that in addition to these transactions, he has, during the week, bought tea and sugar from the cash in the till but he is not sure how much he has spent. He now asks you to start off his financial records for him and work out how much he has spent on tea etc.
Note.

(a) You should enter his tea and sugar in his accounting record in the same way that you enter any of his other business expenses.

(b) The amount that is in his cash register at the close of the business on 17 September 19–1 was £332.00.

(c) You should extract a trial balance at the end of the assignment to test the accuracy of your entries.

6. The trading and profit and loss account

We have so far developed our ledger so that it will tell us:

1. How much cash we have.
2. How much our sales are.
3. How much our purchases are.
4. How much our expenses are in each category of expense.

One very important question which our ledger has not yet answered is 'How much profit have we made?'. Referring to Chapter 1, we know that there are two descriptions of profit:

1. Gross profit – the difference between the sales and the cost of sales.
2. Net profit – how much is left of gross profit after we have deducted the expenses of running the business.

Since our ledger now contains information which relates to sales – the sales account – and information which relates to the cost of goods sold – the purchases account and the stock account – it only remains to bring these pieces of information together in the ledger to find gross profit. Further, if our ledger shows gross profit and since our ledger also contains a record of all expenses, we can bring together these pieces of information to find net profit.

6.1 The Trading Account

The trading account is the name we give to the ledger account where we bring together all the information which is related to the gross profit (sales less the cost of the sales). Since it is a ledger account, when we enter a transaction we must be careful to obey the rules of double entries (one debit; one credit). At this stage we will assume that the only three items of information which relate to gross profit are sales, purchases and stock. The complete ledger and trial balance which you should have produced for A. Johnson (see **A5.1**) is illustrated below.

A. JOHNSON LEDGER

Date	Particulars	Fol. No.	£	p	Date	Particulars	Fol. No.	£	p
				CA$H (1)					
Jan 1	Capital	2	100	—	Jan 2	Purchases	4	60	—
Jan 4	Sales	6	90	—	Jan 3	Haulage	5	10	—
Jan 6	Sales	6	100	—	Jan 5	Advertising	7	3	—
Jan 7	Sales	6	60	—	Jan 6	Wages	8	15	—
					Jan 7	Drawings	9	20	—
					Jan 7	Advertising	7	2	—
					Jan 7	Haulage	5	15	—
					Jan 7	Balance		225	—
			350	—				350	—
Jan 8	Balance		225	—					
				CAPITAL (2)					
					Jan 1	Cash	1	100	—
					Jan 1	Stock	3	45	—
				STOCK (3)					
Jan 1	Capital	2	45	—					
				PURCHASES (4)					
Jan 2	Cash	1	60	—					

Date	Particulars	Fol. No.	£	p	Date	Particulars	Fol. No.	£	p
				HAUL	AGE (5)				
Jan 3	Cash	1	10	–					
Jan 7	Cash	1	15	–					
				SAL	ES (6)				
					Jan 4	Cash	1	90	–
					Jan 6	Cash	1	100	–
					Jan 7	Cash	1	60	–
				ADVERT	ISING (7)				
Jan 5	Cash	1	3	–					
Jan 7	Cash	1	2	–					
				WAG	ES (8)				
Jan 6	Cash	1	15	–					
				DRAW	INGS (9)				
Jan 7	Cash	1	20	–					

A. JOHNSON
TRIAL BALANCE 7 JANUARY 19–1

		Dr			Cr
Cash		225	–		
Capital				145	–
Stock		45	–		
Purchases		60	–		
Haulage		25	–		
Sales				250	–
Advertising		5	–		
Wages		15	–		
Drawings		20	–		
		395	–	395	–

6.2 Preparing the Trading Account

The four accounts which relate to this procedure are:

1. The trading account itself.
2. The sales account.
3. The purchases account.
4. The stock account.

These accounts for A. Johnson are produced below in isolation:

SALES ACCOUNT			PURCHASES ACCOUNT		
	Cash	90	Cash	60	
	Cash	100			
	Cash	60			

STOCK ACCOUNT		TRADING ACCOUNT	
Capital	45		

We must transfer the balances of the sales account, purchases account and the stock account by double entry.

Step 1

To transfer the balance of the stock account to the trading account:

(a) Calculate the balance of the stock account − it is a debit balance of £45.
(b) Credit the stock account and debit the trading account with £45.
(c) Rule off stock account (since there is only one item, no need for total).

Note. The writing in the particulars column must describe the account where the double entry appears.

The relevant part of the ledger now appears:

SALES ACCOUNT				PURCHASES ACCOUNT		
	Cash	90		Cash	60	
	Cash	100				
	Cash	60				

STOCK ACCOUNT				TRADING ACCOUNT		
Capital	45	Trading		Stock	45	
‗		Account	45			
		‗				

Step 2

(a) In a similar way transfer the balance of the purchases account to the trading account and rule off the purchases account.

(b) Since there is no stock on hand on 7 January (all pianos have been sold) the sum of the purchases and stock represents the cost of goods sold.

(c) Enter the cost of goods sold in trading account.

The ledger now appears:

SALES ACCOUNT				PURCHASES ACCOUNT			
	Cash	90		Cash	60	Trading	
	Cash	100		‗		Account	60
	Cash	60				‗	

STOCK ACCOUNT				TRADING ACCOUNT		
Capital	45	Trading		Stock	45	
‗		Account	45	*Add*		
		‗		Purchases	60	
				Cost of	–––	
				Sales	105	

Step 3

(a) Transfer the balance of the sales account to the trading account. Note that this time the sales account is debited and the trading account credited.

(b) If the cost of goods is £105 and the sales £250 the gross profit is £145. Therefore, the balance of the trading account

is the same as the gross profit.
(c) Write in the gross profit on the trading account and rule off.

The ledger now appears:

SALES ACCOUNT

Trading		Cash	90
Account	250	Cash	100
		Cash	60
	250		250

PURCHASES ACCOUNT

Cash	60	Trading	
		Account	60

STOCK ACCOUNT

Capital	45	Trading	
		Account	45

TRADING ACCOUNT

Stock	45	Sales	250
Add			
Purchases	60		
Cost of			
Sales	105		
Gross			
Profit	145		
	250		250

You will notice that the sales account, the purchases account and the stock account now all have nil balances – the balances having been transferred to the trading account.

You will also notice that we have followed the rules of double entry for each entry in the trading account with the exception of gross profit. The credit entry for gross profit must appear in the profit and loss account which now follows.

6.3 Preparing the Profit and Loss Account

The accounts which relate to this procedure are:

1. The trading account in so far as it contains gross profit.
2. The accounts of the various business expenses. Care must be taken in identifying which accounts are the accounts of business expenses.

An examination of the ledger at this stage reveals the following:

1. Cash account: merely a record of cash received and paid – not the account of an expense

and therefore not relevant to the profit and loss account.

2. Capital account: merely a record of what the owner has lent the business and not an expense account and not related to the profit and loss account.

3. Stock account: contains no balance – transferred to trading account.

4. Purchases account: contains no balance – transferred to the trading account.

5. Haulage account: quite clearly an expense account and therefore related to profit and loss account.

6. Sales account: contains no balance – transferred to trading account.

7. Advertising account: an expense account and related to profit and loss account.

8. Wages account: an expense account and related to profit and loss account.

9. Drawings account: related to the owner's drawings for personal use and therefore not a business expense and not related to profit and loss account.

The accounts related to A. Johnson's profit and loss account are produced in isolation below:

TRADING ACCOUNT

Stock	45	Sales	250
Add			
Purchases	60		
Cost of			
Sales	105		
Gross Profit	145		
	250		250

HAULAGE ACCOUNT

Cash	10	
Cash	15	

ADVERTISING ACCOUNT

Cash	3	
Cash	2	

PROFIT AND LOSS ACCOUNT

WAGES ACCOUNT

Cash	15	

Step 1. Enter the gross profit in the credit side of the profit and loss account – this completes the double entry of gross profit.

Step 2. Transfer the balances of all expense accounts to the debit side of the profit and loss account.

After completion of the above steps, the ledger appears as follows:

TRADING ACCOUNT				HAULAGE ACCOUNT			
Stock	45	Sales	250	Cash	10	Profit	
Add				Cash	15	and Loss	25
Purchases	60				25		25
Cost of							
Sales	105						
Gross Profit	145			**ADVERTISING ACCOUNT**			
	250		250	Cash	3	Profit	
				Cash	2	and Loss	5
PROFIT AND LOSS ACCOUNT					5		5
Haulage		Gross					
Account	25	Profit	145				
Advertising				**WAGES ACCOUNT**			
Account	5						
Wages				Cash	15	Profit	
Account	15					and Loss	15

Since net profit is equal to the difference between gross profit and the expenses of running the business, the balance of the profit and loss account is net profit, (£145 − [£25 + £5 + £15]), i.e. £145 − £45 = £100.

Step 3. The final step in the preparation of the profit and loss account is to calculate the net profit and make double entries for it. The debit entry for net profit must appear in the profit and loss account — the credit entry must appear in the owner's capital account. This is because any profit that the business makes belongs to the owner of the business and therefore increases the business's indebtedness to the owner.

The completed ledger appears at the beginning of the next chapter and you will notice that the drawings have been transferred to the capital account at the same time as the net profit.

The accounting period

In order for our trading and profit and loss accounts to be meaningful, they should contain a statement of the length of the period of time to which they refer. The net profit for the above example is £100. This may be a reasonable profit for one or even two weeks' trading, but if it is for six months or a year then it may be insufficient. A statement of the length of the accounting period will also make possible the comparison of results from one period to another.

In practice, rather than divide up the trading account from the profit and loss account, one heading is used for both. The heading for A. Johnson's trading account and profit and loss account therefore appears;

A. JOHNSON

TRADING AND PROFIT AND LOSS ACCOUNT

FOR THE ONE WEEK ENDING 7 JANUARY 19–1

Dealing with a net loss

If the expenses of the business exceed the gross profit the result is a net loss. In this case credit the profit and loss account with the amount of the loss and debit the capital account — thus reducing the business's indebtedness to the owner.

Example. Suppose Johnson paid £150 for wages instead of £15. The ledger work would appear:

PROFIT AND LOSS

Haulage	25	Gross	
Advertising	5	Profit	145
Wages	150	Net Loss	35
	180		180

CAPITAL

Net Loss	35	Cash	100
		Stock	45

HAULAGE

Cash	10	Profit	
Cash	15	and Loss	25
	25		25

ADVERTISING

Cash	3	Profit	
Cash	2	and Loss	5
	5		5

WAGES

Cash	150	Profit	
		and Loss	150

6.4   Trading and Profit and Loss Account in Vertical Form

An alternative layout for trading and profit and loss accounts frequently used by firms whose accounts may be examined by non-accountants is illustrated below alongside the conventional form used in previous examples. You will notice that instead of a debit side and a credit side the relevant details are listed vertically down the page and entries which would appear as debits are treated as negative quantities and subtracted, and credit entries are treated as positive and added. This alternative method is known as the vertical form:

Conventional Form					*Vertical Form*		

A. JOHNSON TRADING AND PROFIT AND LOSS ACCOUNTS FOR THE WEEK ENDING 7 JANUARY 19–1

A. JOHNSON TRADING AND PROFIT AND LOSS ACCOUNTS FOR THE WEEK ENDING 7 JANUARY 19–1

Conventional Form				Vertical Form		
Stock	45	Sales	250	Sales		250
Add Purchases	60					
				Less		
Cost of Sales	105			Stock at start	45	
Gross Profit	145			Add Purchases	60	
	250		250	Cost of Sales		105
Haulage	25	Gross		Gross Profit		145
Advertising	5	Profit	145			
Wages	15			*Less*		
Net Profit	100			Haulage	25	
	145		145	Advertising	5	
				Wages	15	
						45
				Net Profit		100

6.5   Summary

See Figs. 6.1 and 6.2 for diagrammatic representations of the process of transferring net profit to the capital account and the preparation of the trading and profit and loss account.

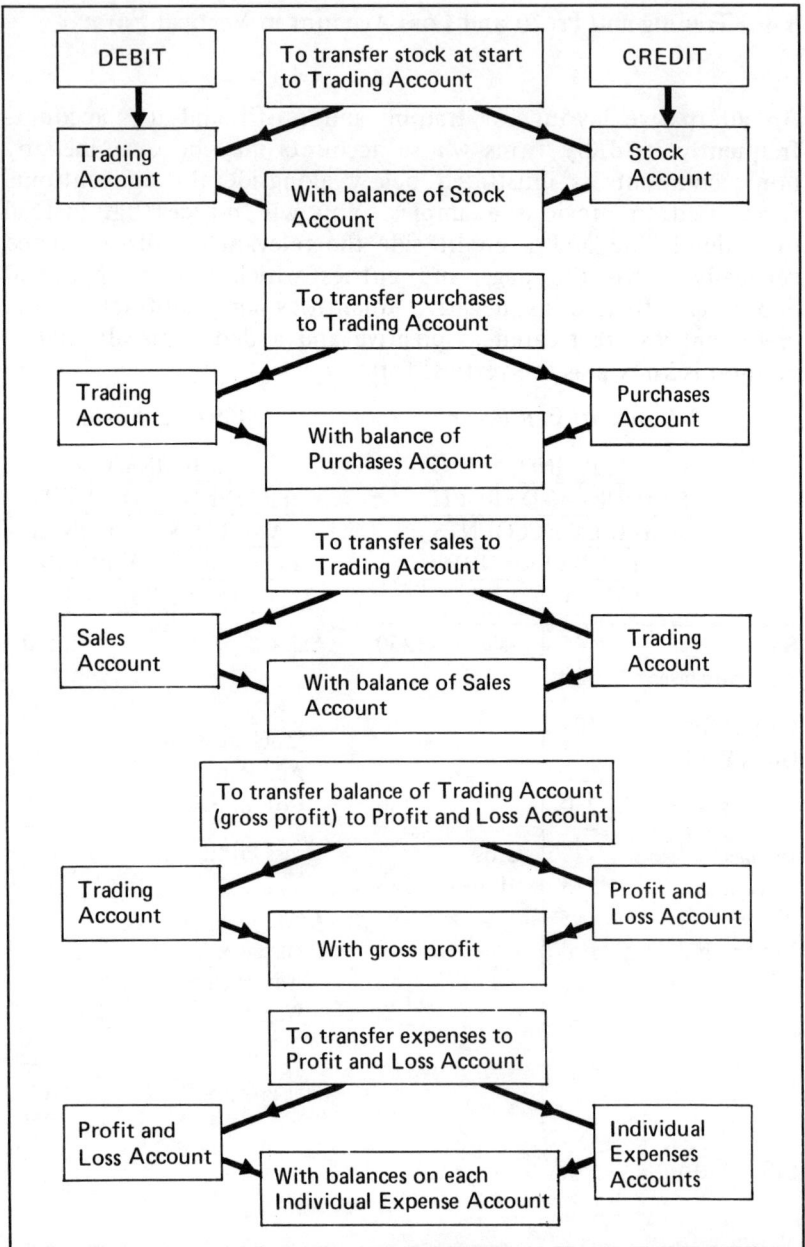

Figure 6.1 *Preparing the trading and profit and loss account*

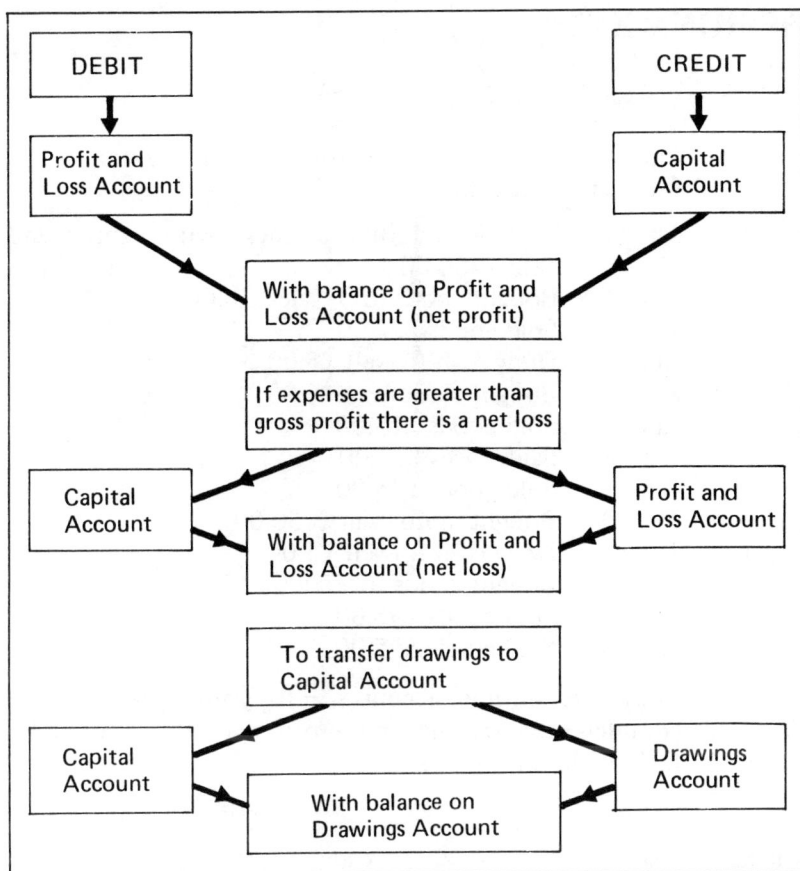

Figure 6.2 *To transfer net profit to capital account. (Finally, balance and rule off capital account bringing the balance down to the start of the next period.)*

ASSIGNMENTS

A6.1   The accounts produced in outline below refer to the following transactions:

Jan 1   B. Good started business with capital and cash £500.00
Jan 2   Bought goods for resale £30.00
Jan 3   Sold goods £25.00
Jan 4   Drew cash for self £5.00
Jan 5   Bought stationery £6.00
Jan 7   Sold goods £15.00
Jan 8   Paid wages £15.00
Jan 9   Sold goods £35.00
Jan 10   Bought motor van £150.00
Jan 11   Drew cash for self £5.00
Jan 12   Bought goods for resale £35.00
Jan 13   Sold goods £45.00
Jan 14   Sold goods £55.00

Copy the outline accounts into your notebook and complete the trading and profit and loss account by making double entries.

CASH

Capital	500	Purchases	30
Sales	25	Drawings	5
Sales	15	Stationery	6
Sales	35	Wages	15
Sales	45	Motor Van	150
Sales	55	Drawings	5
		Purchases	35
		Balance	429
	675		675
Balance	429		

CAPITAL

		Cash	500

PURCHASES

Cash	30		
Cash	35		

SALES

		Cash	25
		Cash	15
		Cash	35
		Cash	45
		Cash	55

DRAWINGS

Cash	5		
Cash	5		

	STATIONERY
Cash	6

	WAGES
Cash	15

	MOTOR VAN
Cash	150

TRADING AND PROFIT
AND LOSS ACCOUNT

A6.2 Enter the following transactions into appropriate ledger accounts. Extract a trial balance and then produce a trading and profit and loss account for the month of July.

July 1 D. Layham started business with capital in the following forms:

Premises £10 000.00
Stock £150.00
Cash £2 000.00

July 2 Bought goods for resale £90.00
July 3 Bought goods for resale £80.00
July 5 Paid for advertising £15.00
July 7 Cash sales £120.00
July 12 Cash sales £90.00
July 15 Paid wages £35.00
July 17 Cash sales £65.00
July 20 Bought stationery £5.00
July 22 Cash sales £150.00
July 28 Paid wages £35.00
July 30 Cash sales £90.00

A6.3 Re-draft the following trading and profit and loss account into vertical form.

D. CARR
TRADING AND PROFIT AND LOSS ACCOUNT
FOR THE YEAR ENDED 31 DECEMBER 19—1

Stock (1 Jan—1)	1 500	Sales	14 350
Add Purchases	7 300		
Cost of Sales	8 800		
Gross Profit	5 550		
	14 350		14 350
Wages	1 500	Gross Profit	5 550
Rent	800		
Electricity	50		
Advertising	120		
Telephone	80		
Stationery	20		
Net Profit	2 980		
	5 550		5 550

7. The balance sheet

7.1 The Balance Sheet in the Accounting Cycle

The order of work which we have adopted for our accounting records has been;

Stage 1. Ledger work – recording by double entry financial transactions.

Stage 2. Trial balance – extraction of information in summary from the ledger and checking the accuracy of the ledger.

Stage 3. Trading account – making double entries in the ledger to transfer information related to gross profit.

Stage 4. Profit and loss account – making double entries in the ledger to transfer information related to net profit.

The final stage in the accounting cycle is:

Stage 5. Production of a balance sheet – extraction of information in summary from the ledger.

7.2 Producing the Balance Sheet

You will notice that Stage 2, the trial balance, and Stage 5, the balance sheet, are very similar. Indeed, the balance sheet is just like a trial balance in a different form but it takes into account the effect of the ledger entries which have taken place at Stage 3 and Stage 4. The balance sheet, then, is merely two lists of accounts which appear in the ledger with the amount of the balance of each account. One list is for accounts with debit balances – *assets*; and the other list is for accounts with credit balances – *liabilities*. If an account has no balance then there is no need to list it in the balance sheet. The balance sheet, like the trial balance, is not part of the ledger. It is merely a description of it. No double entries are required.

The completed ledger for A. Johnson is shown below and an examination of the ledger reveals that there are only two accounts that have balances.

These are: cash account – debit balance of £225
    capital account – credit balance of £225

A. Johnson's balance sheet appears as shown on page 62.

Date	Particulars	Fol. No.	£	p	Date	Particulars	Fol. No.	£	p
				CASH (1)					
Jan 1	Capital	2	100	–	Jan 2	Purchases ·	4	60	–
Jan 4	Sales	6	90	–	Jan 3	Haulage	5	10	–
Jan 6	Sales	6	100	–	Jan 5	Advertising	7	3	–
Jan 7	Sales	6	60	–	Jan 6	Wages	8	15	–
					Jan 7	Drawings	9	20	–
					Jan 7	Advertising	7	2	–
					Jan 7	Haulage	5	15	–
					Jan 7	Balance		225	–
			350	–				350	–
Jan 18	Balance		225	–					
				CAPITAL (2)					
Jan 7	Drawings	9	20	–	Jan 1	Cash	1	100	–
					Jan 1	Stock	3	45	–
Jan 7	Balance		225	–	Jan 7	Net Profit		100	–
			245	–				245	–
					Jan 8	Balance		225	–

Date	Particulars	Fol. No.	£	p	Date	Particulars	Fol. No.	£	p
				STOCK (3)					
Jan 7	Capital	2	45	—	Jan 7	Trading Account		45	—
				PURCHASES (4)					
Jan 2	Cash	1	60	—	Jan 7	Trading Account		60	—
				HAULAGE (5)					
Jan 3	Cash	1	10	—	Jan 7	Profit and Loss Account		25	—
Jan 7	Cash	1	15	—					
			25	—				25	—
				SALES (6)					
Jan 7	Trading Account		250	—	Jan 4	Cash	1	90	—
					Jan 6	Cash	1	100	—
					Jan 7	Cash	1	60	—
			250	—				250	—
				ADVERTISING (7)					
Jan 5	Cash	1	3	—	Jan 7	Profit and Loss Account		5	—
Jan 7	Cash	1	2	—					
			5	—				5	—
				WAGES (8)					
Jan 6	Cash	1	15	—	Jan 7	Profit and Loss Account		15	—
				DRAWINGS (9)					
Jan 7	Cash	1	20	—	Jan 7	Capital	2	20	—

A. JOHNSON
TRADING AND PROFIT AND LOSS ACCOUNT
FOR THE WEEK ENDING 7 JANUARY 19–1

Jan 7	Stock	45	–	Jan 7	Sales		250	–
	Add Pur-chases	60	–					
	Cost of Sales	105	–					
	Gross Profit	145	–					
		250	–				250	–
				Jan 7	Gross Profit		145	–
Jan 7	Haulage	25	–					
	Advertising	5	–					
	Wages	15	–					
	Net Profit to Capital Account	100	–					
		145	–				145	–

A. JOHNSON
BALANCE SHEET AS AT 7 JANUARY 19–1

Assets	£	Liabilities	£
Cash	225	Capital	145
		Less Drawings	20
			125
		Add Net Profit	100
	225		

7.3 Notes to the Balance Sheet

1. The heading is 'Balance Sheet As At' and the date when the balance sheet is produced. The balance sheet can only be a

statement of how the ledger appears at one moment in time, unlike the profit and loss account which explains how we have *accumulated* a profit or loss *over a period of time*. The balance sheet is rather like a photograph of the firm when it has arrived at a given point. The profit and loss account is rather like a movie film of the journey.

2. *Assets* are *what the firm owns* and usually appear on the left-hand side of the balance sheet. The expression 'debit side of the balance sheet' is inappropriate since it is not part of the ledger.

3. *Liabilities* are *what the firm owes* and usually appear on the right-hand side of the balance sheet.

4. Students often have difficulty in understanding why capital is a liability. Remember that it is the balance sheet of the firm and not the owner. *Capital* represents the amount the owner has 'lent' to the firm.

5. You will notice that capital is itemized, i.e. shown as:

	£	
Capital	145 —	this represents the balance of capital at the start of the financial period (stock £45 + cash £100).
Less Drawings	20 —	this represents the capital withdrawn during the period by the owner in anticipation of profit.
	125 —	this represents the capital left after taking into account drawings.
Add Net Profit	100 —	net profit as per profit and loss account.
	225 —	the new balance of the capital account for the start of the next financial period.

It is conventional to break down the capital balance in this way so that comparison of return (net profit) on capital can be easily made. In this case the net profit of £100 represents a return of 69% on the capital at the start.

6. If a net loss has occurred a similar layout for capital should be adopted to 5 above but the net loss should be deducted.

ASSIGNMENTS

A7.1   Produce B. Good's balance sheet using the information given in **A6.1**.

A7.2   On 1 June A. Salter started business with capital in cash £500. During the following month the following transactions took place:

June 2   Bought goods for resale £50.00
June 4   Paid rent £10.00
June 6   Paid wages £15.00
June 8   Cash sales £30.00
June 9   Bought goods for resale £20.00
June 12   Sold goods for cash £40.00
June 14   Sold goods for cash £60.00
June 18   Paid wages £15.00
June 19   Paid rent £10.00
June 20   Bought stationery £5.00
June 22   Paid for advertisement £5.00
June 23   Cash sales £80.00
June 25   Cash sales £70.00
June 26   Paid rent £10.00
June 27   Paid wages £15.00
June 28   Cash sales £85.00
June 30   Cash sales £95.00

(a)   Enter these transactions into appropriate ledger accounts.
(b)   Extract a trial balance.
(c)   Produce the trading and profit and loss account for the month of June.
(d)   Produce a balance sheet as at June 30.

Assume that A. Salter has sold all the goods which he has purchased for resale.

8. Stock

8.1 Stock at Close

At the end of the trading period in the previous example, the trader is left with no stock on hand. In practice it would be a coincidence if the trader were to run out completely of the item in which he was dealing at the end of his financial period. Indeed, most traders will try to organize their purchases in such a way that they never completely run out of stock. If a trader holds a quantity of stock at the end of a financial period it must be taken into account in the calculation of the cost of sales when the trading account is produced. See Fig. 8.1.

Example. During his first accounting period a trader buys three boxes of goods for £5 each. During the same period he sells two of these boxes at £7 each. It can be seen from Fig. 8.1 that the:

Cost of Goods Bought – Stock at Close = Cost of Goods Sold
(at cost)

The trading account for the example above may be set out, there-fore, as shown below:

A. TRADER
TRADING ACCOUNT

3 boxes at £5 each →	Purchases	15	Sales	14 ← 2 boxes at £7 each
1 box at £5 →	Less Stock at Close	−5		
Purchases *less* stock at close →	Cost of Sales	10		
The difference between sales and the cost of sales →	Gross Profit	4		
		14		14
			Gross Profit	4

8.2 Stock at Close and Double Entries

You will notice that in the above trading account there is now an entry on the debit side for stock at close. In order to comply with the rules of double entry, another entry for this transaction must be made in the ledger. The important point to understand and remember however when dealing with stock at close in the ledger, is that although the entry for stock at close appears on the debit side of the trading account, *it is in fact a credit entry* since *it is being deducted from the debit side*. The double entry for this item must appear in a stock account and it must appear in the debit side of the stock account as follows:

STOCK ACCOUNT

Trading Account	5	

Thus, stock is double entered in the ledger and appears twice on the debit side but the trading account entry, although on the debit side, is a credit entry.

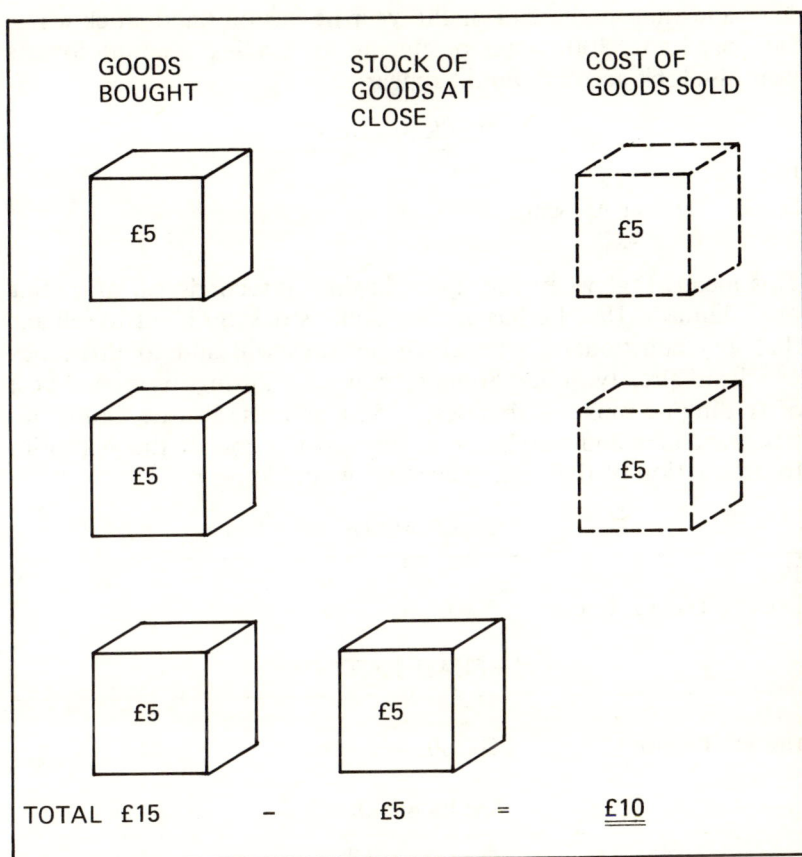

GOODS BOUGHT	STOCK OF GOODS AT CLOSE	COST OF GOODS SOLD
£5		£5
£5		£5
£5	£5	
TOTAL £15	– £5	= £10

Figure 8.1 *Calculating the cost of sales taking into account stock at close of trading period*

8.3 Stock at Close and the Balance Sheet

When a trader has stock at close we have seen that this gives rise to the stock account. The balance on the stock account represents an asset and should appear on the asset side of the balance sheet.

8.4 Stock at Start

Suppose that a trader's accounting year ends on the 31 December

19-1 and that at the end of the year he has on hand stock which has cost him £300. After producing his trading account for the year his stock account would appear:

STOCK ACCOUNT

19-1	
Dec 31 Trading Account 300.00	

This means that when the trader begins his second year of trading on 1 January 19-2 he has already some stock on hand to sell and that any additional goods which he buys will add to this stock which he already holds. Suppose now that during his second year of trading he makes purchases, £1500, and his sales are £2000, his stock account and purchases account at the end of the year prior to production of the trading account would appear:

STOCK ACCOUNT

19-1	
Dec 31 Trading Account 300.00	

PURCHASES ACCOUNT

19-2	
Dec 31 Balance 1500.00	

SALES ACCOUNT

	19-2
	Dec 31 Balance 2000.00

If the trader's stock on hand at the end of his second year amounted to £450, his cost of sales during the year is:

Stock at Start + Purchases − Stock at Close = Cost of Sales
£300.00   + £1500.00 −   £450.00   =   £1350.00

To produce a trading account where there is both stock at start and stock at close the following procedure should be adopted (see Fig. 8.2 for a diagrammatic representation):

Step 1. Transfer the opening stock (balance of stock account) to the trading account − stock at start.
Step 2. Transfer the purchases (balance of purchases account) to the trading account − add purchases.

Step 3. Add together in the trading account stock at start and purchases. The resultant figure should be entered in the trading account. There is no need for a double entry of this figure since it is just a summary of the preceding figures.

Step 4. Enter stock at close into the ledger. Remember that this entry must be made as a deduction from the debit side in the trading account and as a straightforward debit entry in the stock account.

Step 5. Deduct stock at close to find cost of sales in the trading account.

Step 6. Calculate and enter gross profit.

The ledger entries for the above example would therefore appear as follows:

STOCK ACCOUNT

19-1			19-2		
Dec 31	Trading Account	350.00	Dec 31	Trading Account	350.00
19-2					
Dec 31	Trading Account	450.00			

PURCHASES ACCOUNT

19-2			19-2		
Dec 31	Balance	1500.00	Dec 31	Trading Account	1500.00

SALES ACCOUNT

19-2			19-2		
Dec 31	Trading Account	2000.00	Dec 31	Balance	2000.00

TRADING ACCOUNT FOR THE YEAR ENDED 31 DECEMBER 19-2

19-2			19-2	
Dec 31	Stock at Start	350.00	Dec 31 Sales	2000.00
	Add Purchases	1500.00		
		1850.00		
	Less Stock at Close	450.00		
	Cost of Sales	1400.00		
	Gross Profit	600.00		
		2000.00		2000.00

Fig. 8.2 provides a summary of the book-keeping entries for the trading account.

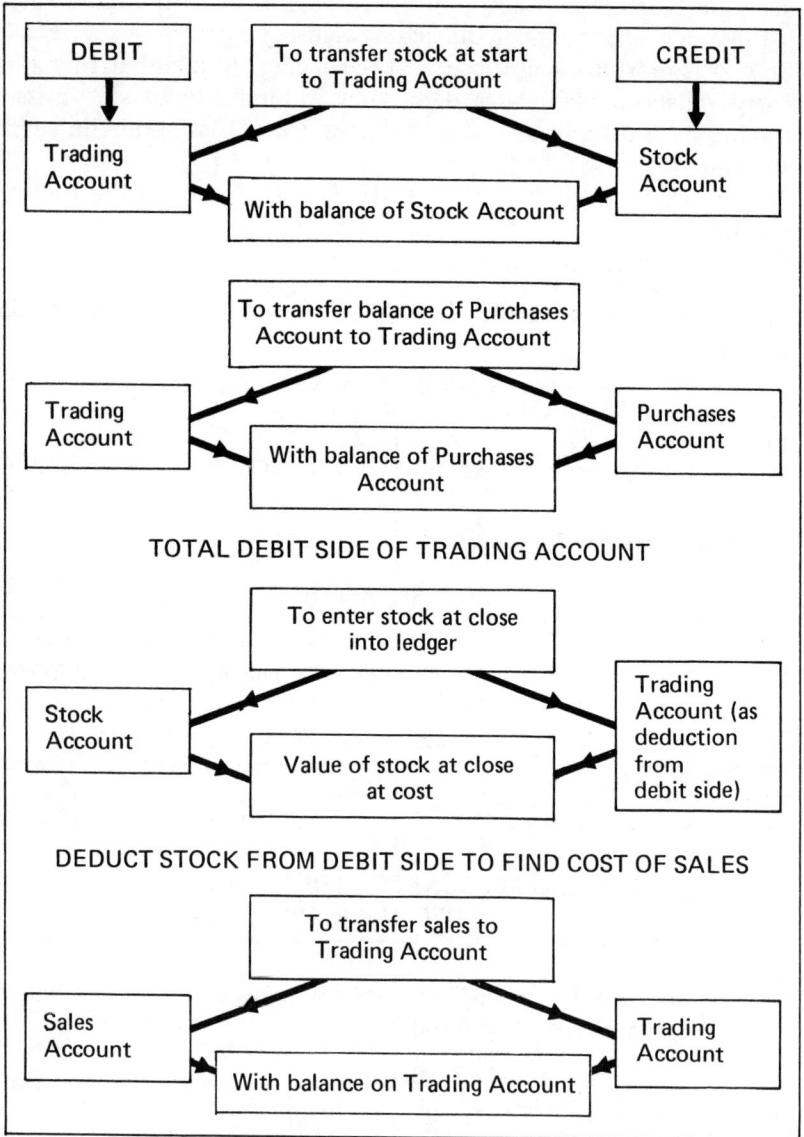

Figure 8.2 *Summary of book-keeping entries for trading account. Note: each period's stock at close will therefore become the following period's stock at start*

8.5   Stock Valuation

In practice the owner of the business will establish the value of stock at close by a physical stocktaking. He will count each item of stock and value it at cost or market value, whichever is the lower. The figure which is established from this stocktaking is the one that will be entered in the ledger.

8.6   Average Stock

To find average stock add together the value of stock at start and stock at close valued at cost and divide by two.

8.7   Rate of Stock Turnover

A trader will wish to satisfy himself that the volume of stock that he holds is appropriate to the nature and size of his business. If too much stock is held, it means that goods are held in the business for a longer period of time than necessary which increases the chance of the stock going out of fashion or going bad. If too little stock is held, it means that the trader runs the risk of running out of stock and thus losing sales. An indication of how quickly stock is sold can be obtained by calculating rate of stock turnover:

$$\text{Rate of Stock Turnover} = \frac{\text{Cost of Sales}}{\text{Average Stock}}$$

Rate of stock turnover will vary greatly from one kind of business to another so that a dairy or newsagent would expect a rate of stock turnover of 365 times a year, since they would have fresh milk and newspapers each day, whereas a business such as a furniture store may have a rate of stock turnover as low as 2 times per year, where items of furniture are held in stock for an average of six months.

8.8   Control of Stock

Where the rate of stock turnover of a business is too high it means that the amount of stock held by the business, on average, is too small compared with the amount of activity in the business. In such a case traders run the risk of losing business by not being able to satisfy their customers' demands quickly. On the other hand, where the rate of stock turnover is low too much stock is being held. Since this stock is at risk from deterioration, change of fashion or theft, and since this will represent a significant pro- portion of the owners' capital being tied up inactively, action will be required to reduce the amount of stock held to a more appro- priate level.

8.9   Minimum Stock Level

The minimum level of stock of any particular item that should be held is that level which ensures that the item is never completely sold out. The two factors which combine to determine this minimum stock level are:

1.   The weekly usage of the item.
2.   The length of time that the supplier takes to deliver an order.

Example. All Parts Ltd sell grommits, and they usually sell two dozen grommits each week. Their supplier, Rubber Mouldings Ltd, usually takes three weeks to deliver any order. Since in three weeks All Parts Ltd will sell six dozen grommits the minimum stock level is six dozen.

It should be noted that both the weekly usage of an item and the length of time taken by a supplier to deliver orders may vary from the norm. These variations may be due to a variety of reasons such as:

1.   *Seasonal variations.* Sale of swimwear will be greater during the summer months than in the winter months. Similarly rainwear sales will fall during the summer. These seasonal variations

may affect both the firms' own sales of these items and the manufacturers' ability to fulfil orders promptly.

2. *Industrial action.* A supplier may have difficulty in fulfilling an order because of strikes amongst the firm's work force or the work force of the suppliers or delivery firm.

3. *External factors.* It may be that a manufacturer uses an imported raw material such as cotton from India. Manufacture will be disrupted if for reasons such as a crop failure or civil disturbance in India the supply is disrupted. Similarly announcement by the Health Council that swimming is good for you may increase customer demand for swimwear.

The above factors should be taken into account when adjusting the minimum stock level.

8.10 Re-Order Level

It is prudent to re-order an item of stock before the minimum level is reached and the re-order level should be fixed above the minimum stock level. If, subsequent to the goods being re-ordered, the minimum level is reached it may be a good time to check with the supplier to ensure that the order is in the process of being completed. The difference between the re-order level and the minimum level acts as a buffer in the event of unforeseen delays by suppliers.

8.11 Maximum Level

Fixing a minimum and re-order level of stock for each item held should ensure that the rate of stock turnover is not too low. Fixing a maximum level should ensure that the rate of stock turnover is not too high. In fixing the maximum level consideration should again be given to factors which may affect both the demand of customers and the reliability of suppliers. In addition, recognition should be given to the possibility of negotiating discounts for a large order as opposed to several smaller orders (bulk discount). The trader should nevertheless not be tempted into overstocking because of attractive-looking bulk discounts. Manufacturers who are aware that their product will soon be superseded by a superior product will wish to dispose of as much of their soon-to-be-obsolete stock as quickly as possible.

8.12   Stock Records

The most usual way of ensuring that the stock held is within the normal limits of minimum and maximum is by completing a stock record card for each item of stock. The stock record card for All Parts Ltd's grommits is shown in Fig. 8.3.

Notes to stock record card

1.   Details are recorded which describe in detail the item of stock including the unit in which it is held in stock, i.e. box of 10, pack of 100, litre, 28 kilo pack, etc.
2.   Details are recorded of the main supplier and, since it is not advisable to be totally reliant on a single supplier, alternative sources of supply are given. Alternative suppliers can also be useful in negotiating the best possible price for orders.
3.   Re-order, minimum and maximum stock levels are recorded as are any notes which may affect the quantity and timing of re-ordering.
4.   To avoid duplication of orders any order which is made is recorded in the ordered column.
5.   As items are received into stock the stock record card is amended to show the quantity received as well as the supplier so that orders and deliveries can be matched.
6.   As items are sold, or issued for internal use, the quantity is recorded. If the item is issued for internal use a requisition form should be completed and signed by a person in authority. The requisition number is then recorded on the stock record card.
7.   A running balance is kept of the quantity in stock so that proper control over re-ordering and stocking can be kept.

ALL PARTS LTD
STOCK RECORD CARD

1 ITEM Grommit	SIZE Standard	TYPE Rubber	UNIT Dozen

MAIN SUPPLIER Rubber Mouldings Ltd
Heath Lane
Wolding Ham
Phone:

RE-ORDER LEVEL	10
MINIMUM LEVEL	6
MAXIMUM LEVEL	30

ALTERNATIVE SUPPLIERS

Howe Products, Weybridge
Rubber Things, Croydon

Note 5% discount on orders over £50

Rubber Mouldings close for two weeks' holiday in August.

ORDERS			RECEIVED			ISSUED			BALANCE
DATE	FROM	QTY	DATE	FROM	QTY	DATE	REQ.	QTY	QTY
1/5/84	Balance							25	
30/5/84	Rubber	20				2/5	Sales	5	20
	Mouldings					3/5	539	7	13
						30/5	Sales	4	9
						4/6	Sales	6	3
			6/8	Rubber	20			23	
				Mouldings					
						12/6	Sales	5	18

Figure 8.3

8.13   The Stock Card and Stocktaking

It should be noted that the quantity recorded on the stock card represents the number of items that should be in stock and not necessarily the number of items that are in stock. A discrepancy can be caused either by poor record keeping or by losses of stock through theft or unauthorized use. The stock record card is not a substitute for physical stocktaking but is a useful tool in identifying items of stock which are at risk. Semi-random checks should go on throughout the year reconciling the stock cards with the physical stock. Obviously those items of stock which are most at risk should be checked more frequently than those which have little risk. Providing that the stock cards are accurate their existence can allow the calculation of interim stock figures for the purpose of interim accounts or budgeting.

8.14   Computer-assisted Stock Controls

The issuing, re-ordering and receiving of stock is a fairly repetitive function and therefore lends itself fairly easily to operation by computer. A wide range of programs are available for this function, the most simple of which merely replaces the manual recording of stock movements on a stock card with a computer-based record. Most of these simpler programs will indicate when stock has fallen to the re-order level and many will, in addition, print out a new order for an appropriate amount of stock. The more sophisticated stock control programs will form part of an integrated system and will automatically record and re-order stock on the basis of the sales and purchases which have been recorded.

8.15   Review of Stock Levels

Since so many factors, internal and external, can affect the appropriate level of an item of stock it is vital that whatever system is used to record stock it should be kept under constant review to take account of changing circumstances. A system which merely shows that a firm has run out of stock of some items and overstocked others will be of little consolation to the proprietor who has a reduced profit.

ASSIGNMENTS

A8.1 Produce a trading account to calculate gross profit or loss in each of the following cases.

(a)	Stock at start	£50	Stock at close	£150
	Purchases	£450	Sales	£550
(b)	Stock at start	£735	Stock at close	£625
	Purchases	£7 250	Sales	£8 900
(c)	Stock at start	£1 050	Stock at close	£920
	Purchases	£23 480	Sales	£34 950
(d)	Stock at start	£1 095	Stock at close	£2 395
	Purchases	£14 320	Sales	£15 480

A8.2 G. Tar started business as a musical instrument dealer on 1 January with capital in cash £500. During the month of January the following transactions took place:

Jan 2   Bought instruments for cash £200.00
Jan 3   Paid for advertising £12.00
Jan 8   Bought instruments for cash £50.00
Jan 12   Paid delivery expenses £5.00
Jan 16   Cash sales £150.00
Jan 18   Cash sales £70.00
Jan 25   Bought stationery £5.00
Jan 26   Paid for advertising £15.00
Jan 31   Cash sales £20.00

Stock at 31 Jan valued at cost £75.00.

(a) Produce the ledger accounts necessary to record the above transactions.
(b) Extract a trial balance.
(c) Produce trading profit and loss accounts.
(d) Produce a balance sheet.

A8.3 A trader's stock at the start of the year valued at cost is £4350 while the figure at the end of the year is £5380. During the year his purchases amounted to £12 300.

(a) Calculate his rate of stock turnover.
(b) Assume that he is a greengrocer. Do you think that this rate of stock turnover is too high, too low, or about right for the type of business? Explain why.

9.   Fixed assets

In all the previous examples that we have examined, the business has purchased goods and services which it will expend almost immediately — stationery, wages, electricity are either used almost as soon as they are bought or indeed in the case of electricity is used as it is bought and paid for later. We must now examine the situation where the business purchases items which are not 'used up' in the same way as stationery, wages and electricity, but which are intended to be kept in the firm for a long period of time for use by the firm. Items which are bought for use by the firm over a period of time are called fixed assets. Fixed assets will include items such as the premises themselves, the firm's delivery vehicles, the firm's furniture and fittings and office equipment. Because of the more permanent nature of fixed assets we will need to account for them in our ledger in a slightly different way from expenditure on other items, but first we must be able to recognize when an item that we have bought is a fixed asset.

9.1   Fixed Asset or Current Asset

The general rule to use when deciding whether an item is a fixed asset is *if the item is to remain the property of the firm for more than one year then it is a fixed asset.* If the firm buys premises then it can be assumed that it intends to hold and use these premises for more than one year and that it is therefore a fixed asset. Similarly, a new delivery van or typewriter will have this capacity for an extended period of use and are fixed assets. If the firm buys a stock of goods at the start of the year which it intends to resell during the year this is not a fixed asset. As we have seen in the previous chapter, the firm may well still hold a quantity of stock at the end of the year, but we can assume that it will comprise different items of stock from those at the start of the year, so it is not a fixed asset. Similarly, the firm will have cash balances at the start and the close of the year but we can assume that the notes and coins held at the year end are different to those held at the start of the year. If the asset that is acquired is not a fixed asset it is called a current asset. Current assets are changing constantly in the normal course of business trading.

9.2 Capital and Revenue Expenditure

When the business resources are expended in the acquisition of a fixed asset this is called *capital expenditure*. If a firm buys premises or a motor van or a typewriter, capital expenditure is taking place. If the business resources are expended in the acquisition of current assets, stock, stationery, etc. this is called *revenue expenditure*. It can be seen then that distinguishing between capital and revenue expenditure and distinguishing between fixed and current assets often requires the same approach, although it is not exactly the same thing. See Fig. 9.1 for clarification of the distinction between capital and revenue expenditure.

However, an exception to this generalization occurs when a fixed asset is acquired as a replacement for one which already exists. Under these circumstances, providing that the replacement is of a similar type and value to the fixed asset that it replaces, the expenditure that has taken place is revenue expenditure and should be treated in the ledger in the same way as other items of revenue expenditure such as wages, stationery, etc. If the replacement is an improvement on the fixed asset which it replaces, the expenditure should be allocated on the basis of:

cost of replacing — revenue expenditure
cost of improving — capital expenditure.

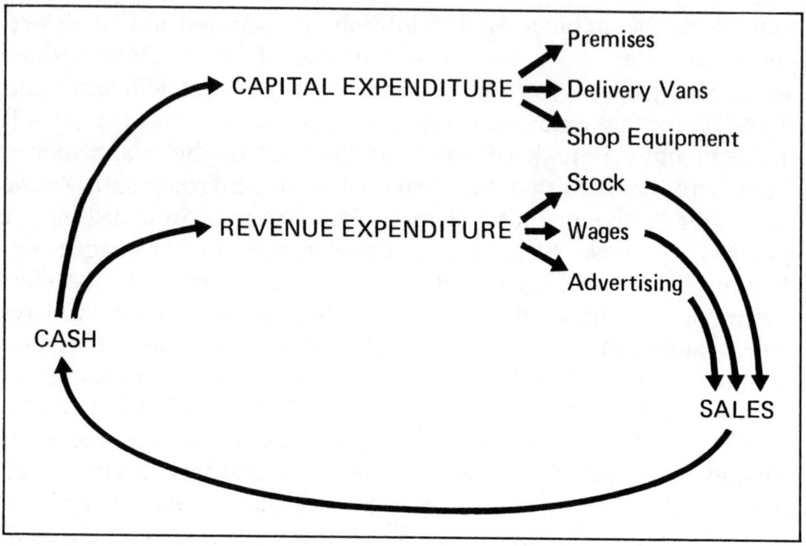

Figure 9.1 *The distinction between revenue and capital expenditure. Capital expenditure is expenditure on items which remain in the firm. Revenue expenditure is expenditure on items which circulate through the firm*

Examples of capital and revenue expenditure

1. A firm buys a new delivery van for £7000 – capital expenditure.
2. A firm buys a typewriter for £50 – capital expenditure.
3. A firm buys petrol for its delivery van – revenue expenditure.
4. A firm buys a new typewriter ribbon for £2 – revenue expenditure.
5. A firm has its motor van repaired after a breakdown at a cost of £500 – revenue expenditure.
6. A firm replaces a manual typewriter worth £50 with an electric typewriter costing £200 – revenue expenditure £50
   – capital expenditure £200

   Total $\overline{\underline{£250}}$

9.3 Fixed Assets and the Ledger

When fixed assets are initially purchased the cash account should be credited and an appropriate ledger account should be debited in much the same way that any other kind of expenditure is recorded. However, as we have seen, it is the nature of a fixed asset that it is not 'used up' and that at the end of the year it retains its value (we will initially assume that our fixed assets retain all their value indefinitely). Since the fixed assets remain in the firm at the end of the accounting period and have not been used up, it means that it would be incorrect to transfer this expenditure to the profit and loss account as a charge against gross profit. These accounts of fixed assets should therefore merely be balanced and ruled off at the end of the year in the same way as the cash account. The balances of the fixed asset accounts should appear in the balance sheet on the asset side, with separate listing of each class of fixed asset. Separate sub-headings and sub-totals should be made on the balance sheet for: (a) fixed assets; and (b) current assets. All assets should appear in the balance sheet in order of liquidity, that is to say, those which are most easy to change into cash appear last.

Example. Suppose that at the end of his financial year on 31 December 19—1 B. Birches' ledger contains the following assets. Show how they would appear in his balance sheet.

Cash, £120.
Stock, £300.
Premises, £10 000.

Delivery van, £600.
Furniture and fittings, £300.

B. RICHES
BALANCE SHEET AS AT
31 DECEMBER 19—1

Fixed Assets	£	£
Premises	10 000	
Delivery Van	600	
Furniture and Fittings	300	10 900
Current Assets		
Stock	300	
Cash	120	420
		11 320

Example. Ivor Price began business on 1 January 19-- with the following assets representing capital:

Premises	£7000
Motor van	£1500
Furniture and fittings	£700
Stock	£80
Cash	£3200

During the following month the following transactions took place:

Jan 1	Bought goods for resale £50.00
Jan 2	Sold goods for cash £80.00
Jan 3	Bought goods for resale £20.00
Jan 4	Bought stationery £5.00
Jan 5	Paid wages £15.00
Jan 6	Bought typewriter £30.00
Jan 10	Bought franking machine £40.00
Jan 11	Sold goods for cash £120.00
Jan 12	Bought additional motor van £450.00
Jan 15	Bought goods for resale £15.00
Jan 17	Sold goods for cash £80.00
Jan 20	Paid wages £15.00
Jan 20	Sold goods for cash £120.00
Jan 24	Paid electricity bill £8.00

Stock at close valued at cost £98.00

CAPITAL (1)

				Jan 1	Premises	7000	—	
					Motor Van	1500	—	
					Furniture and			
					Fittings	700	—	
					Stock	80	—	
Jan 31	Balance	12480	—		Cash	3200	—	
		12480	—			12480	—	
				Jan 31	Balance	12480	—	
Jan 31	Balance	12770	—	Jan 31	Net Profit	290	—	
		12770	—			12770	—	
				Feb 1	Balance	12770	—	

PREMISES (2)

Jan 1	Capital		7000	—				

MOTOR VAN (3)

Jan 1	Capital	1500	–				
Jan 12	Cash	450	–	Jan 31	Balance	1950	–
		1950	–			1950	–
Feb 1	Balance	1950	–				

FURNITURE AND FITTINGS (4)

Jan 1	Capital	700	–

STOCK (5)

				Jan 31	Trading		
Jan 1	Capital	80	–		Account	80	–
Jan 31	Trading						
	Account	98	–				

CASH (6)

Jan 1	Capital	3200	–	Jan 1	Purchases	50	–
Jan 2	Sales	80	–	Jan 3	Purchases	20	–
Jan 11	Sales	120	–	Jan 4	Stationery	5	–
Jan 17	Sales	80	–	Jan 5	Wages	15	–
Jan 20	Sales	120	–	Jan 6	Office		
					Equipment	30	–
				Jan 10	Office		
					Equipment	40	–
				Jan 12	Motor Van	450	–
				Jan 15	Purchases	15	–
				Jan 20	Wages	15	–
				Jan 24	Electricity	8	–
				Jan 31	Balance	2952	–
		3600	–			3600	–
Feb 1	Balance	2952	–				

PURCHASES (7)

Jan 1	Cash	50	–				
Jan 3	Cash	20	–				
Jan 15	Cash	15	–	Jan 31	Trading		
					Account	85	–
		85	–			85	–

SALES (8)

				Jan 2	Cash	80	–
				Jan 11	Cash	120	–
				Jan 17	Cash	80	–
Jan 31	Trading Account	400	–	Jan 20	Cash	120	–
		400	–			400	–

STATIONERY (9)

Jan 4	Cash	5	–	Jan 31	Profit and Loss	5	–

WAGES (10)

Jan 5	Cash	15	–				
Jan 20	Cash	15	–	Jan 31	Profit and Loss	30	–
		30	–			30	–

OFFICE EQUIPMENT (11)

Jan 6	Cash	30	–				
Jan 10	Cash	40	–	Jan 31	Balance	70	–
		70	–			70	–
Feb 1	Balance	70	–				

ELECTRICITY (12)

Jan 24	Cash	8	–	Jan 31	Profit and Loss	8	–

IVOR PRICE
TRADING AND PROFIT AND LOSS ACCOUNT
FOR THE MONTH ENDING 31 JANUARY 19--

Jan 31	Stock at Start	80	–	Jan 31	Sales	400	–
	Add Purchases	85	–				
		165	–				
	Less Stock at Close	98	–				
	Cost of Sales	67	–				
	Gross Profit	333	–				
		400	–			400	–

Jan 31	Stationery	5	—	Jan 31	Gross Profit	333	—
	Wages	30	—				
	Electricity	8	—				
	Net Profit	290	—				
		333	—			333	—

IVOR PRICE
BALANCE SHEET
AS AT 31 DECEMBER 19--

Fixed assets			*Capital*	12 480	
Premises	7 000		Net Profit	290	12 770
Motor Van	1 950				
Furniture and					
Fittings	700				
Office Equipment	70	9 720			
Current assets					
Stock	98				
Cash	2 952	3 050			
		12 770			12 770

Notes to ledger work

Jan 6   The typewriter bought on this date is a fixed asset — office equipment — an appropriate account is therefore opened and debited.

Jan 10   The franking machine is another piece of office equipment and is therefore debited to the account opened on Jan 6 — there is no need for a separate account since it is the same *kind* of item as the typewriter.

Jan 12   This motor van is debited to the motor van account which is already open on the books. It increases the cost of motor vans held by the firm from £1500 to £1950.

Notes to trading and profit and loss accounts

As we know, these accounts contain only revenue expenditure and income.

Notes to balance sheet

Again each account with a balance is listed with debit balances on asset side and credit balances on liabilities side. Note also the sub-heading and sub-totals. The omission of the appropriate sub-headings and sub-totals IS INCORRECT.

ASSIGNMENTS

For each of the following assignments you should open ledger accounts and enter the transactions. You should then produce (a) a trial balance; (b) a trading and profit and loss account; and (c) a balance sheet.

A9.1
Jan 1 E. Earlson started business with capital in cash of £350.00
Jan 2 Bought goods for resale £50.00
Jan 3 Bought stationery £10.00
Jan 4 Bought cash register £20.00
Jan 5 Sold goods for cash £90.00
Jan 6 Sold goods for cash £30.00
Jan 7 Bought scales for use in shop £15.00
Jan 8 Paid wages £10.00
Jan 9 Sold goods for cash £30.00

Stock at close valued at cost £20.00

A9.2
Jan 1 F. Clark started business with capital in cash £500 and goods for resale worth £50.00
Jan 2 Bought goods for cash £90.00
Jan 3 Sold goods for cash £70.00
Jan 4 Bought stationery £10.00
Jan 5 Sold goods for cash £30.00
Jan 6 Bought adding machine £30.00
Jan 7 Paid wages £15.00
Jan 8 Bought delivery van £120.00
Jan 9 Sold goods for cash £50.00
Jan 10 Bought stationery £15.00
Jan 11 Sold goods for cash £100.00

Stock at close valued at cost £65.00

A9.3   Jan 1   E. Smith started business with capital in cash
                       £700 and goods valued at cost £65.00
          Jan 2   Bought goods for cash £30.00
          Jan 3   Bought goods £35.00
          Jan 4   Sold goods for cash £45.00
          Jan 5   Bought stationery £5.00
          Jan 6   Paid wages £15.00
          Jan 7   Sold goods for cash £35.00
          Jan 8   Bought cash register £25.00
          Jan 9   Bought scales £20.00
          Jan 10   Bought delivery van £150.00
          Jan 11   Sold goods £25.00
          Jan 12   Paid wages £15.00
          Jan 13   Sold goods for cash £38.00

          Stock at close valued at cost £10.00

10. Credit transactions

10.1 Credit Purchases and Credit Sales

We have up to now only accounted in our ledger for goods which are sold for cash. In the modern commercial world transactions are rarely carried out on a 'cash on the nail' basis. A trader may sell goods to a customer and give the customer time to pay. This is called a credit sale. You should note that this is different from an HP sale, since with a credit sale the customer becomes the new owner of the goods immediately the bargain is struck, even though he does not pay for the goods until later. Alternatively, a trader may buy goods from his suppliers and pay for them later, i.e. credit purchases. Many traders will be concerned with both buying and selling goods on credit.

10.2 Selling Goods on Credit

Suppose that we wished to record the following transaction in the books of a business :

Jan 1 Sold goods to A. Red £50 cash.

If this transaction was for cash, the book-keeping entries would appear as follows:

CASH ACCOUNT		SALES ACCOUNT	
Jan 1 Sales 50			Jan 1 Cash 50

However, suppose that the transaction to be recorded *was not*:

Jan 1 Sold goods to A. Red £50, *but was*:
Jan 1 Sold goods to A. Red £50, *on credit*.

An alternative set of ledger entries is required in this situation. What these entries are becomes clear if we examine how the second transaction differs.

The key difference is that the goods are sold *on credit*, i.e. no cash has been received. Nevertheless, the goods have been sold. We can conclude therefore, that this transaction is correctly recorded above in the credit side of the sales account but since no cash has been received the debit entry in the cash account is invalid.

In order to decide where to place the debit entry we should ask ourselves 'what is the effect of selling the item on credit'.

1. Sales have been made, £50.
2. A. Red owes £50.

The debit entry must therefore record that A. Red owes £50 and we must therefore open a personal account for A. Red and place the debit in his account. The correct entries are:

CASH ACCOUNT		SALES ACCOUNT		A. RED ACCOUNT	
			Jan 1 A. Red 50	Jan 1 Sales 50	

Note that the description of the entry in the sales account is 'A. Red' and the description in Red's account is 'sales' and the debit balance of £50 on A. Red's account shows that he owes £50 – he is a debtor. Each time that we sell goods to customers on credit we should credit sales and debit the personal account of the customer. We shall then need a separate personal account for each of our credit customers.

10.3   Receiving Money from Customers

Following through the example above, suppose that on 7 January the following transaction took place:

Jan 7   A. Red paid his account in full £50

What is the effect of this transaction?

1. Cash £50 is received.
2. A Red's debt to the firm is reduced by £50.

We must therefore debit cash account with £50 in respect of (1) cash received and credit A. Red's personal account in respect of (2) the reduction of debt.

The position therefore appears:

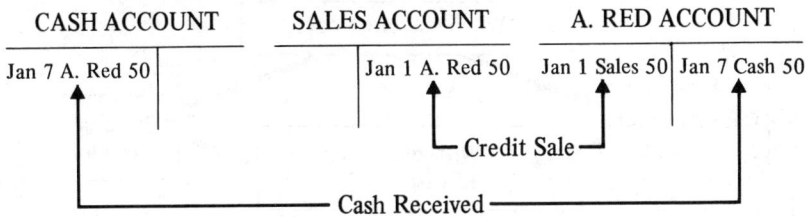

CASH ACCOUNT	SALES ACCOUNT	A. RED ACCOUNT
Jan 7 A. Red 50	Jan 1 A. Red 50	Jan 1 Sales 50 | Jan 7 Cash 50

Credit Sale

Cash Received

The entries above should be followed whenever credit sales occur and whenever a customer pays — however much he pays.

10.4   Summary

The entries for credit sales can be summarized as shown in Fig. 10.1.

Before continuing with Section 10.5 you should attempt A10.1 at the end of the chapter.

10.5   Credit Purchases

In the same way that we will allow our customers to buy goods from us on credit our suppliers may allow us to buy goods from them on credit. The book-keeping procedure for credit purchases is very similar to that used for credit sales. Follow through the example below:

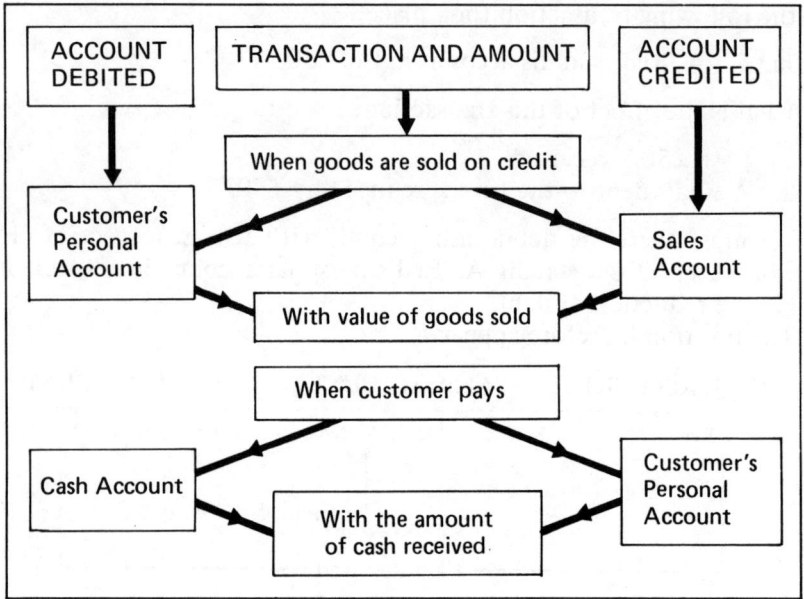

Figure 10.1 *Summary of entries for credit sales*

Example. On Jan 1 a business buys from A. Oak goods worth £50 on credit and goods from B. Ash worth £25 on credit. Note that the business has purchased the goods and is the new owner but no money has changed hands. Instead the firm owes A. Oak £50 and B. Ash £25.

The ledger entries therefore appear as follows:

CASH ACCOUNT | | PURCHASES ACCOUNT

Jan 1 A. Oak 50
Jan 1 B. Ash 25

A. OAK | | B. ASH

Jan 1 Purchases 50 | | Jan 1 Purchases 25

No cash has been paid therefore no entry in cash account

Goods purchased amount to £75

The credit balances in these accounts show that we owe A. Oak £50 and B. Ash £25. They are creditors.

10.6   Cash Paid to Suppliers

Suppose now that in the above example the additional transactions shown below take place:

Jan 4 The business pays cash £50 to A. Oak.
Jan 5 The business pays cash £15 on account to B. Ash.

The ledger entries appear as follows:

CASH ACCOUNT		PURCHASES ACCOUNT	
	Jan 4 A. Oak 50	Jan 1 A. Oak 50	
	Jan 5 B. Ash 15	Jan 1 B. Ash 25	

A. OAK		B. ASH	
Jan 4 Cash 50	Jan 1 Purchases 50	Jan 5 B. Ash 15	Jan 1 Purchases 25

A. Oak's account now has a nil balance and the business owes him nothing.

The business only paid B. Ash £15 of what it owed him. The credit balance on the account shows that he is still owed £10.

10.7   Summary

The entries for credit purchases can be summarized as shown in Fig. 10.2.

10.8   Getting the Side Right

Students very often have difficulty in deciding which account to debit and which to credit when dealing with credit purchases and credit sales. To get the side right assume to start with that the transaction is not for credit but for cash. In this way you will be able to establish the correct side in the sales or the purchases account.

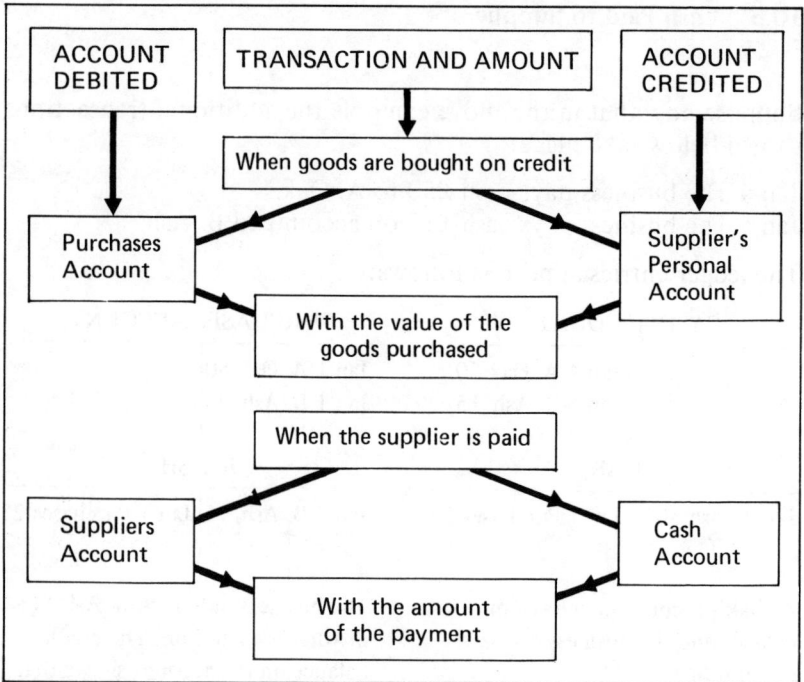

Figure 10.2 *Summary of entries for credit purchases*

10.9 Creditors and Debtors in the Balance Sheet

Creditors and debtors are not 'business expenses' they are merely current liabilities (creditors) and current assets (debtors). Outstanding accounts at the end of the financial period will not therefore be transferred to the trading or profit and loss account but will appear in the balance sheet. You should merely add together the balances of all debtors and show them as a single item under current assets – debtors. Similarly, add together creditors and show them as a single item under current liabilities – creditors.

10.10 The Reason for Credit Transactions

If businessmen sell goods they normally prefer their customers to pay immediately. If, however, the choice is between allowing a customer credit or not making a sale the businessman will, providing that he is reasonably sure that the customer will eventually pay, allow a period of credit. In addition, if a businessman makes frequent sales to the same customer, the businessman may come to an arrangement with the customer to settle his account monthly as a matter of convenience. The reason for credit transactions can therefore be summarized:

1. Allowing credit may increase sales.
2. Allowing credit may be more convenient than settling up individually for many small transactions.

The businessman will carefully weigh against the additional profitability of allowing credit sales the cost of allowing credit before he takes the decision to trade in this way. The direct costs that can be involved with credit transactions are:

1. The risk of people dishonouring the debts — bad debtors. These will be treated as an additional expense just like wages or stationery expenses.
2. The costs of the additional paperwork involved in recording the credit sales and payments from customers.

In addition to these direct costs, if a large proportion of the businessman's sales are on credit to slow payers, the businessman's ability to renew the stock which he has sold will be seriously affected since until the debtors pay up he will not have the cash to buy more stock — unless, of course, he renews his stock *on credit from his suppliers.*

Example. A businessman starts with cash £100:

BALANCE SHEET

Cash	£100	Capital	£100
	£100		£100

He buys stock with £100:

BALANCE SHEET

Stock	£100		
Cash	—	Capital	£100
	£100		£100

He sells his stock for £120 on credit (profit £20):

BALANCE SHEET

Stock	—	Capital	£100
Debtors	£120	Add profit	£ 20
Cash	—		£120
	£120		£120

Now until his customer pays him the £120 he cannot buy any more stock or make any additional sales unless he buys on credit. He buys more stock, £100 *on credit*:

BALANCE SHEET

Stock	£100		
Debtors	£120	Capital	£120
Cash	—	Creditors	£100
	£220		£220

Since the chain of production in commerce can be a fairly lengthy one we can begin to see how each link in the chain relies on credit from the previous link.

10.11   Bad Debts

As we mentioned in 10.8 above, a trader may occasionally allow credit to a customer who eventually dishonours the debt. Where it is considered that the debit balance on a customer's account can never be recovered it becomes necessary to 'write off' the balance to a 'bad debts account'. The bad debts account will be used to record all debts written off in this way and as it is an expense account similar to wages, postage, etc. its balance at the end of the accounting period is transferred to the profit and loss account.

Example.   On February 2 a trader sold goods on credit to I. du Flit for £150. On February 8 the trader discovered that I. du Flit had left the country for an undisclosed destination and that the debt was irrecoverable. The trader's entries recording these transactions appear opposite.

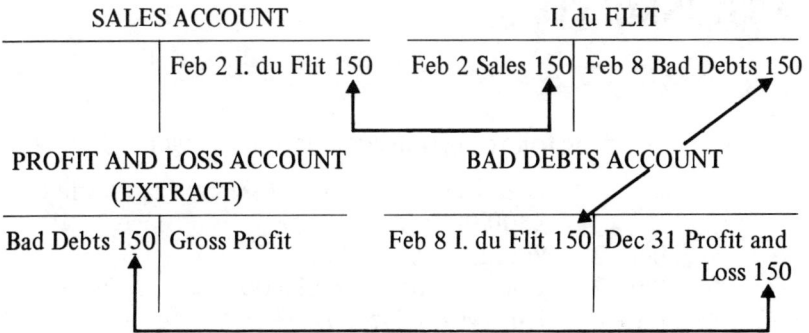

```
        SALES ACCOUNT                              I. du FLIT
              | Feb 2 I. du Flit 150    Feb 2 Sales 150 | Feb 8 Bad Debts 150
              |                                          |
              |           ←——————————————————┘          ↗
   PROFIT AND LOSS ACCOUNT                   BAD DEBTS ACCOUNT
         (EXTRACT)
  Bad Debts 150 | Gross Profit        Feb 8 I. du Flit 150 | Dec 31 Profit and
              ↑                                            |           Loss 150
              └————————————————————————————————————————————→
```

10.12 Summary

Fig. 10.3 summarizes the entries for bad debts.

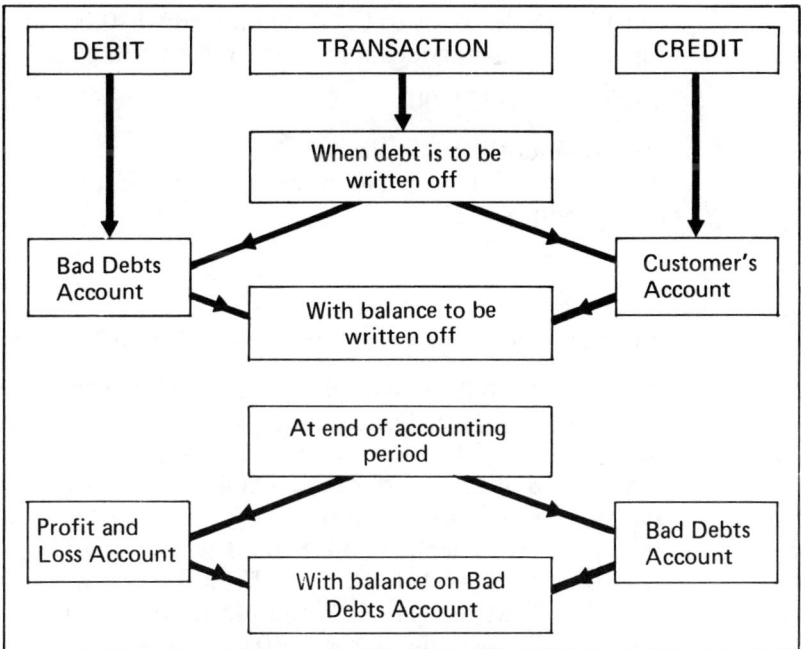

Figure 10.3 *Summary of bad debts*

ASSIGNMENTS

A10.1 Enter the following transactions in the ledger of J. Bloggs:

Jan	1	J. Bloggs started business with capital in cash £300.00
Jan	2	Purchases £30.00
Jan	3	Bought stationery £10.00
Jan	4	Paid wages £15.00
Jan	5	Bought new cash register £70.00
Jan	6	Sold goods for cash £30.00
Jan	7	Sold goods to A. Red £15.00 on credit
Jan	8	Sold goods to B. Blue £10.00 on credit
Jan	9	Sold goods to A. Red £20.00 on credit
Jan	10	A. Red settled his account in full
Jan	11	Sold goods to B. Blue on credit £25.00
Jan	12	B. Blue paid £5.00 on account
Jan	13	Sold goods to C. White on credit £20.00
Jan	14	Bought goods for resale for cash £30.00

Stock at close £35.00

(a) Extract the trial balance.
(b) Produce a trading and profit and loss account.
(c) Produce a balance sheet.

A10.2 Enter the following transactions in the ledger of T. Smith:

Jan	1	T. Smith started business with capital in cash £300.00
Jan	2	Bought goods for resale £50.00
Jan	3	Sold goods for cash £60.00
Jan	4	Paid wages £16.00
Jan	5	Paid telephone bill £16.00
Jan	6	Sold goods to B. Black £30.00 on credit
Jan	7	Sold goods to C. White £15.00 on credit
Jan	8	Sold goods for cash £30.00
Jan	9	Bought goods for resale £35.00
Jan	10	Sold goods to C. White £10.00 on credit
Jan	11	B. Black paid £20.00 on account

Jan 12   Sold goods to B. Black £30.00 on credit
Jan 13   Paid wages £16.00

Stock at close at cost £45.00

(a)   Extract a trial balance.
(b)   Produce a trading and profit and loss account.
(c)   Produce a balance sheet.

A10.3   Enter the following transactions into the ledger of A. Angler. Bring down balances remaining on accounts to the next period where appropriate.

Jan 1   A. Angler started business with the following assets representing capital:

             Cash £900.00
             Premises £11 000.00
             Motor van £600.00
             Stock £200.00
             Shop equipment £300.00

Jan 2   Bought goods for resale from B. Line £65.00 on credit
Jan 3   Bought goods for resale from C. Float £75.00 on credit
Jan 4   Bought additional motor van £300.00
Jan 5   Sold goods to S. Pike £80.00 on credit
Jan 6   Sold goods to T. Bream £95.00 on credit
Jan 7   Paid wages £15.00
Jan 8   Bought stationery £5.00
Jan 9   Bought goods from D. Sinker £55.00 on credit
Jan 10   Sold goods to U. Rudd £45.00 on credit
Jan 11   Cash sales £120.00
Jan 12   Paid B. Line £45.00 on account
Jan 13   Bought goods for resale £35.00 from C. Float on credit
Jan 14   Sold goods to V. Salmon £25.00 on credit
Jan 15   Paid wages £15.00
Jan 16   S. Pike settled his account in full
Jan 17   V. Salmon declared bankrupt
Jan 18   Drew cash for personal use £15.00

Jan 19   U. Rudd paid £20.00 on account
Jan 20   Bought goods for resale from B. Line £20.00 on credit
Jan 21   Bought goods for resale paid cash £20.00

Stock at close valued at cost £270.00

(a)   Extract a trial balance.
(b)   Produce a trading and profit and loss account.
(c)   Produce a balance sheet.

A10.4   Enter the following transactions in the ledger of T. Singh:

Jan 1   T. Singh started business with capital in cash £300.00
Jan 2   Bought goods for cash £35.00
Jan 3   Bought goods from A. Ash £20.00 on credit
Jan 4   Bought goods from E. Elm £30.00 on credit
Jan 5   Sold goods to A. Red £35.00 on credit
Jan 6   Sold goods to B. Blue £25.00 on credit
Jan 7   Paid wages £15.00
Jan 8   Paid rent £30.00
Jan 9   Sold goods for cash £35.00
Jan 10   Bought goods for cash £15.00
Jan 11   Paid A. Ash £10.00 on account
Jan 12   A. Red settled his account in full
Jan 13   Sold goods to P. Pink £40.00 on credit
Jan 14   Bought goods from O. Oak £15.00 on credit

Stock at close at cost £65.00

(a)   Extract a trial balance.
(b)   Produce a trading and profit and loss account.
(c)   Show a balance sheet.

Continue for a second period:

Jan 15   Settled E. Elm's account in full
Jan 16   Sold goods for cash £80.00
Jan 17   Bought goods from E. Elm £65.00 on credit
Jan 18   Paid wages £15.00
Jan 19   Paid rent £30.00

Jan 20   Sold goods to P. Pink £60.00 on credit
Jan 21   Sold goods to A. Red on credit £15.00
Jan 25   Sold goods to P.Pink £20.00 on credit
Jan 27   P.Pink paid £60.00 on account
Jan 28   Bought cash register £70.00 cash

Stock at close at cost £70.00

(d)   Extract a trial balance.
(e)   Produce a trading and profit and loss account.
(f)   Show a balance sheet.

11. Bank accounts

11.1 The Advantages of a Bank Account

Many businessmen find that it is convenient to open a separate account at the bank for use by the business. The existence of a business bank account has many immediate advantages to the business.

1. The businessman can avoid holding large quantities of cash on the business premises which may be insecure.
2. Payments to suppliers by cheque, particularly if delivered by post, is more convenient and secure than cash. It may also provide additional proof that payment has been made.
3. Many of the business's customers may wish to pay their accounts by cheque. The existence of the business bank account allows for the collection of debts in this way.
4. An account at the bank makes more readily available to the business the other bank services that are available such as loans and overdrafts, safe custody of valuables, expert advice on a wide range of business problems.

11.2 The Current Bank Account

A current account at a bank is an account into which money can be paid and from which money can be withdrawn without any prior notice. The operation of the current account can best be illustrated with an example.

Suppose I. Havalot, a general trader, finds that he is holding £1500 in cash in his premises (see Fig. 11.1). He may recognize that this is not a very secure way of keeping money so he opens an account at the Greedy's Bank and pays into the bank £1400, keeping just £100 in the premises for day to day transactions (see Fig. 11.2).

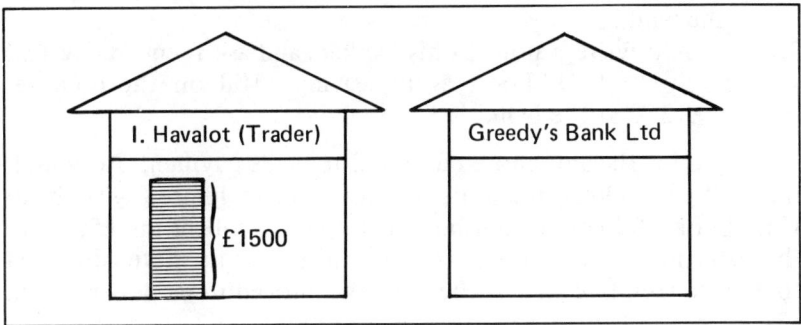

Figure 11.1 *Stage 1 — I. Havalot keeps a pile of cash £1500 on his premises*

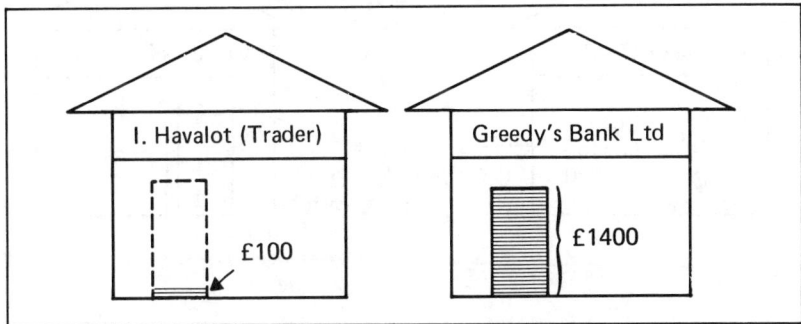

Figure 11.2 *Stage 2 — I. Havalot pays £1400 into bank*

I. Havalot still owns £1500 but now he is keeping it in two different localities, £1400 at the bank and £100 on his own premises. What I. Havalot has done, in fact, is to lend Greedy's Bank £1400, but he can demand repayment of all or any part of this money at a moment's notice. Since the bank owe I. Havalot £1400 they are a debtor to him.

Making payments by cheque

Suppose now that I. Havalot has a supplier called U.O. Loot to whom he owes £50. I Havalot could pay U.O. Loot in one of the following ways:

1. He could pay cash out of the £100 he holds on his premises, leaving £50 on the premises and £1400 at the bank.
2. He could withdraw £50 in cash from the bank and give this £50 to U.O. Loot, leaving £100 on his premises and £1350 at the bank.
3. He could write a note to his bankers and ask them to pay £50 directly to U.O. Loot, again leaving £100 on the premises and £1350 at the bank.

Suppose I. Havalot chose method 3 to make payment. He would, rather than deliver the note to his bankers himself give it to U.O. Loot who could then be relied upon to collect the £50 from the bank in exchange for the note. In this case the note addressed to the banker is called a cheque. The procedure is illustrated in Fig. 11.3.

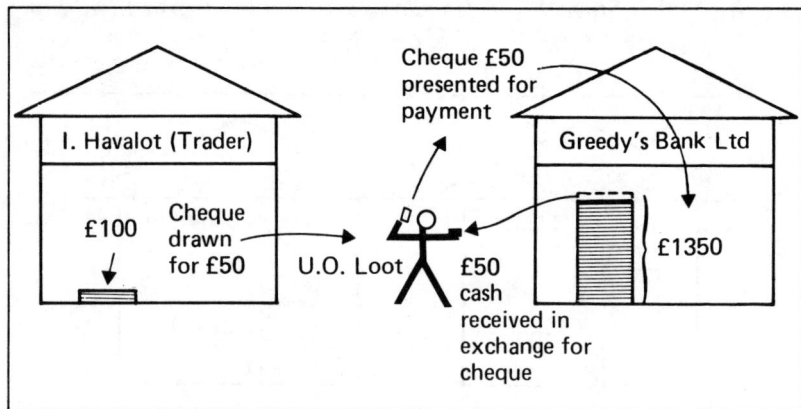

Figure 11.3 *Making payments by cheque*

Receiving payments by cheque

In the same way that I. Havalot may settle his debts by drawing cheques in favour of his creditors, people who owe him money, his debtors, may settle their debts by writing cheques.

Suppose that one of I. Havalot's customers, A. Big-Buyer owes him £75. Suppose that A. Big-Buyer pays by a cheque drawn on Grasping's Bank with whom he banks. I. Havalot, rather than collect the cash personally from Grasping's Bank will merely pay the cheque into his account at Greedy's Bank. Greedy's Bank will then collect the £75 on behalf of I. Havalot from Grasping's Bank. (See Fig. 11.4.)

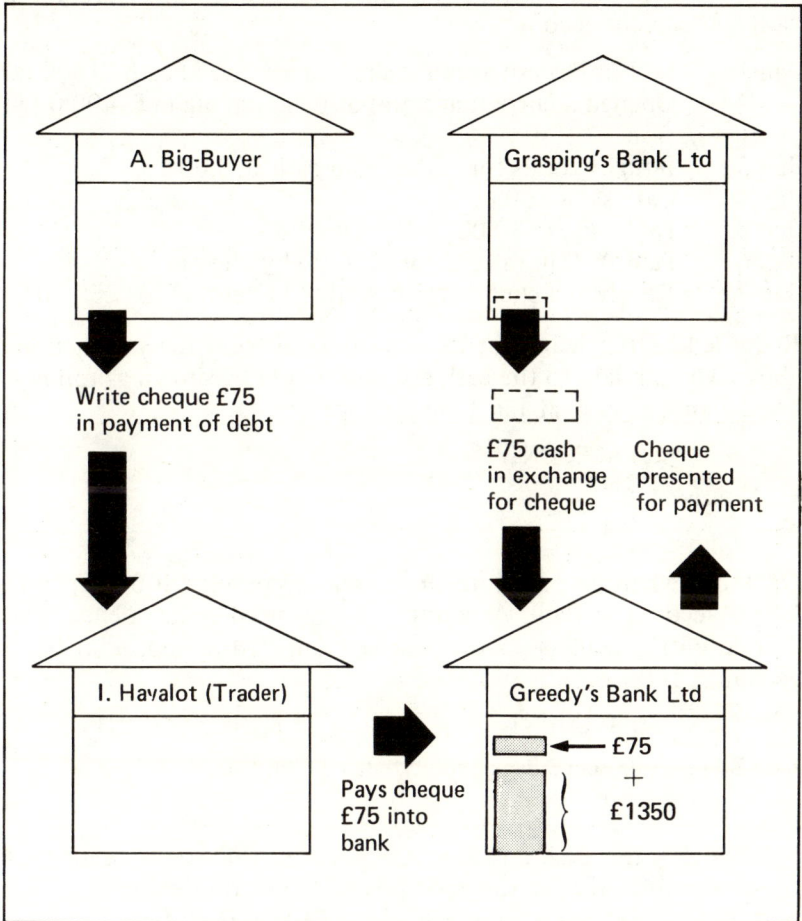

Figure 11.4 *Receiving payment by cheque*

11.3   The Current Account and the Ledger

Having dealt with the mechanics of paying money into and out of the bank current account we must now turn our attention to making our ledger reflect the movements of cash. Consider how the following transactions may be recorded in the cash account (the double entries are ignored for the purpose of illustrating the cash and current account).

Jan 1	D. Ford's cash account shows a balance of cash £1500.00
Jan 2	Opened a current account at bank paying in £1400.00 in cash
Jan 3	Bought goods for resale, paid cash £20.00
Jan 4	Cash sales £60.00
Jan 5	Paid wages £30.00 cash
Jan 6	Paid A. Oak (a creditor) £50.00 by cheque
Jan 7	Received a cheque from A. Red (a debtor) for £30.00

Recorded in the ledger in its conventional form the transactions above which relate to the cash account would be shown as follows. The balance in cash at Jan 1 would appear:

CASH ACCOUNT

Jan 1 Balance 1500|

On Jan 2 when he pays into his current account £1400 a separate ledger account − Bank Account − would need to be opened. The double entries will be credit cash account £1400 and debit bank account £1400:

CASH ACCOUNT		BANK ACCOUNT	
Jan 1 Balance 1500	Jan 2 Bank 1400	Jan 2 Cash 1400	

Balancing the cash and bank accounts at this stage means that these accounts record the true position, i.e. that there is a cash balance of £100 and a bank balance of £1400. Each time that cash (notes and coins) is received or paid from cash in hand the transaction will be recorded in the cash account on the appropriate side, and each time that cash (cheques) is received or paid from the bank the transaction will be recorded in the appropriate side in the bank account. Double entries will of course usually be made in the ledger but for the purposes of this example the double entries are omitted.

CASH ACCOUNT		BANK ACCOUNT	
Jan 1 Balance 1500	Jan 2 Bank 1400	Jan 2 Cash 1400	
↑	↑	↑	↑
Cash (notes and coins) received	Cash (notes and coins) paid	Cash (usually cheques) paid into bank	Cash (cheques drawn) paid out of bank

The way in which the remainder of the transactions may appear in these two accounts is shown below:

CASH ACCOUNT				BANK ACCOUNT			
Jan 1 Balance	1500	Jan 2 Bank	1400	Jan 2 Cash	1400	Jan 6 A. Oak	50
Jan 4 Sales	60	Jan 3 Purchases	20	Jan 7 A. Red	30	Jan 7 Balance	1380
		Jan 5 Wages	30		1430		1430
		Jan 7 Balance	110				
	1560		1560	Jan 8 Balance	1380		
Jan 8 Balance	110						

11.4 Bank and Cash — an Alternative Approach

As an alternative to the two quite separate ledger accounts used in the example above many traders record their cash and bank transactions on the same sheet side by side. The advantages of using this method evolves from the fact that cash at bank and cash in hand are almost the same asset, and transactions will frequently occur which will affect both accounts. You should keep in mind nevertheless that although these two accounts may be kept on the same sheet they are separate accounts. You should also bear in mind that although the cash and bank accounts may be physically separated from the rest of the ledger in a single 'cash book', it is still part of the ledger and requires double entries.

Treble-column cash book

The paper which appears in the cash book for the cash and bank account is specially ruled. The most commonly used ruling is called 'treble-column cash' — see the example overleaf.

DEBIT SIDE

CASH BOOK

CREDIT SIDE

Example 11.1

Debit side:

Date	Particulars	Fol No.	Discount £ p	Cash £ p	Bank £ p

Credit side:

Date	Particulars	Fol No.	Discount £ p	Cash £ p	Bank £ p

Example 11.2

Debit side — Cash received (notes and coins) — Cheques received

Date	Particulars	Fol No.	Discount £ p	Cash £ p	Bank £ p

Credit side — Cash paid (notes and coins) — Cheques paid

Date	Particulars	Fol No.	Discount £ p	Cash £ p	Bank £ p

Example 11.3

Debit side:

Date	Particulars	Fol No.	Discount £ p	Cash £ p	Bank £ p
Jan 1	Balance	✓		1500 —	
Jan 2	Cash				1400 —
Jan 4	Sales			60 —	
Jan 7	A. Red				30 —

Credit side:

Date	Particulars	Fol No.	Discount £ p	Cash £ p	Bank £ p
Jan 2	Bank	✓		1400 —	
Jan 3	Purchases			20 —	
Jan 5	Wages			30 —	
Jan 6	A. Oak				50 —

You will notice that like other parts of the ledger the cash book is divided down the centre into a debit side and a credit side. Columns for date, particulars, folio numbers and three cash columns for discount, bank and cash (we shall ignore the discount columns for the time being) appear on both sides. As with the simple cash account, the debit side is used to record receipts and the credit side payments. If cash (notes and coins) is received, the transaction should be entered on the debit side of the cash book, date in the date column, description in the particulars column and amount in the cash column. If a cheque or cash is paid into the bank, the details should similarly be recorded in the debit side of the cash book but the amount should appear in the bank column. It can be seen that both cash and cheques received are recorded in the date, particulars and folio numbers columns, but that the amounts are analysed into their respective cash columns. In a similar way, payments are recorded in the credit side of the cash book. Both cash and cheques share the same columns for date, particulars and folio numbers, but have separate columns for cash and bank. (Example 11.1.)

Using these parallel accounts the transactions for the example above would appear in these accounts as follows. Double entries are not shown except where both entries appear in the cash book. (Example 11.2.)

Notice that Jan 2 cash is paid into the bank — this means that cash is being paid out (notes and coins), credit cash account and, as cash is being paid into the bank, debit bank account. Where both the credit and debit entries appear in the same account this is called a *contra entry* and is denoted by a ✓ or a ✗ in the folio column. (Example 11.3.)

11.5   Balancing the Cash Book

We will require to balance and 'rule off' our cash and bank accounts from time to time in the same way that we would if they were kept separately. Balancing the cash book is done in the following way.

Step 1. Calculate the balance of cash — difference between the totals of the debit cash column and the credit cash column.

CASH BOOK

Date	Particulars	Fol No.	Discount £ p	Cash £ p	Bank £ p	Date	Particulars	Fol No.	Discount £ p	Cash £ p	Bank £ p
Jan 1	Balance	✓		1500 —		Jan 2	Bank	✓		1400 —	
Jan 2	Cash				1400 —	Jan 3	Purchases			20 —	
Jan 4	Sales			60 —		Jan 5	Wages			30 —	
Jan 7	A. Red				30 —	Jan 6	A. Oak				50 —
						Jan 7	Balance			110 —	
				1560 —						1560 —	
Jan 8	Balance			110 —							

Balancing the cash account

Example 11.4

CASH BOOK

Date	Particulars	Fol No.	Discount £ p	Cash £ p	Bank £ p	Date	Particulars	Fol No.	Discount £ p	Cash £ p	Bank £ p
Jan 1	Balance	✓		1500 —		Jan 2	Bank	✓		1400 —	
Jan 2	Cash				1400 —	Jan 3	Purchases			20 —	
Jan 4	Sales			60 —		Jan 5	Wages			30 —	
Jan 7	A. Red				30 —	Jan 6	A. Oak				50 —
						Jan 7	Balance			110 —	1380 —
				1560 —	1430 —					1560 —	1430 —
Jan 8	Balance			110 —	1380 —						

Example 11.5

Step 2. Enter the balance on the 'light' side.
Step 3. Rule off, re-add columns and carry balance forward. (Example 11.4.)
Step 4. Calculate the balance at bank — difference between the totals of the debit bank column and credit bank column.
Step 5. Enter the balance on the 'light' side.
Step 6. Rule off, re-add columns and carry balance forward. (Example 11.5.)

Notice that in the above example there is no need to write the date and balance separately for bank and cash since they appear on the same line. Notice also that as always the totals appear on the same line.

11.6 Bank Overdrafts and Loans

Since it is not possible to spend more cash (notes and coins) than you actually have, the cash account will always have a debit balance. This is not the case with the bank account. The businessman may occasionally find himself short of cash for a variety of reasons and, providing that the business is quite sound, the bank may be quite willing to make some of its money available to the business usually in the form of a loan or an overdraft.

The overdraft

If the bank allows an overdraft it quite simply means that the bank will allow the businessman to draw more out of his current account than he has paid in up to some agreed limit. When the overdraft is negotiated *no special book-keeping* entries are required. However, when the account becomes overdrawn (when more has actually been drawn from the account than paid in) the bank account in the cash book will have a credit balance, reflecting the fact that the bank has become a creditor of the business rather than a debtor and that the bank has lent resources to the business. In such a situation the cash book would be as shown below when balanced and ruled off. (Example 11.6.)

CASH BOOK

Date	Particulars	Fol No.	Discount £ p	Cash £ p	Bank £ p
Jan 1	Balance			50 —	80 —
Jan 4	Sales			10 —	
Jan 8	A. Red				10 —
Jan 8	Balance				75 —
				60 —	165 —
Jan 9	Balance			35 —	

Date	Particulars	Fol No.	Discount £ p	Cash £ p	Bank £ p
Jan 2	Purchases			5 —	15 —
Jan 3	Wages			20 —	55 —
Jan 4	A. Oak				50 —
Jan 5	B. Elm				45 —
Jan 6	C. Ash				
Jan 7	A. Oak				
Jan 8	Balance			35 —	165 —
				60 —	
Jan 9	Balance				75 —

£35 cash in hand
Debit balance
Asset in balance sheet

£75 more paid out of bank than paid in
Credit balance
Liability in balance sheet

Balance sheet as at January 9 (extract)

Current liabilities	*Current assets*
Bank overdraft £75	Cash in hand £35

should be other way around

Example 11.6

The bank loan

The alternative method by which a bank will sometimes lend its resources to a business is a loan. If a loan is the method adopted then the bank will pay into the business's current account the amount of the loan, e.g. £2000. This will mean that if the business's current account before the loan was a surplus of £75 this surplus on the current account will increase to £2075. At the same time that the bank pays into the current account the amount of the loan (£2000) the bank will open an additional account for the business called a 'loan account' in which the debt will be recorded.

11.7   The Bank Loan and the Ledger

Unlike the bank overdraft the bank loan will require special ledger entries when the loan takes place. The double entries to record the loan in the business ledger can be best understood if we consider carefully what the bank has done and how this affects the business's relationship with the bank.

Firstly, the bank has increased the balance on current account by the amount of the loan therefore one entry in the business ledger must be debit current account. Secondly, the bank has lent the amount paid into the current account and has in this aspect become a creditor, therefore, open an additional account in the ledger — a 'bank loan account' — the second entry must be credit bank loan account.

Where there is at the end of a financial period a bank loan account, the amount of the loan would appear in the balance sheet under the heading of current liabilities. At the same time the current account will usually have a debit balance by virtue of the loan and should appear under current assets. This is illustrated below.

Example. On 30 December 19-1 J. Singh, a general trader, had £70 cash in hand and £50 cash at bank in current account. On 31 December his bank made a loan of £1200 to be paid into his current account. J. Singh's ledger appears as shown in Example 11.7.

Dec 30 Balance	70	50	Dec 31 Balance
Dec 31 Loan		1200	
	70	1250	
Jan 1 Balance	70	1250	

	70	1250	
	70	1250	
	—	—	

Bank Loan Account

Dec 31 Current Account £1200

J. Singh Balance Sheet as at 31 December 19-1 (extract)

Current Liabilities
Bank Loan £1200

Current Assets
Current Account £1250

Cash £70

Example 11.7

11.8   The Bank Deposit Account

The business may find itself in the position where it has more cash in the current account than it requires for the near future; since it is a feature of current accounts that banks do not usually pay interest on the balance, the surplus in the current account represents an idle resource. In these circumstances the business-man may consider transferring some of his surplus from the current account, where it earns no interest, into a deposit account, where it will earn interest. The book-keeping entries to record the transfer from current account to the deposit account are as follows.

As cash is transferred out of the current account, credit the current account and as cash is transferred into the deposit account, debit a bank deposit account.

Unlike the current account, a period of notice must be given to the bank before withdrawal from a deposit account takes place. The period of notice varies and will be the subject of an agree-ment between the bank and the depositor. Generally though, the higher the rate of interest earned, the longer will be the period of notice required.

Example. D. Patel found on 31 December that his cash in hand amounted to £80 and cash at bank on current account amounted to £3000. On this date he arranged to open a deposit account with a transfer from current account of £2500 (Example 11.8).

11.9   Bank Interest and Charges

If the business has an overdraft or loan from the bank it will be charged interest on the amount outstanding. Indeed, the firm will usually be charged by the bank for the maintenance of the current account. The bank will usually charge the firm by deducting the amount due from the current account. Interest payable and bank charges are a business expense and should be recorded in an expense account in the same way as any other expense.

Since interest and charges represent a deduction in current account balance (cash paid out) the current account should be credited with the interest on the overdraft account, interest on

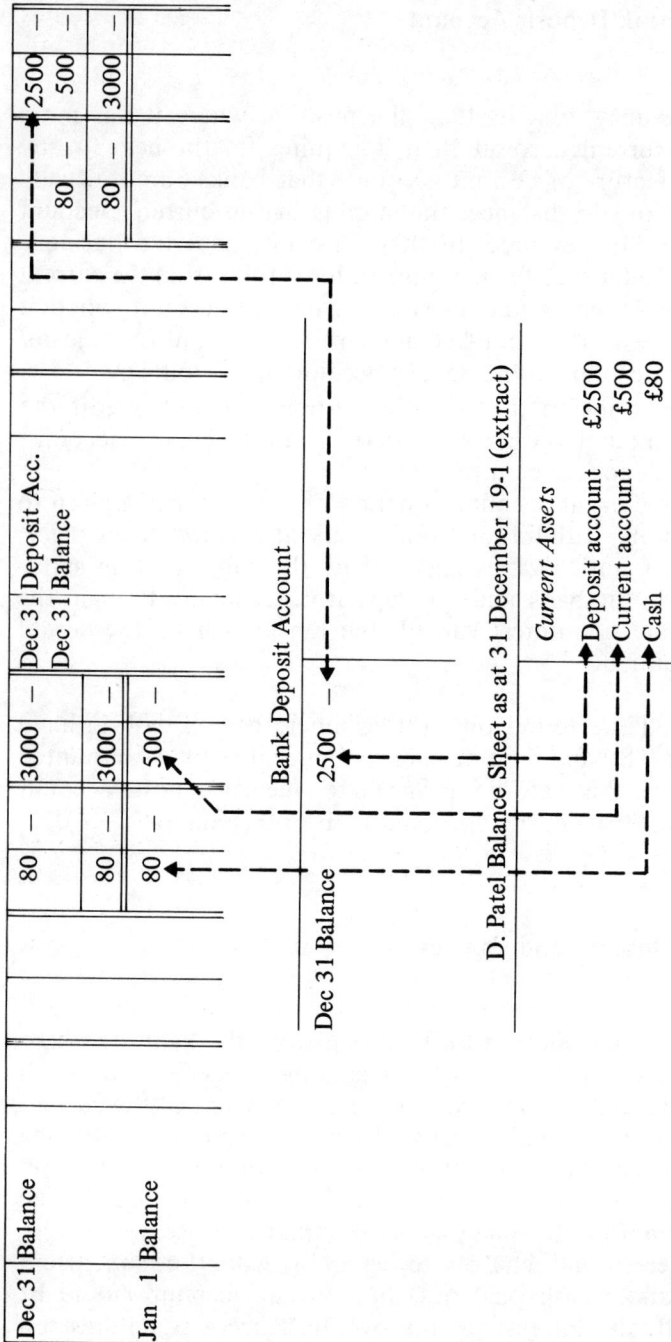

	80			2500	
Dec 31	Deposit Acc.			500	
Dec 31	Balance			3000	
	80			3000	

		80		3000	–
Dec 31 Balance		80		3000	–
Jan 1 Balance		80		500	–

Bank Deposit Account

Dec 31 Balance 2500

D. Patel Balance Sheet as at 31 December 19-1 (extract)

Current Assets

Deposit account	£2500
Current account	£500
Cash	£80

Example 11.8

the loan account; the bank charges account should be debited as appropriate. These expenses should be transferred to the profit and loss account at the end of the financial period in the same way as any other business expense.

Example. J. Evans's ledger on 31 December 19-1 showed that he had cash in hand £40, a balance on current account of £120, and a bank loan of £2000. On this date he received a statement from his bank which included bank charges £3 and interest on loan £15. (Example 11.9.)

Note. The bank may occasionally add the interest on a loan to the amount already outstanding. In this case the bank loan account rather than the current account should be credited. The debit entry under these circumstances should still appear in a bank interest account. An arrangement of this sort is rather unusual and unless there is information to the contrary you should assume that interest is charged to the current account.

Bank interest receivable

Where there is in existence a deposit account the business will be entitled to receive interest. The bank will periodically notify the firm of how much interest is receivable and the firm will then make the double entries to record this interest. Since interest receivable increases the balance at the bank the account should be debited and an interest receivable account should be credited. Usually interest receivable is added to the balance in the current account but occasionally it is added to the balance on the deposit account. You should assume that unless you have information to the contrary it is the current account which is affected, and therefore you should normally debit the current account rather than the deposit account.

Interest receivable and the profit and loss account

In a sense interest receivable is the opposite of interest payable and in the same way that the balance on the interest payable account is transferred to profit and loss so will be the balance on the interest receivable account. You will notice that the interest

Date	Particulars	Fol No.	Discount	Cash £ p	Bank £ p	Date	Particulars	Fol No.	Discount	Cash £ p	Bank £ p
Dec 31	Balance			40 —	120 —	Dec 31	Interest				15
						Dec 31	Charges				3
				40 —	120 —	Dec 31	Balance			40 —	102 —
Jan 1	Balance			40 —	102 —					40 —	120 —

BANK LOAN

Balance 2000

BANK INTEREST

Bank 15.00	Profit and Loss 15.00

BANK CHARGES

Bank 3.00	Profit and Loss 3.00

PROFIT AND LOSS ACCOUNT
FOR THE YEAR ENDING 31 DECEMBER 19-1
(EXTRACT)

Bank Interest 15	Gross Profit
Bank Charges 3	

Example 11.9

receivable account bears a credit balance. When this credit balance is transferred to the profit and loss account, providing that you follow the rules of double entry, you will notice that it will appear on the credit side of the profit and loss account, next to gross profit. Interest receivable then quite logically increases net profit.

Example. On 31 December 19-1 D. Jones' ledger shows cash in hand £80, cash at bank £200, deposit account £1500. On this date he receives from the bank a statement which shows that interest received in respect of his deposit account – £15 – had been added to his current account. (Example 11.10.)

11.10   Bank Reconciliation Statements

In the previous sections we have shown that when we receive a statement of account from the bank it may include certain items which have, until the time of the receipt of the statement, been unrecorded in our ledger. This means that the balance that the cash book shows and the balance that the statement from our bank shows will differ. It will be necessary to make sure that the difference is not a result of either an error on the part of the bank or an error on the business's books, but that the difference merely represents the omission from one or the other of the balances of items such as interest receivable, interest payable, bank charges. In other words, we will want to reconcile (make agree) the bank statement balance with the cash book balance. The way in which this reconciliation is carried out is discussed later. But we must first examine some other sources of differences between the cash book and bank statement and also the way in which the bank statement will be presented to us.

11.11   Standing Orders

If the business requires to make regular payments for an item such as rent, the business may save itself the trouble of remembering to write a cheque and send it to the landlord each month by making a standing order at the bank to pay rent. The bank will then automatically pay the landlord the same amount of money

CASH BOOK

Dec 31	Balance	80	—	200	—	Dec 31 Balance	80	—	215	—
Dec 31	Interest			15						
		80	—	215	—		80	—	215	—
	Balance	80	—	215	—					

DEPOSIT ACCOUNT

Dec 31 Balance   1500

INTEREST

Dec 31 Profit and Loss	15	Dec 31 Bank	15

PROFIT AND LOSS ACCOUNT
YEAR ENDING 31 DECEMBER 19-1
(EXTRACT)

Gross Profit
Interest received   15

Example 11.10

each month until further notice from the business. This means that since a cheque for rent is not prepared by the firm each month the rent paid will be unrecorded in the cash book. When the business receives its statement it will check that the rent has been paid correctly in accordance with instructions and then make the necessary double entries in the ledger.

11.12   Direct Debits

A direct debit is almost identical to a standing order except that it is used where the amount of the payment due varies from one period to the next, e.g. rates. In order to save the business the trouble of frequently altering the amount due on a standing order the business gives authority to the recipient of the payment to change the amount paid. A direct debit then is a standing order the amount of which can be altered by the receiver.

11.13   Credit Transfers

In the same way that payments may be made out of the business bank account without the direct knowledge of the business by means of direct debits and standing orders, the business may receive into its account revenue from a variety of sources in addition to interest receivable. The business may receive regular payments such as rent from property owned by the business and dividends from investments. When such items appear on the bank statement, after checking that the amounts are correct, the appropriate double entries should be made in the business ledger, i.e. debit cash book (bank column) and credit some other account such as rent receivable account, dividend from investment account, etc., as appropriate.

11.14   Cheques not yet Presented for Payment

When the business receives its statement we will frequently find that several cheques which we have already drawn in favour of our suppliers will be omitted from the statement. These cheques will be entered into the credit side of the cash book as they are drawn but there will be a delay in the payment being made out of the business account since: (a) the cheque has first to be delivered to the supplier; (b) the supplier may not pay the cheque into his account immediately; and (c) when the supplier pays the cheque into his bank it will take a few days to 'clear' the cheque, that is to say, it will take a few days for the supplier's bankers to present the cheque to the business's bankers for payment. The effect of cheques not yet presented for payment is to make the figure that appears as the balance on the bank statement appear larger than the figure which appears as the balance in the bank column of the cash book.

11.15 Cheques not yet Cleared

In a similar way that cheques recently drawn in favour of our suppliers may not appear on the bank statement, so may cheques recently received and paid into the business account from our customers be omitted from the bank statement. These cheques received will be entered in the business ledger as they are received but as with cheques not yet presented there may be a delay in the business presenting the cheque for payment at our customer's bank. The business's bank will not enter into our account amounts received from customers until the bank has actually received the transfer from the customer's account. The effect of cheques not yet cleared will be that the figure which appears as the balance on the bank statement will be smaller than the figure which appears as the balance in the business cash book.

11.16 The Bank Statement

We have seen that under normal circumstances (with no overdrafts) the bank is the business's debtor, i.e. the bank owes money to the firm. Looking at this relationship from the bank's point of view the business is the bank's creditor. Since the bank produces its statement of account from its own point of view the business account will be a 'mirror' version of the business bank book. Cheques paid into the bank appear as a credit, cheques paid out appear as debits and under normal circumstances show a credit balance. Bank statements are usually prepared by machine and use the more modern layout of the ledger with a cash column for debits, a cash column for credits and a column for a running balance. This layout is illustrated in Fig. 11.5.

11.17   Bank Statement and Cash Book Compared

The cash book which relates to the above statement may appear as shown below. For the sake of simplicity only the bank columns are shown:

CASH BOOK (BANK COLUMNS)

May 30	Balance		321	81	June 2	E. Elder		45	60
June 12	Cash		50	—	June 2	A. Oak		23	24
June 13	B. Green		33	90	June 3	B. Elm		63	90
June 25	A. Red		40	—	June 7	C. Ash		45	20
June 26	B. Blue		15	20	June 8	D. Rowan		33	90
					June 9	E. May		46	28
					June 10	F. Holly		35	20
					June 12	D. Yew		36	28
					June 16	B. Elm		23	90
					June 17	H. Privet		19	80
					June 26	Balance		87	61
			460	91				460	91
June 27	Balance		87	61					

Notes to bank balance and cash book

1. You will notice that the amounts which appear in the debit side of the cash book appear in the credit column in the bank statement and vice versa.
2. The amounts are not necessarily in the same order in the bank statement as they are in the cash book.

FIRM'S
NAME AND
ADDRESS

839241
A. Smith Ltd.,
198 Lavender Drive,   In account with
Wembley,   Grasping's Bank Ltd
Middx.
                       WEMBLEY

Date	Details	Debit	Credit	Balance
30 May	Balance Forward			321.81
4 June	893291	45.60		276.21
8 June	893289	23.24		252.97
9 June	893290	63.90		189.07
11 June	893294	33.90		155.17
11 June	893292	45.20		109.97
12 June	D/V Cash/Cheque		50.00	159.97
13 June	Cheque		33.90	193.87
14 June	893295	46.28		147.59
14 June	893296	35.20		112.39
15 June	I.C.I. Dividend		24.30	136.69
17 June	Interest on deposit		33.20	169.89
21 June	893298	36.28		133.61
23 June	D.D.Wembley C.C.	13.00		120.61
24 June	Charges	3.00		117.61
25 June	S.O. Ruby Insurance	2.00		115.61

Abbreviations   **D.D.** Direct Debit **S.O.** Standing Order **D.V.** Dividend

DATE OF TRANSACTION
(DATED ACCORDING
TO THE DAY OF
ENTRY INTO
BANK'S LEDGER)

DETAILS
(USUALLY JUST
CHEQUE NUMBERS
IN THE CASE
OF DRAWINGS)

DEBITS

CREDITS

BALANCE OF
ACCOUNT
AFTER EACH
TRANSACTION

Figure 11.5   *Analysis of a bank statement*

3. Certain items which appear in the cash book are not recorded in the bank statement and vice versa.
4. The closing balances differ.

Adjusting the cash book balance

As we know when the bank statement is received and compared with the cash book there will appear several items which do not tally between the two. As an aid to identifying these sources of difference those items which *can be agreed* should be marked with a small tick in both the bank statement and the cash book. In the example shown in Fig. 11.6 those items which remain un-ticked after this process have been circled.

The items which remain unticked in the bank statement should consist of bank charges, direct debits, standing orders, and credit transfers. When these amounts have been checked they should be entered in the ledger in the way described previously. This means that in the above example the cash book will be credited with bank charges (£3.00), standing order (£2.00) and direct debit (£13.00), reducing the cash book's debit balance by a total of £18.00 and that the cash book will then be debited with the credit transfer from ICI (£24.30) and interest received on deposit account (£33.20) increasing the cash book debit balance by a total of £57.50. The corrected cash book balance is therefore:

Calculation of cash book balance

						£	£
Unadjusted cash book balance as at 27 June							87.61
Less	Bank charges	..	..	..	..	3.00	
	Standing order	..	..	..	..	2.00	
	Direct debit	..	..	..	..	13.00	18.00
							69.61
Add	Credit transfers						
	ICI dividend	..	..	..	..	24.30	
	Interest on deposit	..	..	..	..	33.20	
							57.50
Adjusted cash book balance							127.11

Date	Details	Debit	Credit	Balance
30 May	Balance Forward			321.81 ✓
4 June	893291	45.60 ✓		276.21
8 June	893289	23.24 ✓		252.97
9 June	893290	63.90 ✓		189.07
11 June	893294	33.90 ✓		155.17
11 June	893292	45.20 ✓		109.97
12 June	D/V Cash/Cheque		50.00 ✓	159.97
13 June	Cheque		33.90 ✓	193.87
14 June	893295	46.28 ✓		147.59
14 June	893296	35.20 ✓		112.39
15 June	I.C.I. Dividend		(24.30)	136.69
17 June	Interest on deposit		(33.20)	169.89
21 June	893298	36.28 ✓		133.61
23 June	D.D.Wembley C.C.	(13.00)		120.61
24 June	Charges	(3.00)		117.61
25 June	S.O. Ruby Insurance	(2.00)		115.61

839241
A. Smith Ltd.,
198 Lavender Drive,
Wembley,
Middx.

In account with
Grasping's Bank Ltd

WEMBLEY

Abbreviations   **D.D.** Direct Debit **S.O.** Standing Order **D.V.** Dividend

Cash Book (Bank Columns)

MAY	30	BALANCE	321	81 ✓	JUNE	2	E. ELDER	45	60 ✓
JUNE	12	CASH	50	– ✓	JUNE	2	A. OAK	23	24 ✓
JUNE	13	B. GREEN	33	90 ✓	JUNE	3	B. ELM	63	90 ✓
JUNE	25	A. RED	(40)	–	JUNE	7	C. ASH	45	20 ✓
JUNE	26	B. BLUE	(15	20)	JUNE	8	D. ROWAN	33	90 ✓
					JUNE	9	E. MAY	46	28 ✓
					JUNE	10	F. HOLLY	35	20 ✓
					JUNE	12	D. YEW	36	28 ✓
					JUNE	16	B. ELM	(23	90)
					JUNE	17	H. PRIVET	(19	80)
					JUNE	26	BALANCE	87	61
			460	91				460	91
JUNE	27	BALANCE	87	61					

Figure 11.6 *Bank statement and cash book compared*

The adjusted cash book then appears as follows:

CASH BOOK (BANK COLUMNS)

May 30	Balance		321	81	June 2	E. Elder			45	60
June 12	Cash		50	–	June 2	A. Oak			23	24
June 13	B. Green		33	90	June 3	B. Elm			63	90
June 25	A. Red		40	–	June 7	C. Ash			45	20
June 26	B. Blue		15	20	June 8	D. Rowan			33	90
					June 9	E. May			46	28
					June 10	F. Holly			35	20
					June 12	D. Yew			36	28
					June 16	B. Elm			23	90
					June 17	H. Privet			19	80
					June 26	Balance			87	61
			460	91					460	91
June 27	Balance		87	61	June 27	Rates				
June 27	Dividend on					(Wembley CC)			13	–
	Statement		24	30	June 27	Bank Charges			3	–
June 27	Interest on				June 27	Insurance			2	–
	Deposit		33	20	June 27	Balance			127	11
			145	11					145	11
Balance			127	11						

11.18   The Reconciliation Statement

Having brought the cash book up to date the balance (£127.11) will still vary from that which appears on the bank statement (£115.61) by a difference represented by the unticked items in the cash book, i.e. cheques not yet presented for payment (Elm £23.90, Privet £19.80) and cheques not yet cleared (Red £40.00, Blue £15.20). The bank reconciliation statement is not part of the double entry system, and merely says 'this is the balance which the cash book shows', 'this is the balance which the bank statement shows', 'the difference between these two figures can be accounted for by these items'. The layout which we adopt for the statement is shown below and reconciles the two statements in the example above.

A. SMITH LTD

BANK RECONCILIATION STATEMENT AS AT 27 JUNE 19—

		£	£
Balance as per bank statement		–	115.61
Add *Cheques* not yet cleared			
	A. Red	40.00	
	B. Blue	15.20	
			55.20
			170.81
Less *Cheques* not yet passed for payment			
	B. Elm	23.90	
	M. Privet	19.80	
			43.70
BALANCE AS PER CASH BOOK			127.11

Notes to reconciliation statement

1. Two sub-headings and the relevant sub-totals appear on the statement for the two different classes of items.
2. If the balance as per cash book differs from that which is calculated in the reconciliation statement, an error has occurred either in the bank reconciliation statement or the cash book or the bank statement. This error must be found and corrected.

ASSIGNMENTS

A11.1 Jan 1   D. Peters started business with £2000.00 in cash

Jan 2   He opened a current account at bank paying in £1900.00

Jan 3   Bought goods paid cash £50.00

Jan 4   Bought goods paid for by cheque £110.00

Jan 5   Cash sales £200.00

Jan 6   Sales paid by cheque £190.00

Jan 7   Paid cash into bank £150.00

Jan 8   Paid electricity bill by cheque £80.00

Jan 9   Cash sales £80.00

Jan 10 A. Red, a customer, settled his outstanding account by cheque £120.00

Jan 11 Paid wages by cheque £120.00

Jan 12 Drew cash for self £20.00

Enter the above transactions into D. Peter's cash book, balance and rule off. Do *not* make double entries.

A11.2 Enter the following transactions into J. Finn's cash book. Do *not* make double entries to ledger accounts.

Jan 1   J. Finn started business with capital in cash £12 000.00

Jan 2   Opened a current account at the bank paying in £11 500.00

Jan 3   Bought premises paid by cheque £7500.00

Jan 4   Bought goods paid cash £250.00

Jan 4   Cash sales £300.00

Jan 5   Bought goods paid by cheque £120.00

Jan 6   Received cheque from D. Smith, a customer, £35.00

Jan 7   Cash sales £400.00

Jan 8   Paid cash into bank £620.00

Jan 9   Took cash for personal use £20.00

Jan 10 Bought goods paid by cheque £10.00

Jan 11 Paid wages by cheque £150.00

Jan 12 Cash sales £45.00
Jan 13 Paid J. Johnson, a supplier, £15.00 by cheque
Jan 14 Bought motor van paid by cheque £150.00

Balance cash book, carry down balance, continue:

Jan 15 Bought additional premises paid by cheque £5000.00
Jan 16 Cash sales £20.00
Jan 17 Withdrew cash from bank for office use £30.00
Jan 18 Bought stationery by cheque £40.00
Jan 19 Bought goods paid cash £100.00
Jan 20 Cash sales £150.00
Jan 21 D. Finch (a customer) paid his account £30.00 by cheque

Balance the cash book and carry down the balance.

A11.3   A. Portley started business on Jan 1 with the following assets:

	£
Premises	10 000
Motor van	500
Equipment	200
Stock	50
Cash at bank	1 100
Cash in hand	250

Calculate his capital and open his ledger accounts and record the following transactions.

Jan 2 Bought goods from B. Elm £80.00 on credit
Jan 3 Bought goods from A. Oak £90.00 on credit
Jan 4 Cash sales £60.00
Jan 5 Sold goods to A. Red £90.00 on credit
Jan 6 Paid B. Elm £80.00 by cheque
Jan 7 Paid wages by cheque £30.00
Jan 8 Cash sales £90.00
Jan 9 A. Red paid £50.00 on account by cheque
Jan 10 Cash sales £30.00
Jan 12 Paid cleaner by cash £10.00
Jan 14 Cash sales £30.00

(a)   Balance the cash book.
(b)   Extract a trial balance.
(c)   Produce a trading and profit and loss account for the two weeks. (Stock at close valued at cost £85.00.)
(d)   Produce a balance sheet as at Jan 14.

A11.4   J. Wood's bank statement shows a balance at the bank of £320. A comparison with his cash book reveals the following:

(a)   Cheques drawn by Wood in favour of his suppliers not yet presented for payment:

      A. Oak   £35
      B. Elm   £25
      C. Ash   £40

(b)   Cheques recently paid into Wood's account at the same bank but not recorded on the statement:

      A. Red   £20
      B. Blue   £40
      C. Yellow   £25

Calculate by producing a bank reconciliation statement the balance on J. Wood's cash book.

A11.5   K. Roads' bank statement balance and cash book balance disagree. A closer examination reveals:

(a)   The following items appear on the bank statement but not in his cash book:

      Bank charges £3.00
      Rent paid by standing order £14.00
      Interest on deposit account received £23.00

(b)   The following items appear in his cash book but not on his bank statement:

      Cheques paid out not yet presented amounted to £53.00
      Cheques received not yet cleared from payment £92.00

If his cash book balance appeared prior to any adjustments as £1429.00 what was the balance on the bank statement?

Draw up a bank reconciliation statement for K. Roads.

12. Journals

In practice the book-keeper of a business will gather his information from a variety of sources. Two of the most important sources of information will be those documents which relate to credit sales and credit purchases. These will consist of copies of invoices sent to credit customers in the case of credit sales, and invoices received from suppliers demanding payment for goods purchased on credit.

12.1 Dealing with Suppliers' Invoices

When goods are purchased on credit from suppliers the information for the ledger entries will be taken from the suppliers' invoices. The book-keeping entries will be:

Debit purchases account — credit suppliers' personal accounts

with invoiced amount

Many businesses may receive hundreds of invoices from their suppliers each day and if both the debit and credit entry for each individual invoice is separately made, the process of entering credit purchases into the ledger will be slow and laborious. In order to speed the process many businesses make use of a purchases journal in addition to the ledger and then adopt the following procedure for credit purchases:

1. Details of invoices from suppliers are copied into the journal (this will represent a listing of credit purchases and is not a ledger entry).
2. Details of the value purchased from suppliers are credited individually to the personal account of the supplier from the journal on a daily basis. (This will represent many relatively small credit entries each day.)
3. At the end of each week (or other convenient time period) the purchases journal is totalled and the total is entered in the debit side of the purchases account. (The total of the journal debit to the purchases account will equal the sum of the individual entries made to the credit of the individual suppliers' accounts – so the double entry is completed in summary and the books balance at the end of each week.)

This procedure (outlined in Fig. 12.1) represents a more efficient way of making entries into the ledger in respect of credit purchases since:

1. The task of making entries into the ledger is broken up into simple component parts, each of which can be carried out by people with little specialist book-keeping knowledge.

    (a) Copying invoice details into the purchases journal would normally be the task of a fairly junior employee with very little knowledge or experience.

    (b) Making the ledger entries in the suppliers' personal accounts from the journal is a fairly simple and repetitive task requiring little more of the employee than above.

    (c) The weekly totalling and entering into the purchases account of the purchases journal total represents a clear saving in the number of entries and therefore the amount of time spent making individual entries in the purchases account.

2. The process of specializing ledger tasks will eventually facilitate more than one person working on the ledger at one time.

12.2 Making Journal Entries – Purchases Journal

An example of the type of ruling used for journals is shown on page 136. Since one of the functions of the journals is to describe more fully the entries which take place in the ledger and not to form part of the ledger, you will notice that there is not a debit side and credit side, merely columns for date, particulars, folio numbers and two cash columns.

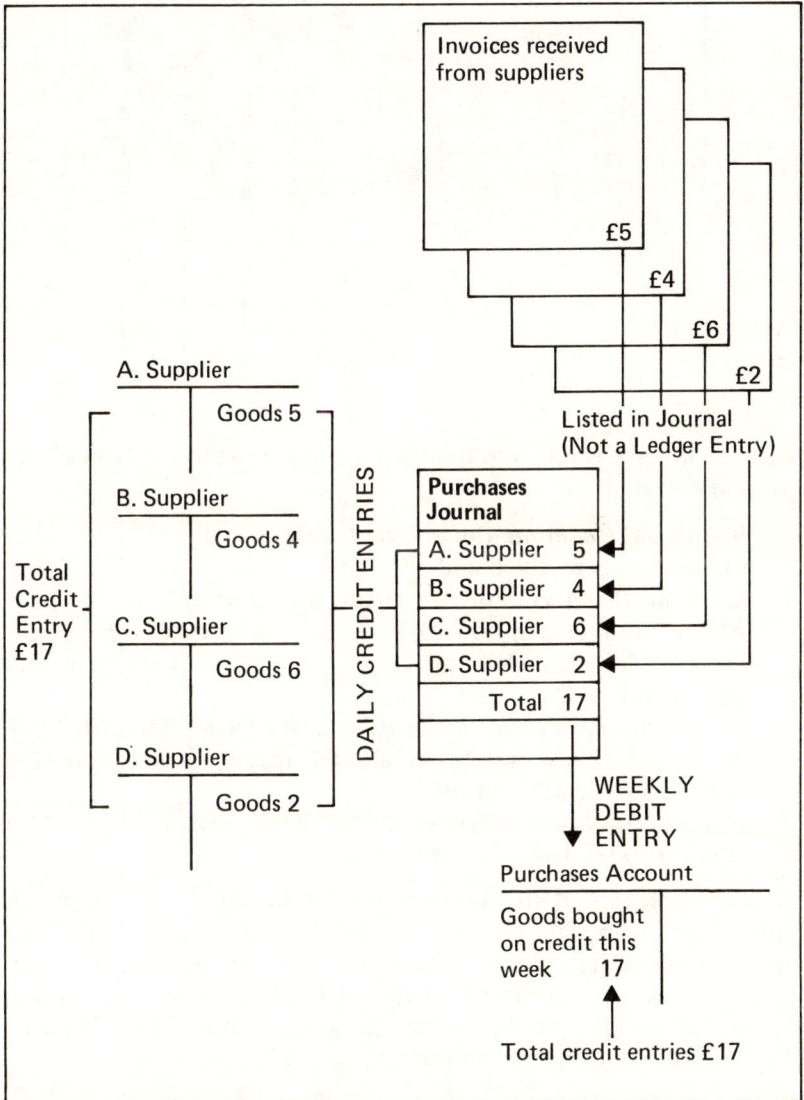

Figure 12.1 *The use of the purchases journal*

Date	Particulars	Fol No.	£	p	£	p

As each invoice is received a separate entry is made in the purchases journal showing:

1. *In the date column* the relevant date, usually the date when the invoice is received and entered.
2. *In the particulars column* the name and address of the supplier. Also a brief description of each type of article purchased — separate line for each different type. This description may also include price.
3. *In the first cash column* the total cost of each kind of article purchased. These sub-totals should appear on the same line as the relevant description.
4. *In the second cash column* the total invoice value, i.e. the total amount to be paid to the supplier.

It is important that the amount due to the supplier — the whole total — only appears in the second cash column since: (a) this is the amount which the supplier's account will be credited with; and (b) this column must be totalled for the purpose of entering total credit purchases to the purchases account. You will notice that no folio numbers are entered at this stage.

The example below shows how an invoice may appear in the purchases journal of A. Byer:

No. B00031	INVOICE						
A. Byer					53 Lavender Hill		
103 Canterbury Road					Wembley		
Caterham					Middx		
Surrey				VAT No. 8394876			
				1st Feb 19–1			
Bought of J. Celler							
Terms:							

Qty	Description	Price		Item		Total	
10	Size 12 Grommit Extractors		69	6	90		
15	Size 15 Lue Loppers	1	20	18	00		
20	Size 28 Rebate Rippers	1	12	22	40		
						47	30

PURCHASES JOURNAL

Date	Particulars	Fol No.	Details		Total	
Feb 5	J. Celler 53 Lavender Hill Wembley					
	10 size 12 Grommit Extractors @ £0.69		6	90		
	15 size 15 Lue Loppers @ £1.20		18	–		
	20 size 28 Rebate Rippers @ £1.12		22	40		
					47	30
Feb 5	Z. Callit 86 The Mail Croydon					
	5 Tyre Levers @ £0.30		1	50		
	6 Oil Valves @ £0.25		1	50		
	10 Pressure Hoppers @ £3.20		32	–		
					35	–
Feb 5	J. Losemore 5 Railway Cuttings					

Note. As an alternative to the above some businesses stamp incoming invoices with sequential numbers and merely note in the journal the date, name of the supplier, relevant sequential number and the invoice total. The invoices are then carefully filed and the sequential number which appears in the journal can be used for referencing the invoice should the description be required at a later date.

12.3   From Journal to Ledger — Suppliers' Account

The purchases journal as we know represents a listing of goods purchased on credit. The details which appear in the journal must subsequently be entered into the ledger, a process sometimes called *posting*. The person who is responsible for the accounts of creditors will at the end of each day take the relevant page of the purchases journal and credit the account of each named supplier with the amount which appears in the invoice total column. As he makes each entry he will enter into the purchases journal the folio number of the supplier's account where he has made the entry to show that the entry has been made. The folio numbers which appear in the personal ledger accounts will reference the relevant page number of the purchases journal.

```
J. Celler    Page 10
                    Feb 5 Goods PJ12 £47.30
                    Feb 7 Goods PJ12 £29.30


Z. Callit    Page 14
                    Feb 5 Goods PJ12  £35.00
                    Feb 6 Goods PJ12  £36.50


J. Losemore    Page 16
                    Feb 5 Goods PJ12    £8.00


B. Cauller    Page 20
                    Feb 6 Goods PJ12 £14.00
```

As can be seen from the above example, at the end of this stage credit entries only have been made in the ledger.

	PURCHASES JOURNAL					
			Page 12			
Feb 5		c/f			125	–
Feb 5	J. Celler 53 Lavender Hill Wembley					
	10 size 12 Grommit Extractors @ £0.69		6	90		
	15 size 15 Lue Loppers @ £1.20		18	–		
	20 size 28 Rebate Rippers @ £1.12		22	40		
		10			47	30
Feb 5	Z. Callit 86 The Mall Croydon					
	5 Tyre Levers @ £0.30		1	50		
	6 Oil Valves @ £0.25		1	50		
	10 Pressure Hoppers @ £3.20		32	–		
		14			35	–
Feb 5	J. Losemore 5 Railway Cuttings					
	10 size 15 Grommit Extractors @ £0.80		8	–		
		16			8	–
Feb 6	B. Cauller The Pit Clapham					
	10 size 15 Grommit Extractors @ £0.80		8	–		
	10 size 10 Grommit Extractors @ £0.60		6	–		
		20			14	–
Feb 6	Z. Callit 86 The Mall Croydon					
	15 Tyre Levers @ £0.30		4	50		
	10 size 15 Lue Loppers @ £1.20		12	–		
	10 size 20 Lue Loppers @ £2.00		20	–		
		14			36	50
Feb 7	J. Celler 53 Lavender Hill Wembley					
	10 size 12 Grommit Extractors @ £0.69		6	90		
	10 size 28 Rebate Rippers @ £1.12		22	40		
		10			29	30

This account credited with this amount

12.4   From Journal to Ledger — the Purchases Account

In order to complete the double entries for the many small credit entries in suppliers' accounts at the end of the week, the purchases journal is totalled and posted to the debit side of the purchases account:

				PURCHASES JOURNAL		Page 12			
				c/f				125	–
Feb 5	J. Celler 53 Lavender Hill Wembley								
					6	90			
					18	–			
					22	40			
								47	30
Feb 7	J. Celler 53 Lavender Hill Wembley								
	10 size 12 Grommit Extractors @ £0.69				6	90			
	10 size 28 Rebate Rippers @ £1.12				22	40			
				10				29	30
				5				295	10

PURCHASES ACCOUNT   Page 5

Goods bought on credit this week 295.10	

Total of purchases journal including previous pages carried forward debited to purchases account

The summary of procedure for credit purchases:

1. Details of invoices entered into purchases journal.
2. Individual credit entries made from purchases journal to suppliers' personal accounts.

3. One large debit entry — the total of the purchases journal — is made to the debit of the purchases accounts.

Other names of purchases journal:

> purchases daybook
> bought daybook
> bought journal

Cash paid to suppliers and cash purchases will be entered into the ledger in the same way as usual, i.e. directly entered into the cash book and suppliers' or purchases account.

12.5 Dealing with Customers' Invoices — the Sales Journal

In the same way that the use of a purchases journal can improve the efficiency of the book-keeping process in respect of credit purchases, the use of a sales journal will aid entries related to credit sales. The principle of listing in the journal and posting to the ledger is the same but since, in the case of copies of the business invoices sent to customers, we are dealing with credit sales, the sides of the entries are opposite. The method of using the sales journal in conjunction with the ledger is contrasted with the use of purchases journals below (Fig. 12.2):

Summary of procedure for credit sales:

1. Details of invoices sent to customers entered into sales journal.
2. Individual debit entries made from sales journal to customer's personal account.
3. One large credit entry — the total of the sales journal — is made to the credit of the sales account.

Other names for the sales journal:

> sales daybook
> daybook
> sales book

Cash received from customers and cash sales will be entered into the ledger in the same way as usual, i.e. directly into the cash book and the customers' or sales account.

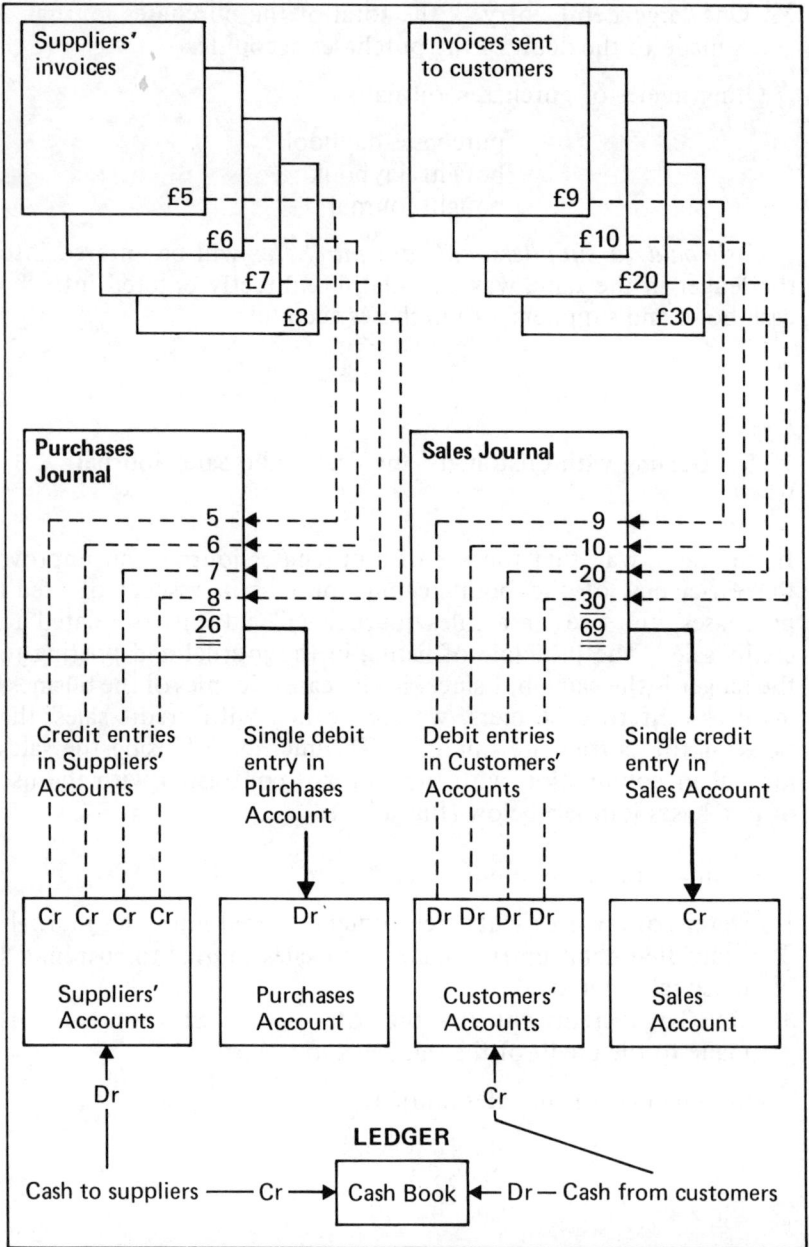

Figure 12.2 *The use of the sales journal in conjunction with the ledger contrasted with the use of the purchases journal*

12.6   Goods Returned

Sales returns

It may be that a business occasionally has returned to it goods which were sold but were subsequently found to be not of the quality demanded or faulty in some way. If the complaint is just-ified, the business will have no choice but to either make a refund, if originally a cash sale, or issue a credit note in the case of a credit sale.

Cash sales returns

When goods are sold for cash the ledger entries are: debit the cash account and credit the sales account.

Example. Goods were sold for cash to a customer on Jan 10, £30.

CASH BOOK	SALES
Jan 10 Sales 30.00	Jan 10 Cash 30.00

In a sense if these goods are subsequently returned and a refund made, the book-keeping entries should be a reversal of the former entries.

Example. Some of the goods sold to the customer on Jan 10 were subsequently returned and £5 was refunded to the customer on Jan 12.

CASH BOOK		SALES	
Jan 10 Sales 30.00	Jan 12 Sales 5.00	Jan 12 Cash 5.00	Jan 10 Cash 30.00

Goods sold on Jan 10   Goods returned Jan 12

The ledger entries above have the correct effect on the accounting records in as much as the returns reduce the cash balance and the sales account balance by £5. However, making entries in this way infringes the book-keeping rules, which state that each different class of transaction must have a separate account. Since goods which are returned are not sales but sales returned, the correct ledger entries for cash sales returned are: *credit cash book* and *debit sales returns account* so that the ledger in the above example appears as shown below.

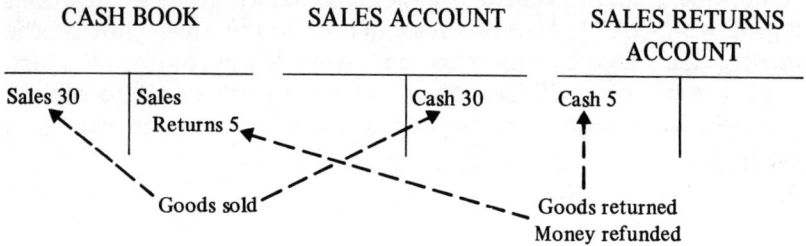

CASH BOOK		SALES ACCOUNT	SALES RETURNS ACCOUNT
Sales 30	Sales Returns 5	Cash 30	Cash 5
	Goods sold		Goods returned Money refunded

Credit sales returned

When a credit customer returns goods, instead of refunding cash, the business usually issues a credit note. The ledger entries required to record this are similar to those illustrated above but since no cash has been refunded the credit entry cannot appear in the cash book, but must instead appear in the customer's personal account.

Example. On Jan 1, a business sold to B. Fare goods for £55 on credit. On Jan 4, B. Fare returned £20 of these goods damaged in transit. A credit note was duly issued.

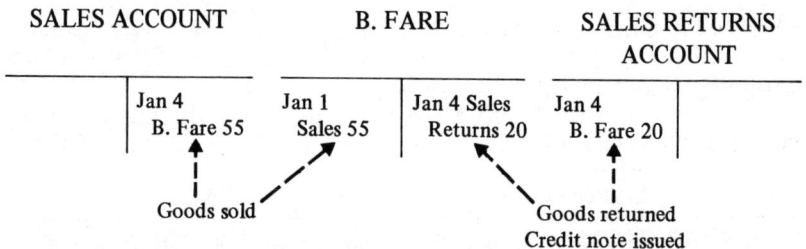

SALES ACCOUNT	B. FARE		SALES RETURNS ACCOUNT
Jan 4 B. Fare 55	Jan 1 Sales 55	Jan 4 Sales Returns 20	Jan 4 B. Fare 20
Goods sold			Goods returned Credit note issued

Even if B. Fare had in the intervening period paid the full amount (£55), the entries to record the issue of the credit note are correct. This may, of course, mean that in the short term B. Fare's account will have a credit balance but this credit balance will be off-set by goods which are subsequently purchased by him.

12.7 Purchases Returns

In the same way that a business's customer may from time to time return goods, the business itself may have occasion to return goods to suppliers – *purchases returns*. In such a situation the ledger entries required are similar to those relating to sales returns and depend upon whether the cash is returned or a credit note issued.

In either case a 'purchases returned account' should be credited and either the cash book (if cash is returned) or the supplier's personal account (if a credit note is issued) should be debited. This is illustrated in the following example.

Example 1. On 1 June a business purchased goods for cash £80. It was subsequently found that a proportion of the goods were defective and on 5 June they were returned in exchange for £20.

CASH BOOK	PURCHASES ACCOUNT	PURCHASES RETURNS ACCOUNT

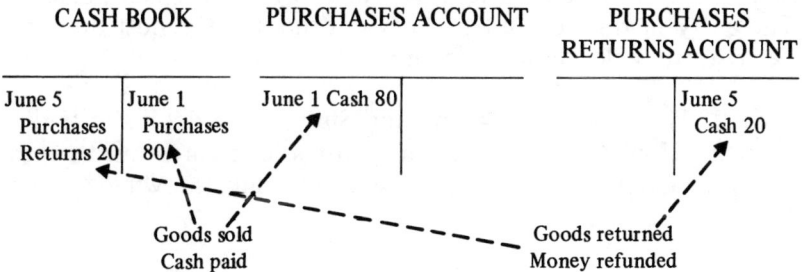

Example 2. On 1 August a business purchased goods from I. Dunyoo on credit for £90. On 6 August £25 of these goods were returned as defective and a credit note issued.

PURCHASES ACCOUNT	I. DUNYOO	PURCHASES RETURNS

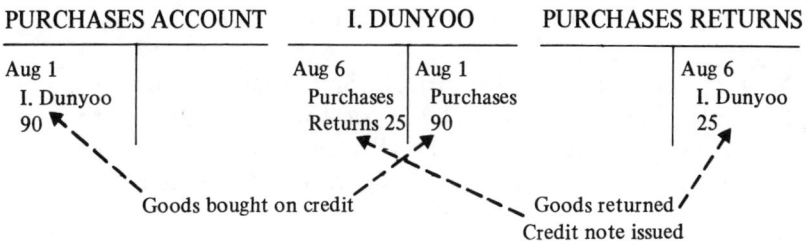

It makes no difference to the ledger entries recording the returned goods if I. Dunyoo has in the intervening time been paid, although it does, of course, mean that his account is temporarily thrown into a debit balance.

12.8   Returns and the Trading Account

As we know the trading account should contain all items which relate to gross profit. Both purchases returns and sales returns affect gross profit, since the effect of sales returned is to reduce the quantity of goods sold and the effect of purchases returns is to affect the quantity of goods purchased. These effects must be shown in the trading account by transferring the balance of these accounts to the trading account at the end of the accounting period. The transfer of these accounts should be done in the following way.

Sales returns

Step 1. The sales returns account will always show a debit balance. The entry in this account to carry out the transfer must therefore be credit the sales returns account.

Step 2. The logical follow-on from Step 1 is to debit the trading account. However, the debit entry for sales returns must appear as a deduction from sales in the credit side, showing a single figure as net sales.

Purchases returns

Step 1. The purchases returns account will always show a credit balance. An entry in this account to carry out the transfer must therefore be: debit the purchases returns account.

Step 2. The logical follow-on from Step 1 is to credit the trading account. However, the credit entry for purchases returns must appear as a deduction from the purchases in the debit side of the trading account, showing a single figure as net purchases.

Example

SALES RETURNS ACCOUNT		PURCHASES RETURNS ACCOUNT	
Dec 31 Balance 50	Dec 31 Trading Account 50	Dec 31 Trading Account 80	Dec 31 Balance 80

TRADING ACCOUNT FOR THE YEAR ENDING 31 DECEMBER 19–1

Stock at Start		100	Sales	5800	
Add Purchases	4500				
			† Sales Returns	50	5750
Less Purchases					
Returns	80	4420			
		4520			
Less Stock at Close		100			
Cost of Sales		4420			
Gross Profit		1330			
		5750			5750

*An entry on the debit side as a deduction has the same effect as a credit entry.

†An entry on the credit side as a deduction has the same effect as a debit entry.

12.9 Purchases Returns Journals

In the same way that a business may make use of journals for recording large numbers of credit purchases and credit sales, the business may initially record purchases returned and sales returned in a 'purchases returns journal' and 'sales returns journal' respectively. These returns journals will be concerned with returns where the original transactions were on credit and will have as their source of information either credit notes received from suppliers or copies of credit notes sent to customers. Their method of use is as follows:

SALES RETURNS
JOURNAL

PURCHASES RETURNS
JOURNAL

As credit notes are sent to customers the relevant details are recorded in the sales returns journal

As credit notes are received from suppliers the relevant details are recorded in the purchases returns journal

These journal entries are copied out in exactly the same way as the journal entries are made in the purchases journal and sales journal, except that they should in addition include a brief description of the reason for the return

Each day the relevant amounts are posted to the *credit side* of the particular *customers' accounts*
(Many small credit entries in the ledger)

Each day the relevant amounts are posted to the *debit side* of the particular *suppliers' accounts*

(Many small debit entries in the ledger)

Single entry in ledger made at this stage

At the end of the week (or other convenient period) the total of the sales returns journal is posted to the *debit side* of the *sales returns account*
(One big debit entry)

At the end of the week (or other convenient period) the total of the purchases returns journal is posted to the *credit side* of the *purchases returns account*
(One big credit entry)

Double entry completed

ASSIGNMENTS

A12.1   The following details relate to A. Bird's credit purchases for the first two weeks of January. The essential details of his suppliers' invoices have been listed below. You should list these details (date, supplier's name, invoice number, amount payable) in A. Bird's journal. Use a separate sheet of journal paper for each week. You should in addition post, at the end of each day, the entries to the relevant supplier's personal account and at the end of each week post the total to the purchases account.

Date	Supplier	Invoice Number	Amount Payable
Week 1			
Jan 1	A. Wren	001	23.40
Jan 1	B. Sparrow	002	43.90
Jan 1	C. Snipe	003	24.30
Jan 2	D. Eagle	004	12.30
Jan 2	E. Pigeon	005	13.90
Jan 2	F. Crow	006	43.90
Jan 3	B. Sparrow	007	12.30
Jan 4	D. Eagle	008	14.20
Jan 6	A. Wren	009	12.30
Jan 6	B. Sparrow	010	14.50
Week 2			
Jan 8	A. Wren	011	12.30
Jan 8	B. Sparrow	012	14.90
Jan 8	D. Eagle	013	18.20
Jan 10	A. Wren	014	25.90
Jan 10	E. Swift	015	14.90
Jan 10	C. Snipe	016	12.90
Jan 11	D. Eagle	017	14.20
Jan 12	E. Pigeon	018	28.90
Jan 13	B. Sparrow	019	14.20

A12.2   The following details relate to Q. Fish's credit sales for the first two weeks of January. The essential details of the invoices sent to customers are shown below. You should list these details (date, customer's name, invoice number, amount payable,) in Q. Fish's sales journal, posting each day to the relevant customer's account and each week to the sales account.

Date	Customer	Invoice Number	Amount
Week 1			
Jan 2	A. Trout	001	53.90
Jan 2	B. Bream	002	42.80
Jan 2	C. Pike	003	63.80
Jan 2	D. Rudd	004	75.63
Jan 2	E. Roach	005	82.90
Jan 3	B. Bream	006	7.00
Jan 3	C. Pike	007	12.90
Jan 4	A. Trout	008	14.20
Jan 4	D. Rudd	009	15.30
Jan 5	E. Roach	010	24.30
Week 2			
Jan 8	B. Bream	011	15.00
Jan 8	C. Pike	012	16.20
Jan 8	D. Rudd	013	12.30
Jan 8	E. Roach	014	14.90
Jan 9	C. Pike	015	16.35
Jan 10	B. Bream	016	14.35

13. Divisions of the ledger and book-keeping with computers

13.1 The Ledger Divisions

Although the cash book may be physically separated from the rest of the ledger and may indeed be kept in a separate location, it is still part of the double-entry system. Since the remaining ledger may eventually contain hundreds perhaps thousands of separate accounts, it may itself be split up into sections, each section containing a separate classification of accounts. The way in which these subdivisions of the ledger are made will vary from firm to firm but the most commonly adopted subdivisions are those which follow.

Debtors ledger

Very often the greatest volume of ledger accounts are the personal accounts of customers. Businesses find it useful to keep all these personal accounts of customers together in a separate subdivision of the ledger called the debtors ledger. The debtors ledger may be referred to as the sales ledger since it will contain a great deal of information which relates to goods sold on credit to customers, but you should note that the sales account itself does not appear in the sales or debtors ledger but remains in the general ledger. If the number of personal accounts of customers is very large indeed, it may itself be subdivided into sections either alphabetically (A-D,

E-G, H-L, etc.); by area (South-East, Midlands, East Anglia, etc.) or some other convenient method of classification.

Creditors ledger

In the same way that the accounts of customers may occupy a separate section of the ledger if the business deals with a large number of separate credit suppliers, it may be convenient to place all the personal accounts of suppliers together into a subdivision of the ledger called the creditors ledger. This subdivision is sometimes referred to as the purchases ledger but does not contain the purchases account itself. The creditors ledger may also be subdivided alphabetically or geographically or some other way.

General ledger

The general ledger can be regarded as those accounts which remain after the separation of the cash book, debtors ledger and creditors ledger. The general ledger may be subdivided into nominal ledger and private ledger.

Private ledger

Accounts which appear in the private ledger are accounts of fixed assets such as premises and motor vans, and long-term liabilities such as long-term loans and capital. The accounts which normally appear in the private ledger are those which normally record capital expenditure or receipts.

Private or nominal ledger

The rule to use to decide if an account should appear in the private or nominal ledger is: if the account appears in the trading or the profit and loss account it should be in the nominal ledger. If the account appears in the *balance sheet* only it should be in the private ledger.

The relationship of those sections of the ledger to each other and to their journals is illustrated in Figs. 13.1 and 13.2.

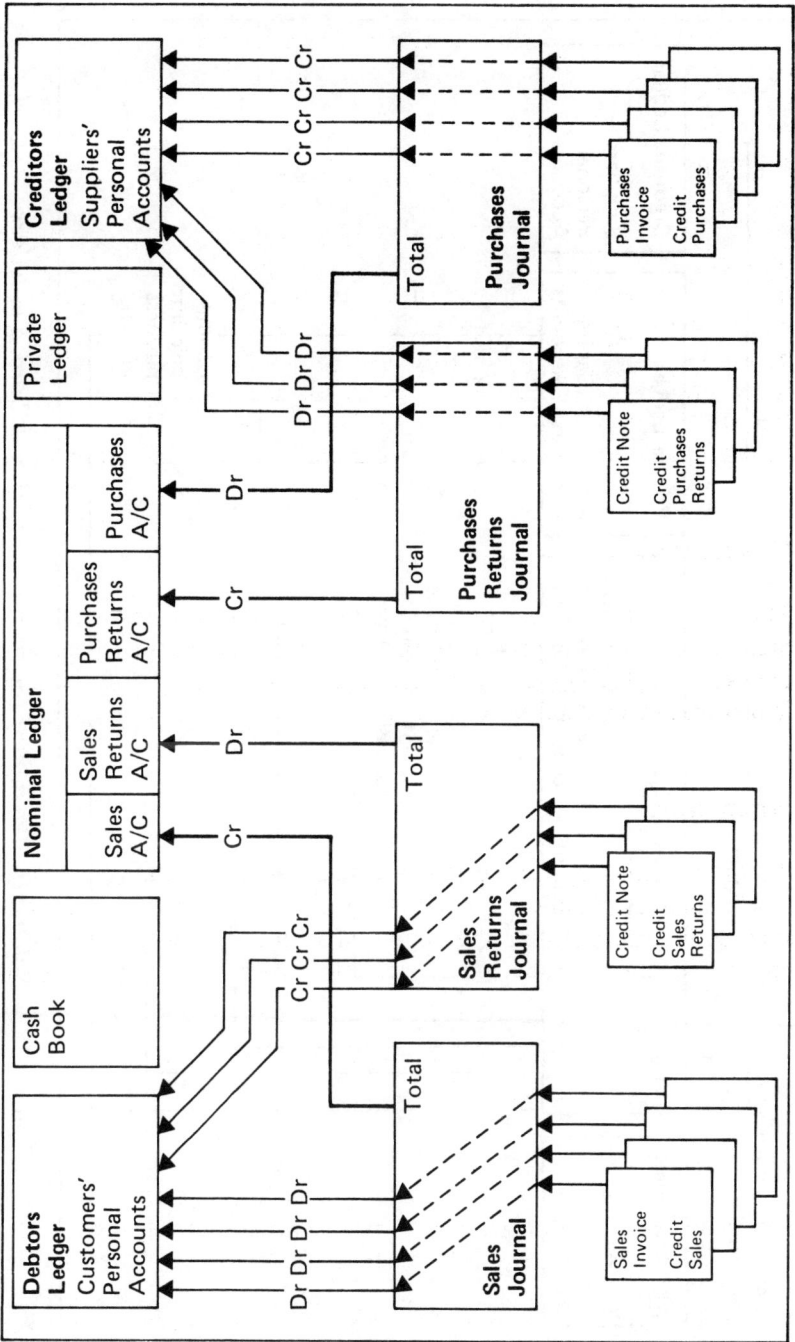

Figure 13.1 *Schematic diagram of the relationships of ledgers and journals*

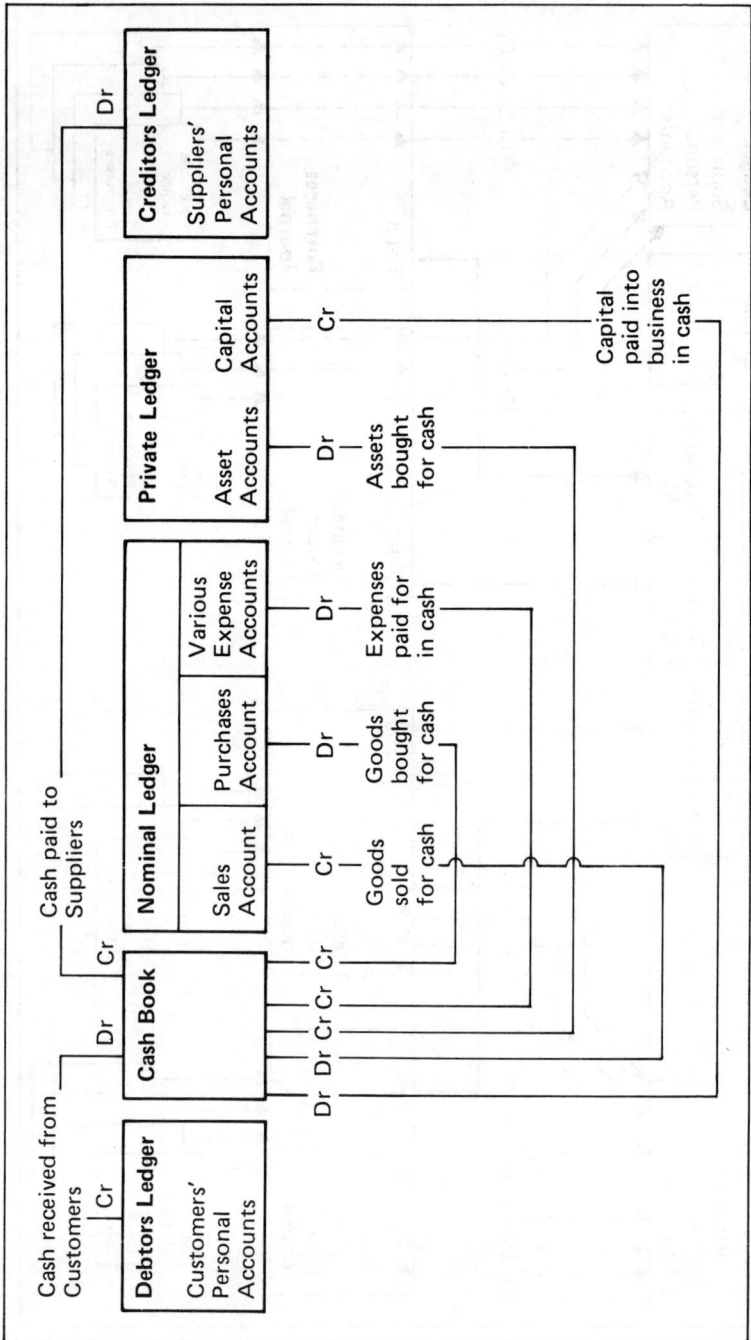

Figure 13.2 *Schematic diagram of the relationship of cash book and ledger*

13.2   Errors not Disclosed by a Trial Balance

You may remember that it is possible for a ledger to contain errors and for the trial balance to still agree. The errors that do not 'show up' on a trial balance can be classified as follows:

1. Error of omission.— *married out debit & credit in both sides*
2. Error of duplication. — *record something twice.*
3. Error of original entry. — *transportive of figures.*
4. Error of commission. = *wrong person.*
5. Error of principle. — *wrong account, fixed assets - Problems*
6. Compensating errors. — *two or more errors are added together & come to the same thing.*

Error of omission

If a transaction is missed out of the ledger, both the debit side and the credit side will be reduced by the same amount and the trial balance will still therefore agree. This type of error is most likely to occur if one of the business documents, e.g. sales invoice, is lost or missing. If it is a sales invoice that is missing, no entry will be made in the sales journal and therefore: (a) no debit entry will be posted to the customer's account and; (b) when the journal is totalled and posted to the credit side of the sales account, the total will be short of the omitted amount. The result is both the debit side and the credit side of the ledger are 'short' of the same amount.

Error of duplication

If a transaction is entered into the ledger twice both the debit side and the credit side of the ledger will be increased by the same amount and the trial balance will agree. If, for example, a new machine, paid for by cash £300, is entered into the ledger twice: (a) cash will be recorded as £300 less than the true figure (reducing the debit side of the ledger by £300) and; (b) machinery will be recorded as £300 more than the true figure (increasing the debit side of the ledger by £300) — the trial balance will agree.

Error of original entry

An incorrect entry into a journal will also distort both the debit and credit sides by like amounts. For example, let us suppose that an invoice received from supplier J. Red for £59.10 is entered into the journal as £10.59. The effect on the ledger will be that J. Red's account is credited with £48.51 too little (i.e. £59.10 − £10.59) and since the total of the journal will also be £48.51 short the debit entry in the purchases account will differ from the correct position by a similar amount.

Error of commission

Where one of the ledger entries is made to the correct kind of account but to the wrong individual account, the ledger will balance and the trial balance still agree although the ledger contains the error. For example, let us suppose that goods valued £25 are sold on credit to A.B. Brown and that the sales account is correctly credited with £25. However, instead of debiting A.B. Brown's account by £25, N.Z. Brown's account is debited. The result is that the ledger has been debited with £25 and credited with £25 but, although the books balance, the personal accounts of A.B. Brown and N.Z. Brown are incorrect.

Error of principle

Where one of the ledger entries is made to the wrong class of account but to the correct side of the ledger the effect will again be that the trial balance agrees although the ledger contains an error. For example, a typewriter purchased for office use at a cost of £385 and correctly credited to the cash account for £385 is debited to the purchases account instead of debiting the office equipment account. The double entry is completed, both debit and credit entries of £385 have been made but both the purchases account and the office equipment account are incorrect.

Compensating errors

It is possible that the ledger contains two or more separate errors which by chance cancel each other out. Examine the table below which illustrates a group of errors which may occur in the same ledger.

	Error	*Effect on Trial Balance*
(a)	A customer's account is debited £10 instead of credited	Debit side increased by £20
(b)	A supplier's account is credited £5 instead of debited	Credit side increased by £10
(c)	Cash received from customer, £7 is correctly credited to his account but cash book debit is omitted.	Debit side decreased by £7
(d)	Machinery purchased for £10 is correctly entered in the cash account but entered as £7 in the machinery account	Debit side decreased by £3

Summary of the effects of errors

The net effect on debit side is an increase of £10 (i.e. £20 − £7 − £3). The net effect on credit side is an increase of £10. The trial balance will therefore still agree.

13.3 The Ledger from the Computer's Viewpoint

As we have seen, the day-to-day operation of a double-entry book-keeping system consists of applying a very limited number of rules to a fairly repetitive series of transactions. Indeed 'the set of books' really consists of a series of lists. A cash account, for instance, is a pair of lists: one list for cash received and another list for cash paid out. Another example is the sales journal, which consists of a list of credit sales, the items in this list merely being transferred to a group of other lists – on the one hand lists of transactions with customers (debtors ledger), and on the other a list of sales that have been made (sales account). As you are probably aware computers are admirable tools for performing repetitive tasks and manipulating lists. It will therefore come as little surprise that as the cost of computers has fallen dramatically over the last few years they have been used increasingly by the smallest of firms in, if not all the book-keeping functions, at least those that are the most repetitive, such as credit sales and credit purchases. The methods of operating most of the smaller computer systems are very similar – as one would expect since the methods of book-keeping are so very similar between businesses.

13.4 How the Computer 'Keeps Books'

It is not necessary for the operator of a well-written computer program to know how the computer works, any more than it is necessary for the driver of a car to know how the car works. However, it may be reassuring for the operator to have a notional model of the mechanics. The notional model described here relates to a typical sales and debtors ledger program or software package. You will see that there is a close resemblance between the way in which the computer accomplishes book-keeping functions and the way in which a traditional system operates. The only real difference is the format of the lists.

13.5 The Computer's Sales Ledger

The following sample list of transactions is used to illustrate the sales ledger:

Transaction number				Transaction type
1	Jan 1	Sold goods on credit to A. Green	£50	1
2	Jan 2	Sold goods on credit to B. Blue	£70	1
3	Jan 3	Sold goods on credit to C. Red	£80	1
4	Jan 3	Sold goods on credit to B. Blue	£40	1
5	Jan 4	Received cash from B. Blue	£40	2
6	Jan 5	Received cash from C. Red	£40	2
7	Jan 6	Sold goods on credit to C. Red	£90	1
8	Jan 7	Sold goods on credit to B. Blue	£20	1

If these transactions were recorded in a traditional set of books they would be recorded in the appropriate accounts as they occurred. This recording of transactions as mentioned above is, in a sense, sorting into lists according to a set of rules — the type of transaction. You will notice that the first four and the last two transactions are of the same nature and will be dealt with in a similar way — debit customer's account, credit sales. You will also notice that transactions 2, 4 and 8 are identical apart from the amount and these would be sorted into the same lists — Blue's account debit side and sales account.

In a computer-based system, when these transactions are recorded an indication of the type of transaction being recorded must be given and a code will be used by the computer so that identification of the type of transaction for future reference can be made easily. This identification code is vital to the computer since the data which are given are not sorted into lists (accounts) until a demand is made. The data above will be sorted in a very similar order to that above and the list of data (called an array) may be held in the form shown below. (A transaction type code of 1 for a credit sale and 2 for a payment by a customer has been used arbitrarily.)

Code			
1	Jan 1	Green	£50
1	Jan 2	Blue	£70
1	Jan 3	Red	£80
1	Jan 3	Blue	£40
2	Jan 4	Blue	£40
2	Jan 5	Red	£40
1	Jan 6	Red	£90
1	Jan 7	Blue	£20

Because the computer has such a rapid rate of sorting it is not necessary for it to sort the above stream of data into lists (accounts) until information is requested from it.

Suppose we now demand from the computer a list of credit sales. The computer will read through its lists and print only those transactions with a code 1 (credit sale). It will skip any transaction with some other code. The terminal screen or print-out will therefore look like this:

Code			
1	Jan 1	Green	£50
1	Jan 2	Blue	£70
1	Jan 3	Red	£80
1	Jan 4	Blue	£40
1	Jan 5	Red	£90
1	Jan 6	Blue	£20

In other words, it will instantly produce a sales journal.

Suppose we now demand a list of all our transactions with Blue. The computer will read through its list and print only those items which mention Blue, i.e.:

Code	Date	Transaction	Amount	Balance
1	Jan 2	Sales	70	70
1	Jan 3	Sales	40	110
2	Jan 4	Cash	40	70
1	Jan 7	Sales	20	90

In other words, it will instantly produce Blue's personal account.

13.6   The System in Use

If the software package being used is just one part of a largely manual book-keeping system, when the program has been loaded the operator will be presented with a set of choices (called a menu) of the kind of transaction which he wishes to enter. The display on the VDU (visual display unit) may appear in the case of a sales ledger as follows:

1.   Enter transaction
2.   Interrogate file
3.   End
Enter choice number

By pressing 1 on the keyboard the operator is indicating that he wants to enter a transaction, 2, that he wants information previously recorded, and 3, that he has finished with the program for the time being.
Assuming that the operator presses the number 1 on the key-board a further set of choices will be displayed:

1.   Credit sale
2.   Cash from customer
3.   Customer returns
4.   Return to main menu
Enter choice number

If the user now presses 1, 2 or 3 he will be required to enter details of the transaction such as date, name of customer, and amount. Pressing 4 will result in the original set of choices (the main menu being displayed again).

With more elaborate systems the range of choice in the main menu will include all the usual double-entry transactions.

14. Discounts

14.1 Trade Discounts

Frequently, manufacturers and wholesalers produce price lists and catalogues for distribution to both retailers and consumers. Obviously, the cost of goods to ..e retailer is below that to the customer (profit margin). This means that the price which appears on the price list is higher than the price that the retailer will have to pay. The retailer, when calculating the price of the goods that he has to pay, will deduct *trade discount* to find the price.

The importance of trade discount is that *it is a reduction in price to be paid*. It does not *therefore require any special ledger entries*.

Example. Suppose that we buy goods on credit from Bicycle Suppliers Ltd at £100 less 25% trade discount. How will this transaction be entered in the ledger?

1. We receive the invoice from Bicycle Suppliers Ltd showing discount.
2. The invoice is entered in the purchases journal.
3. The invoice total only is entered from the journal into the ledger, e.g.:

INVOICE			PURCHASES JOURNAL			PURCHASES	
5 tricycles £20 each less 25% discount	100 25	75	Bicycle suppliers 5 at £20 less discount Total	100 25	75 75	Goods on credit 75	
		75				BICYCLE SUPPLIERS	
							Goods 75

In a similar way the trade discount that we allow to our customers will require no special ledger entries since the price after discount will be the one which is posted from the sales journal.

14.2   Cash Discount

Having sold goods to our customers on credit we shall require them to pay as quickly as possible for the following reasons:

1. As a business principle debtors are an unproductive asset and therefore should be kept to a minimum.
2. The longer that the debt is outstanding the greater becomes the risk that the debt will not be paid.

In order to encourage prompt settlement of debts, we may offer cash discount to our customers. We will say to J. Bloggs who owes us £100, 'pay us within a week and we will accept £90 in full settlement'; in other words we will offer 10% cash discount.
    The ledger work below illustrates this position.

J. BLOGGS		CASH/EXTRACT	
Balance 100	Cash 90 Cash Discount 10	J. Bloggs 90	

DISCOUNT ALLOWED	
J. Bloggs 10	

As we can see from the above ledger work, when J. Bloggs pays £90 in full settlement our ledger will appear initially as if there is a £10 debit balance outstanding on his account. The £10 debit balance must be eradicated by crediting his account with £10 and debiting the discount allowed account. (Note the similarity of ledger work between discount and writing off a bad debt.)

The discount allowed represents our expense of collecting debts and affects net profit rather than gross profit. Discount allowed nould eventually be transferred to the profit and loss account.

14.3 Discount Allowed and the Treble-Column Cash Book

As we know, when a customer pays, the double entry which is involved is debit cash account (cash book) and credit customer's account (debtors ledger). However, if the customer deducts cash discount the entries become more complicated:

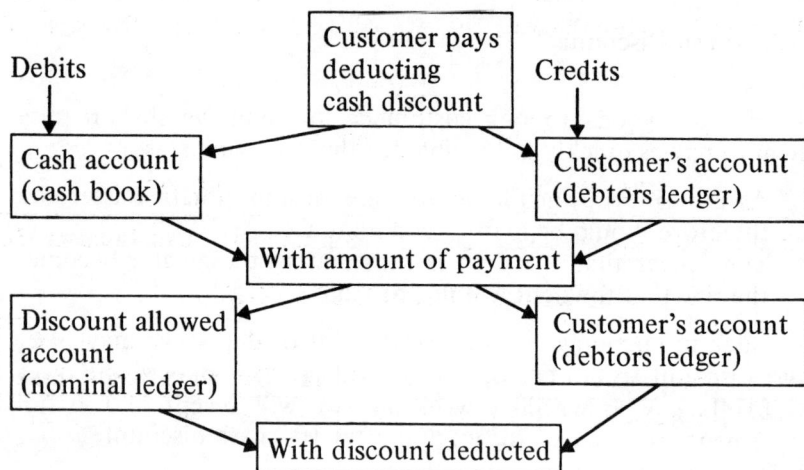

```
                    ┌─────────────────┐
                    │ Customer pays   │
  Debits            │ deducting       │  Credits
    │               │ cash discount   │    │
    ▼               └─────────────────┘    ▼
┌──────────────┐                    ┌──────────────────────┐
│ Cash account │◄──────────         │ Customer's account   │
│ (cash book)  │                    │ (debtors ledger)     │
└──────────────┘          ┌────────────────────────┐
          ──────────►│ With amount of payment │◄──────
                     └────────────────────────┘
┌──────────────────┐                ┌──────────────────────┐
│ Discount allowed │◄──────────     │ Customer's account   │
│ account          │                │ (debtors ledger)     │
│ (nominal ledger) │                └──────────────────────┘
└──────────────────┘    ┌──────────────────────────┐
          ──────────►│ With discount deducted │◄──────
                     └──────────────────────────┘
```

Obviously, four entries in three ledgers for each cash payment involving cash discount is uneconomical of time and effort. The alternative is to use the memorandum column in the treble-column cash book in the way illustrated below:

Example. J. Singh's debtors ledger shows the following accounts with debit balances.

A. White   £30.00
B. Black   £40.00
C. Brown   £50.00
D. Yellow £60.00
E. Green   £20.00

During the week to 7 January 19–0 details of payments were as follows:

Jan 1   A. White settled his account deducting 10% cash discount cheque

Jan 2   C. Brown settled his account deducting 10% cash discount cheque

Jan 3   B. Black paid £40.00 cash, no discount

Jan 4   D. Yellow paid £54.00 cash having deducted 10% cash discount

Jan 5   E. Green settled his account deducting 10% cash discount and paying by cheque

WHITE		YELLOW	
Balance 30	Cash Discount 30	Balance 60	Cash Discount 30

BLACK	
Balance 40	Cash 40

GREEN		BROWN	
Balance 20	Cash Discount 20	Balance 50	Cash Discount 50

CASH BOOK (DEBIT SIDE ONLY)

Date	Particulars	£ Cash Discount	£ Cash	£ Bank
Jan 1	White	3		27
Jan 2	Brown	5		45
Jan 3	Black		40	
Jan 4	Yellow	3	27	
Jan 5	Green	2		18
		13		

DISCOUNT ALLOWED

Discount this week 13	

Notes to ledger entries

1. You will notice that a single entry in the customer's personal account is made including both cash and discount. However, the amount of cash received and discount deducted are recorded separately in the cash book.

2. The discount allowed column in the cash book *is not a ledger entry*. It is merely a memorandum of how much discount has been allowed. When the cash book is balanced there is no need to attempt to 'balance' the discount columns. Just total the discount allowed and post it to the *debit side* of the discount allowed account.
3. The balance of the discount allowed account will ultimately be transferred by double entry to the debit side of the profit and loss account in the same way as any other business expense.

14.4 Discount Received

In the same way that we will be encouraging our debtors to pay promptly by offering them cash discount, our suppliers or creditors will be attempting to extract prompt payment from us. In our ledger we may adopt a similar method of double entry to that which we use when dealing with discount allowed, i.e. when we pay the supplier, debit his account with the full value of the payment including discount. When we make the credit entry in the cash book, it should be analysed in a similar way to discount allowed by use of the discount received column on the credit side of the cash book. At the end of the month the total posted to the credit side of the discount received account is totalled and posted to the credit side of the profit and loss account. Note: in practice, some firms use a single discount account for both discounts received and allowed, posting the balance to the profit and loss account.

Example 1. J. Singh started business in January with a balance of cash £300 and at bank £3000. During the following months the following transactions relating to his cash book took place. You are required to show how his cash book appears for the month of January and illustrate how the discount allowed and discount received accounts would appear after production of the profit and loss account.

Jan	3	Paid A. Red's account £12.00 cheque having deducted £2.00 discount
Jan	4	A. Oak paid £20.00 less £2.00 discount cheque
Jan	5	Paid B. Green £50.00 less £3.00 discount cheque
Jan	6	Paid wages £15.00 cash
Jan	7	Cash sales £35.00

Jan 8   B. Elm paid £70.00 less £5.00 discount cheque
Jan 12   Paid E. Yellow £21.00 less £4.00 discount cash
Example 14.1

Example 2. J. Finch, a trader, makes the following payments with discounts allowed at the rates quoted.

Jan 5   Meeting Ltd   £80.00 less 5% discount
Jan 8   Pricerite   £40.00 less 2½% discount
Jan 12   Hand Bros   £100.00 less 2½% discount

He also receives from customers cheques after allowing discounts at the rates quoted.

Jan 4   J. Vance   £50.00 less 2½% discount
Jan 6   K. Mate   £160.00 less 5% discount
Jan 8   S.C. Brown   £10.00 less 2½% discount
Jan 20   V. Red   £85.00 less 5% discount.

This is shown in the cash book as in Example 14.2.

Notice that the discount columns are not balanced; they are just totalled, and no attempt is made to set one total against another. Thus they are acting as an aid to our memory and not as part of the double entry.
    The personal accounts that have been involved in the transactions listed above would be recorded in the ledger as:

SALES LEDGER

Dr.   J. VANCE   Cr.

Jan 1	Sales	CB	50	—	Jan 4	Bank	CB	48	75
						Discount			
						Allowed		1	25
			£50	—				£50	—

Dr.   K. MATE   Cr.

Jan 1	Sales		160	—	Jan 6	Bank		152	—
						Discount			
						Allowed		8	—
			£160	—				£160	—

CASH BOOK

Date	Particulars	Fol No.	Discount Allowed	Cash	Bank
Jan 1	Balance			300 —	3000 —
Jan 4	A. Oak		2 —		18 —
Jan 7	Sales			35 —	
Jan 8	B. Elm		5 —		65 —
			7 —	335 —	3083 —
Feb 1	Balance			303 —	3024 —

Date	Particulars	Fol No.	Discount Received	Cash	Bank
Jan 3	A. Red		2 —		12 —
Jan 5	B. Green		3 —		47 —
Jan 6	Wages			15 —	
Jan 12	E. Yellow		4 —	17 —	
Jan 31	Balance			303 —	3024 —
			9 —	335 —	3083 —

DISCOUNT ALLOWED

Jan 31 Discount this Month 7	Jan 31 Profit and Loss 7

DISCOUNT RECEIVED

Jan 31 Profit and Loss 9	Jan 31 Discount this Month 9

PROFIT AND LOSS ACCOUNT
FOR MONTH ENDING JAN 31 (Extract)

Discount Allowed 7	Gross Profit
	Discount Received 9

Example 14.1

CASH BOOK

Date	Particulars	Fol No.	Discount Allowed	Cash	Bank
Jan 4	J. Vance		1 25		48 75
Jan 6	K. Mate		8 —		152 —
Jan 8	S.C. Brown		0 25		9 75
Jan 20	V. Red		4 25		80 75
Jan 21	Cash Sales			60 —	
			13 75	60 —	291 25

Date	Particulars	Fol No.	Discount Received	Cash	Bank
Jan 5	Meeting Ltd		4 —		76 —
Jan 8	Pricerite		1 —		39 —
Jan 12	Hind Bros		2 50		97 50
Jan 14	Postage			15 —	
Jan 22	Sundry Expenses			10 —	
Jan 24	Telephone			35 —	
Jan 31	Balance	c/d			78 75
			7 50	60 —	291 25

Example 14.2

The same form of entry would be made in entering S.R. Brown's and V. Red's accounts. Similarly, discount received needs to be recorded in the bought ledger as:

Dr.   MEETING LTD   Cr.

Jan 5	Bank	CB	76	–	Jan 1	Purchases	CB	80	–
	Discount								
	Received		4	–					
			£80	–				£80	–

Dr.   PRICERITE   Cr.

Jan 8	Bank		39	–	Jan 3	Purchases		40	–
	Discount								
	Received		1	–					
			£40	–				£40	–

The same form of entry would be made for Hind Bros. At the end of the month J. Finch would post the total of the discount columns as follows:

Dr.   DISCOUNT ALLOWED ACCOUNT   Cr.

| Jan 31 | Sundries | CB | 13 | 75 | | | | | |

Dr.   DISCOUNT RECEIVED ACCOUNT   Cr.

| | | | | | Jan 31 | Sundries | CB | 7 | 50 |

It is possible that only one discount account is kept, in which case the entry would be as follows:

Dr.   DISCOUNTS ACCOUNT   Cr.

| Jan 31 | Sundries | CB | 13 | 75 | Jan 31 | Sundries | CB | 7 | 50 |

At the end of the financial period the discount allowed and discount received are transferred to the profit and loss account. Note, however, that if discount received exceeds discount allowed, i.e. if the discount account has a credit balance, discount will appear on the credit side of the profit and loss account and will be added to gross profit, thus enlarging Meeting Ltd's net profit.

ASSIGNMENTS

A14.1 M. Samuels sells goods on credit on the following terms:

Payment within 7 days 10% cash discount
Payment within 14 days 7½% cash discount
Payment within 21 days   5% cash discount

He sells the following goods on credit:

Date	Customer	Amount
Feb 1	A. Red	23.90
Feb 3	B. Blue	14.28
Feb 4	C. Yellow	23.90
Feb 8	D. Green	24.90
Feb 10	B. Blue	23.90
Feb 10	D. Green	15.20

If the above customers settle their accounts in full on the dates shown below, how much cash discount will each of them be entitled to deduct from their payment?

Customer	Date of Settlement
A. Red	Feb 7
B. Blue	Feb 23
C. Yellow	Feb 24
D. Green	March 3

A14.2 Enter the following transactions into the treble-column cash book of A. House (no need to show double entries). Balance the cash book and show how the totals of discount received and discount allowed would appear in their respective ledger accounts. Balance at 1 January: cash £500, bank £3500.

Receipts

Jan 1 Cash sales £50.00
Jan 2 J. Slate paid £20.00 less 5% cash discount – cheque
Jan 3 D. Pebble paid £55.00 less 10% cash discount – cheque

Jan 4   A. Rock paid £20.00 less 7½% cash discount – cash

Jan 7   Cash sales £35.00

Jan 8   C. Flint paid £45.00 less 5% cash discount – cheque

Jan 9   D. Pebble paid £20.00 less 5% cash discount – cheque

Jan 13   E. Granite paid £20.00 cheque – no discount

Jan 14   Cash sales £45.00

Payments

Jan 1   Paid A. Rose £35.00 less 10% cash discount – cheque

Jan 2   Paid wages in cash £45.00

Jan 3   Paid electricity bill cheque £95.00

Jan 4   Paid C. Daisy £25.00 less 10% discount – cash

Jan 7   Paid D. Violet £9.00 less 5% cash discount – cheque

Jan 8   Paid for advertising by cheque £15.00

15. Value Added Tax (VAT)

Value Added Tax (VAT) was introduced in this country in 1973. It is a means of raising revenue on a wide range of goods and services that people buy. This form of taxation is known as *indirect*, as opposed to Income Tax which is *direct* taxation and deductible from an individual's salary. The liability of a sole trader, or partnership or any other form of business to pay VAT occurs when turnover exceeds £15 000 per year or £5000 per quarter. Note that these amounts refer to *turnover* and not to profit. VAT is levied (charged) at different rates, all of which can be altered by governments, depending on their policies. This causes considerable variation in the rate of VAT, e.g. since 1973 the standard rate of VAT has been 8%, 10% and 15%. However, some goods and services are zero rated: that is the tax charge is *nil*. A few examples of these goods are: exports of goods, books and newspapers, most food. There is a further category of exempt supplies, where again no tax is paid; examples of this category are insurance, education, banking, services of doctors, dentists.

From this very brief introduction to VAT it is easy to see that it is very complicated and subject to change whenever budget measures are introduced by the government of the day. It is, however, important that you are familiar with VAT calculations and can record VAT in the appropriate books of original entry and transfer the entries to the ledger accounts.

15.1   Calculation of VAT

On all the goods and services that are purchased for the operation of a business, e.g. stock, telephone, stationery, etc., there will be a VAT charge; this is the trader's *input tax*. The VAT that he adds to the price of the goods or services that he sells to his customers is his *output tax*. The balance that is due is to be paid to Customs and Excise is the difference between the two, i.e. OUTPUT TAX – INPUT TAX = VAT payable to Customs and Excise.

In the example below a trader has calculated VAT at the standard rate at 15% for the quarter.

Example 1		2nd Quarter 19–1	
		VAT at 15%	
Sales	£4500	£675	(*output tax*) i.e. received by trader
Purchases	£2900	£435	(*input tax*) i.e. expense to trader
Net Flow	£1600	£240 →	difference between output tax and input tax, payable to Customs and Excise

Example 2

A further example is given of a trader who supplies *zero-rated* goods, i.e. VAT charge is *nil*. However, although he has no *output tax* it is quite possible that he will pay VAT on goods and services that he purchased from other traders in order to carry out his business. In this case he will be refunded by Customs and Excise.

		2nd Quarter 19–1	
		VAT at 15%	
Sales	£5300	–	No VAT chargeable
Purchases	£3400	£510	(*input tax*)
Net Flow	£1900	(£510) →	Trader will be refunded for this amount from Customs and Excise

15.2 VAT Records

VAT records, including zero-rated goods and services, must be kept by the business so that the correct amount of tax is paid or received. Indeed, such records must be kept for three years.

The recording of invoices for input and output tax is very important for the business, since such documents act as evidence of VAT paid and received and may be subject to the inspection of Customs and Excise.

A number of traders record this information by adding extra columns in the cash book (see overleaf).

15.3 VAT Account

It is necessary for the trader to summarize all VAT records so that the *tax due* and the *tax deductible* are shown, and from this the *net amount* that is to be paid or reclaimed is clear. From the figures given in Example 1 above this would be represented as:

Example 2

VAT Account (Period 1 Jan 19–1 to 31 Jan 19–1)

TAX DEDUCTIBLE			TAX DUE		
Input Tax	£		Output Tax	£	
Sundries	6	–	Sundries	24	75
Overdeclarations or			Underdeclarations or		
overpayments	NIL		underpayments	NIL	
TOTAL TAX					
DEDUCTIBLE	6	–	TOTAL TAX DUE	24	75
TAX PAYABLE	18	75			
	24	75			

Note: the sum payable to Customs and Excise is £18.75; this is calculated by using the formula shown at the beginning of this chapter, i.e.

Output (£24.75) – Input (£6.00) = Tax due (£18.75).

CASH BOOK

Date	Particulars	Fol No.	Goods	VAT Rate	VAT Output	Cash		Date	Particulars	Fol No.	Goods	VAT Rate	VAT Input	Cash
Jan 1	Capital	2	—			100 —		Jan 2	Purchases	3	20	15%	3 —	23 —
Jan 4	Sales	4	35	15%	5 25	40 25		Jan 10	Postage	5	—		—	1 —
Jan 8	Sales	4	40	15%	6 —	46 —		Jan 11	Purchases	3	20	15%	3 —	23 —
Jan 15	Sales	4	35	15%	5 25	40 25		Jan 12	Rent	6				10 —
Jan 17	Sales	4	20	15%	3 —	23 —		Jan 28	Postage	5				2 —
Jan 29	Sales	4	35	15%	5 25	40 25		Jan 30	Rent	6				10 —
								Jan 31	Balance					220 75
					24 75	289 75							6 —	289 75
Feb 1	Balance	b/d				220 75								

VAT received or OUTPUT TAX

VAT paid or INPUT TAX

If the trader makes a return to Customs and Excise every three months the VAT account could well take the form indicated:

VAT Account 1 May 19–1 to 31 July 19–1

TAX DEDUCTIBLE			TAX DUE		
Input Tax	£	£	Output Tax	£	£
May	307.67		May	746.03	
June	354.00		June	688.00	
July	519.38		July	593.75	
		1181.05			2027.78
Overdeclarations or overpayments			Underdeclarations or underpayments		
From Customs & Excise	NIL			NIL	
Other	174.36				
		174.36			
Total Tax Deductible		1355.41	Total Tax Due		2027.78
Tax Payable		672.37			
		2027.78			2027.78

In this example the tax due was more than the tax deductible; this means that the difference (£672.37) must be paid to the Customs and Excise. If the tax deductible figure had been the larger amount then the difference would be reclaimed from Customs and Excise.

15.4 VAT Returns

The trader must, after no more than one month, send in his return, referred to as *VAT 100*. This is done at the end of a tax period which is usually every three months.

16. Wages and salaries

16.1 Calculating Gross Pay

Wages and salaries are the reward paid by an employer to an
employee for the contribution that the employee's skill, labour and
effort have made to the profitability of the firm. Traditionally the
term *salary* was used to describe the amount paid to clerical workers whose weekly or monthly payment was calculated as a fraction
of an agreed annual amount. The word *wages* was usually used to
describe the payment made to manual workers whose weekly
payments were calculated according to the number of hours worked
each week. Increasingly as the differences between types of employment and the methods of calculating pay decrease the two terms
are being used as substitutes for each other.

16.2 Gross Pay of Hourly Paid Workers

A typical hourly paid worker's contract of employment will require
the employee to work, as a minimum, a 40-hour week comprising
five days of eight hours each. If employees work on any day for
longer than eight hours they will receive an overtime payment
calculated at an agreed multiple of their usual ordinary rate.
Work on a Saturday or a Sunday is usually rewarded by payment
at an overtime rate except in occupations where weekend working
is the norm.

An extract from Smith Engineering Ltd's conditions of service is shown below and typical of the kind of rules which are applied to calculate the gross wage of hourly paid workers.

1. The employee will work normally a 40-hour week with five days of eight hours each, Monday—Friday.
2. The employee will normally work between the hours of 8 a.m. and 5 p.m. and will take a one-hour break for lunch from either 12 p.m. to 1 p.m. or 1 p.m. to 2 p.m.
3. For each 15 minutes' lateness or part of 15 minutes' lateness 30 minutes' pay will be lost. Employees will not be penalized for three minutes of lateness to allow for clocking on.
4. The first four hours of overtime in any week will be paid at the employee's normal rate plus one quarter of normal rate. The second four hours of overtime in any week will be paid at the employee's normal rate plus one half of normal rate. All remaining overtime together with any Sunday working will be paid at twice the normal rate.
5. Overtime is not paid for less than 30 minutes' work and the number of hours' overtime worked on any one day will be rounded to the nearest quarter-hour below.

Since overtime is not usually worked without the authorization of the supervisor it is not usually used to offset lateness or absence from other work sessions. Therefore an employee who was absent on Tuesday morning but who worked until 9 p.m. on Wednesday would still be entitled to the overtime rate for the extra hours' work on Wednesday.

Time clock card

Where employees are paid on an hourly basis some method of recording the hours worked each day is necessary. This may take the form of a 'clock card' upon which the times of arrival and depart-ure of the employee are recorded either manually or by mechanical means. The design of the clock cards varies but the one shown in Fig. 16.1 for Lindsay Crook, who works for Smith Engineering Ltd, contains the main features required for calculating gross pay.

Notice that although Lindsay Crook usually clocks in a few minutes early and clocks out a few minutes after the official finishing time this does not count as overtime (see Smith Engineer-

NAME Lindsay Crook
WORKS NO. 53
DEPARTMENT Packing
HOURLY RATE £2.00

SMITH ENGINEERING LTD
CLOCK CARD

WEEK ENDING SUNDAY 19 April

DAY	MORNING		AFTERNOON		EVENING		TOTAL	HOURS	
	IN	OUT	IN	OUT	IN	OUT		ORD	O/TIME
MONDAY	7.59	12.01	12.55	17.00			8	8	
TUESDAY	7.59	12.00	12.56	17.01	17.29	18.31	9	8	1
WEDNESDAY	7.59	12.01	12.57	17.00	17.30	21.01	11½	8	3½
THURSDAY	7.59	12.00	13.02	17.00			8	8	
FRIDAY	7.59	12.01	13.00	17.01	17.30	20.01	10½	8	2½
SATURDAY	8.59	13.00					4		4
SUNDAY									
						TOTAL	51	40	11

Hours working	Hours	Rate	Amount
At Ordinary Rate	40	2.00	80.00
At Time and One Quarter	4	2.50	10.00
At Time and One Half	4	3.00	12.00
At Double Time	3	4.00	12.00
Gross Pay			114.00

Figure 16.1

ing Ltd's conditions of service, number 5). Similarly Lindsay Crook is not penalized for being two minutes late back to work on Thursday afternoon (see Smith Engineering Ltd's conditions of service, number 3).

Lindsay Crook worked a total of 11 hours' overtime during the week shown. Of these 11 hours, the first four hours are paid at her normal rate of £2 per hour plus one quarter of her normal rate (£2 + [£2 × ¼] = £2.50 per hour), the next four hours are paid at £2 per hour plus one half of £2 (£2 + [£2 × ½] = £3) and the remaining three hours paid at twice her normal rate (£2 × 2 = £4). Her gross pay for the week then comes to £114.00.

An alternative method of calculating overtime payments is to increase the number of overtime hours by the appropriate factor, 1¼, 1½, etc. and use the standard hourly rate.

16.3   Gross Pay of Employees with an Annual Salary

Where employees have an annual salary their gross pay is calculated as a fraction of the annual figure. If they are paid each calendar month their gross monthly payment will be $\frac{1}{12}$ of the annual figure and if they are paid weekly their gross payment will be $\frac{1}{52}$ of the annual figure.

Example 1. Max Edwards is the Chief Personnel Officer of Smith Engineering Ltd. He is paid monthly and his annual salary is £8520. His monthly gross payment is therefore £8520 ÷ 12 = £710.

Example 2. Valerie Holt is the Chief Personnel Officer of Smith Engineering Ltd. She is paid weekly and her annual salary is £8996. Her weekly gross payment is therefore £8996 ÷ 52 = £173.

16.4   Commission and Bonus

In order to reward employees who give a better-than-usual performance, a payment is sometimes made in addition to salary. This extra reward may take the form of a commission paid, for example to a sales representative for sales above a given figure, or a bonus paid to a production worker for a higher-than-usual level of production (a productivity bonus).

Example 1. Jonathan Ford is employed as a sales representative by the 'Better Trading Company'. In addition to his annual salary of £6000, which is paid monthly, he is paid a commission of 2 per cent on all sales over £20 000 in any one month. His gross pay in a month where his sales are £25 000 will be:

Normal salary £6000 ÷ 12	£500	
Commission on sales over £20 000		
Actual sales – £20 000 = £5000		
£5000 × $\frac{2}{100}$	£100	
Gross pay	£600	for that month.

Example 2. Marion Potter works as pump assembler for D.F. Hydraulics Ltd. She is paid a wage of £60 for a 35-hour week and in addition she is paid a bonus of £0.35 for every pump she assembles in excess of 150 pumps in any one week. Her gross pay for a week in which she assembles 194 pumps is therefore:

Basic wage	£60	
Bonus on [194 – 150] 44 pumps		
44 × £0.35	£15.40	
	£75.40	for that week.

16.5 Calculating Net Pay

Before any employers make payment to their employees they have a responsibility to make certain deductions from the gross pay. In addition to compulsory deductions such as PAYE (Pay as You Earn) income tax and NI (national insurance contribution) the employers will sometimes come to an arrangement with employees to deduct from their gross wage voluntary contributions to such things as the firm's social club levy or employees' trade union contributions.

16.6   PAYE Code Numbers

The amount of PAYE that is deducted from an employee's wage depends upon the amount that the employee earns and the tax code number given to the employee by the Inland Revenue. The code number relates to the amount of income that an individual can receive before becoming liable to taxation. The individual's tax-free pay and code number depend upon his or her circumstances so that a married man with two dependent children will have a higher tax code and therefore a higher level of tax-free pay than, say, a single woman with no dependants. Since his tax-free allowance is higher he will pay less tax on the same income than the single woman.

16.7   Calculating the Tax Deduction

The following items of information are necessary to calculate the tax deductible from an employee's gross pay:

1.   The gross pay for the week.
2.   The total gross pay for all the previous weeks in the current tax year.
3.   The total amount of tax paid to date in the current year.
4.   The employee's code number.
5.   The PAYE-free pay table (known as Table A).
6.   The PAYE-taxable pay table (known as Table B).

The following examples illustrate the way in which the above items of information are used in order to calculate the tax deductible. Relevant tax and national insurance tables appear at the end of the book.

Example 1. The following information relates to Lindsay Crook's PAYE liability:

1.   Her tax code number is 200.
2.   Her gross earnings for week 2 amount to £114.
3.   Her earnings up to week 2 amounted to £80 and the tax paid to date amounts to £12.30.

Calculation of Lindsay Crook's tax deduction, week 2:

Step 1   Turn to week 2 in Table A (Free Pay) and read off against her code number of 200 her free pay to date – £77.28.

Step 2   Calculate her total pay to date by adding her previous gross pay (£80) to her pay for week 2 (£114).

	£
Previous gross pay	80
Add Gross pay this week	114
Gross pay to date	194

Step 3   Deduct from gross pay to date (£194) free pay to date (£77.28) to find taxable pay to date:

	£
Gross pay to date (from Step 2)	194.00
Less Free pay to date (from Step 1)	77.28
Taxable pay to date	116.72

Step 4   Read from Table B (taxable pay tables) the total tax due to date on total taxable pay to date. In this case since taxable pay to date is £116.70, or £116 to nearest £ below total, tax due to date is £34.80.

Step 5   Since total tax due to date is £34.80 and since the tax already paid is £12.30, tax payable this week is £22.50, i.e.:

	£
Tax due to date	34.80
Less Tax paid to date	12.30
Tax payable this week	22.50

Example 1. The following information relates to Max Edward's PAYE liability:

1.   His tax code is 266*.
2.   His gross earnings for week 3 are £145.
3.   His earnings up to week 3 amounted to £290 and the tax paid to date amounts to £56.10.

Calculation of Max Edward's tax deduction, week 3:

Step 1   Tax-free pay, week 3 [code 266] = £153.99 (Table A)

Step 2   Total pay to date:

	£
Up to week 3	290
Add For week 3	145
Total	435

Step 3   Taxable pay to date:

	£
Gross pay to date	435.00
Free pay to date (Table A)	153.99
Taxable pay to date	281.01

Step 4   Tax due on £281.01 = £84.30 (Table B)

Step 5   Tax due this week:

	£
Total tax due	84.30
Less Tax paid to date	56.10
Tax this week	28.20

*Compare Max Edward's high tax code with that of Lindsay Crook. This may be because he has a relative who is dependent upon him and is able to get a higher level of tax-free pay.

16.8   National Insurance Contribution

The amount of national insurance contribution payable is cal-culated by using the national insurance contribution rate tables (CF 391). There are four tables (A;B,C and D) for employees who are not contracted out and the table which applies is decided by the circumstances of the employee. Table A, for example, gives the contribution payable in respect of employees over 16 under pension age whereas table C applies to employees who are over pension age.

The amount payable in any week can be read from the appro-priate table against the gross earnings for the week. Lindsay Crook's contribution in a week when her gross wage was £114, assuming that table A applied, would be £23.36 but notice that of this £23.36 contribution only £10.28 would be a deduction from her salary (employee's contribution payable) while the remaining £13.08 would be contributed by her employer. The maximum contribution under table A is £51.12, made up of £22.50 contrib-uted by the employee and £28.62 contributed by the employer.

16.9   Firm's Own Pension Scheme

Many employers now run their own pension scheme which their employees may join. The employee, by contributing to the firm's pension scheme at the rate of between 4.5 per cent to 6 per cent of his basic gross pay, buys the right to a pension in addition to the state pension. The amount of this additional pension will depend upon the number of years that the employee has paid into the firm's scheme, but for a long-serving employee the pension will usually be between one third and one half of normal salary on retirement. The contribution that the employee makes is frequently called superannuation.

Example. Lindsay Crook contributes to Smith Engineering Ltd's pension scheme, the contribution being 5 per cent of normal gross pay. Lindsay Crook's basic gross pay is £80. Her superannuation will therefore be £4.

Other deductions

The employers may agree to make further small deductions from the employee's wage for payment into such things as the employee's trade union or the firm's social club or for the employee's savings under the Government's SAYE (Save as You Earn) scheme.

Example. Lindsay Crook's trade union contribution is £0.75 per week and her subscription to the firm's social club is £0.25 per week, therefore her total other deductions amount to £1 each week.

16.10   Net Pay: Summary and Examples

Deductions made from gross pay are of two kinds.

1.   Statutory deductions:
     (a)   PAYE income tax;
     (b)   national insurance contributions.

2.   Voluntary deductions.

    (a)   graduated pension;
    (b)   trade union levy;
    (c)   social club subscription.

Example 1. Lindsay Crook's pay slip for week 2 will show the following information:

	£	£	£
Previous gross pay		80.00	
Gross pay this week		114.00	
Total pay to date		194.00	
PAYE:			
Gross pay this week			114.00
Tax due to date	34.80		
Less Tax paid to date	12.30		
Tax due this payment		22.50	
Employee's national insurance contribution		10.28	
Employer's contribution	13.08		32.78
			81.22
Other deductions:			
Superannuation		4.00	
Trade union contribution		0.75	
Social club		0.25	
			5.00
Net pay			76.22

Example 2. Suppose Lindsay Crook's gross pay in week 3 amounted to £120, made up from her basic pay of £80 plus £40 overtime. From the previous examples we know that:

1.   Her tax code is 200.
2.   She contributes 5 per cent of basic pay to pension scheme.
3.   She contributes £0.75 to a trade union and £0.25 to the social club.
4.   Her previous gross earnings were £194.
5.   Her tax paid to date is £34.80.
6.   Table A national insurance contribution applies.

Calculating deductions:

		£	£
1.	PAYE gross pay to date [£194 + £120]	314.00	
	Less Tax-free pay to date [table A, week 3]	115.92	
	Taxable pay to date	198.08	
	Tax due to date on taxable pay table B	59.40	
	Tax paid to date	34.80	
	Tax due this payment		24.60
2.	National insurance contribution		
	Gross pay £120		
	Total contribution [weekly table A]	24.59	
	Of which employer contributes	13.77	
	Employee's contribution		10.82
3.	Superannuation 5 per cent of £80		4.00
4.	Trade union contribution		0.75
5.	Social club subscription		0.25
	Total deductions		40.42

Calculating net pay:

	£
Gross pay	120.00
Total deductions	40.42
Net pay	79.58

16.11 Wages, Salaries and the Ledger

Firms which employ more than a few people use a system of recording details of pay and deductions which allows them to duplicate the individual's pay advice from the main pay record. The system may be a manual one whereby the top sheet consists of perforated strips which form the pay advice and the carbon copy below is for the permanent record of individual employees' payments and deductions. It will show the total amount at the bottom of the page for the total amount paid out in respect of wages, tax, insurance, etc. for posting to the wages and salaries account in the nominal ledger. The significant figures for the firm's accounting purposes will be the total of the gross wages paid to employees and the employer's national insurance contributions.

Alternatively the system may rely upon a computer which will automatically calculate gross pay and deductions, given details of hours worked, commission, bonus, etc., as well as printing pay slips and in some cases preparing cheques or making payments. It may be that the payroll function of the computer is independent of the rest of the accounting system in which case the totals paid will require manual posting to the nominal ledger. Alternatively the payroll may form part of a fully integrated accounting system and make the appropriate postings itself.

ASSIGNMENTS

A16.1 The clock cards for week 3 of the three manual workers of the Nice Ice Cream Company are shown in Figs. 16.2, 16.3 and 16.4. Complete the clock cards and calculate gross pay for each of the workers. Note that the Nice Ice Cream Company uses the same conditions of service as Smith Engineering.

A16.2 The Nice Ice Cream Company employ the following personnel:

(a) Alfred Thomas, a foreman, whose salary is £180 per week, is paid, in addition, a bonus of £0.03 per litre on production over 10 000 litres in a week.

(b) John Sharp, a salesman, who is paid £8000 per annum and receives a commission of 5 per cent on all sales over £10 000 in a week.

(c) Emily Moneypiece, a clerk who is paid £5200 per annum.

(d) Gary Goldberg, the General Manager, who is paid £10 920 per annum.

NB: All employees are paid weekly.

Calculate the gross wage of each of these employees for week 3 when production is 12 000 litres and sales are £12 000.

A16.3   The details below relate to the employees of the Nice
Ice Cream Company:

Name	Tax code numbers	Tax paid up to week 3 £	Gross pay up to week 3 £	Other deductions
John Adams	205	30.00	180	Trade union £0.75
Zoe Patel	210	34.20	196	Trade union £0.75
Fred Pringle	200	48.60	240	Trade union £0.75
Alfred Thomas	250	89.70	396	
John Sharp	180	86.40	358	
Emily Moneypiece	200	36.60	200	
Gary Goldberg	199	102.90	420	

Adams, Patel and Pringle all belong to a trade union
and £0.75 is deducted from their wages each week for
the membership fee. Thomas, Sharp and Goldberg
belong to the firm's own pension scheme and contribute
5 per cent of their basic salary each week to the
scheme. Table A national insurance contribution
applies to all employees.

(a)   Using your calculations of gross pay in assignments A16.1 and A16.2 calculate, for each of the
employees, PAYE, national insurance contribution, and net pay for week 3.
(b)   Calculate the employees' contributions to national
insurance.
(c)   Show how the book-keeping entry for wages and
salaries would appear in week 3. NB: Include
employer's contribution.

NICE ICE CREAM COMPANY
CLOCK CARD

NAME Fred Pringle

WEEK ENDING SUNDAY 26 April

HOURLY RATE £2.40

WORKS NO. 3

DEPARTMENT Manufacturing

DAY	MORNING		AFTERNOON		EVENING		HOURS		
	IN	OUT	IN	OUT	IN	OUT	TOTAL	ORD	O/TIME
MONDAY	7.58	12.00	12.55	17.00	17.30	19.30			
TUESDAY	8.01	12.00	13.00	17.02	17.25	20.00			
WEDNESDAY	8.02	12.00	13.00	17.01	17.25	19.30			
THURSDAY	7.59	12.00	13.00	17.00	17.25	20.00			
FRIDAY	8.00	12.00	13.08	17.03	17.30	19.00			
SATURDAY	9.00	13.01							
SUNDAY						TOTAL			

Hours working	Hours	Rate	Amount
At Ordinary Rate			
At Time and One Quarter			
At Time and One Half			
At Double Time			
Gross Pay			

Figure 16.2

NICE ICE CREAM COMPANY
CLOCK CARD

WORKS NO. 2
DEPARTMENT Manufacturing

NAME Zoe Patel
WEEK ENDING SUNDAY 26 April
HOURLY RATE £2.20

DAY	MORNING		AFTERNOON		EVENING		HOURS		
	IN	OUT	IN	OUT	IN	OUT	TOTAL	ORD	O/TIME
MONDAY	7.58	12.00	13.00	17.00	17.30	19.30			
TUESDAY	7.58	12.00	12.58	17.00	17.30	19.30			
WEDNESDAY	7.58	12.00	12.57	17.00	17.30	19.30			
THURSDAY	7.58	12.00	12.59	17.00	17.30	19.30			
FRIDAY	7.58	12.00	12.59	17.00					
SATURDAY									
SUNDAY					TOTAL				

Hours Working	Hours	Rate	Amount
At Ordinary Rate			
At Time and One Quarter			
At Time and One Half			
At Double Time			
Gross Pay			

Figure 16.3

NICE ICE CREAM COMPANY
CLOCK CARD

NAME John Adams
WEEK ENDING SUNDAY 26 April
HOURLY RATE £2.00

WORKS NO. 1
DEPARTMENT Manufacturing

DAY	MORNING		AFTERNOON		EVENING		HOURS		
	IN	OUT	IN	OUT	IN	OUT	TOTAL	ORD	O/TIME
MONDAY	8.01	12.01	13.00	17.01					
TUESDAY	8.01	12.01	13.00	17.01	17.30	19.30			
WEDNESDAY	8.10	12.00	13.00	17.01					
THURSDAY	7.59	12.01	12.59	17.02					
FRIDAY	7.58	12.00	12.55	17.00					
SATURDAY									
SUNDAY					TOTAL				

Hours Working	Hours	Rate	Amount
At Ordinary Rate			
At Time and One Quarter			
At Time and One Half			
At Double Time			
Gross Pay			

Figure 16.4

A16.4   William Oakland's gross salary during week 14 is £220, and tax paid up to week 13 was £601.50. His tax code number is 237. His gross pay to date is £2600. Table A national insurance contribution applies. Obtain current PAYE tax tables and a national insurance contribution table from your local income tax office and calculate William Oakland's net pay for the week.

17. Business documents

In other sections of your studies you may have become familiar with a range of documents that are used in business transactions. The purpose of this chapter is to describe the key documents.

Any businessman will want to know accurately what the position is regarding:

1. Net sales.
2. Net purchases.
3. Debtors.
4. Creditors.

In the process of buying and selling we may identify these as shown in Fig. 17.1.

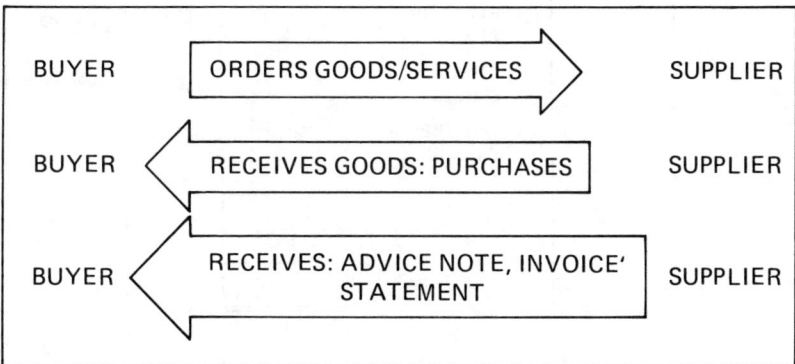

BUYER	ORDERS GOODS/SERVICES	SUPPLIER
BUYER	RECEIVES GOODS: PURCHASES	SUPPLIER
BUYER	RECEIVES: ADVICE NOTE, INVOICE' STATEMENT	SUPPLIER

Figure 17.1   *Identification of the stages in the process of buying and selling*

17.1 Invoices

Invoices will vary in their design and size from company to company. There is, however, basic information common to most organizations and a typical example of such an invoice is shown in Fig. 17.2. It is quite usual for the supplier to issue at least four copies, often in different colours. He may use these different colour copies as advice notes or delivery notes. Often the advice note is sent in advance of the goods, indicating that they are 'on their way'. He will, of course, wish to keep careful records of his customers' accounts and will use copies of the invoice for this purpose.

Galton Industries Ltd, 80 High Street, Perivale, Middlesex VAT Regd No 501 68211 14			Invoice No. 35216 Date: 18th March 19–1		

To: J V Stores Ltd.,
    Station Road,
    Exeter, Devon.					

Terms: Strictly Net 14 days					
Order No	Quantity	Description	Cost £	VAT rate	Vat amount
117	10	Chairs 079 @ £25.50	255.00	15%	38.25
	2	Tables K16 @ £68.70	137.40	15%	20.61
	1	Divan XH25 @ £350.00	350.00	15%	52.50
			742.40 111.36		111.36
			£853.76		

Figure 17.2 *An example of an invoice*

The invoice shown in Fig. 17.2 received from Galton Industries Ltd represents purchases in the books of JV Stores Ltd and sales in the books of Galton Industries. Most traders will receive a number of invoices from different suppliers; these will be filed together to form their own purchases book or for the supplier in the sales book. In this way detailed information is easily available from the filed records of the invoices.

Sales Invoice No. 132   VAT Regd No. 601 6438 19

To: J H Dunburton & Son,
       90 Dean Street, London E17

From:

     H.V. Thomas Ltd.,
     Greer Street, Southampton

Date
31st March 19_1

Quantity	Description and Price	Amount Exclusive of VAT	VAT Rate	VAT Net
		£	%	£
10	Radios, XH5 @ £19.70	197.00		
5	Video Machines, J90			
	@ £450.00	2250.00		
5	Leads, P101 @ £2.00	10.00		
5	Leads, F102 @ £2.70	13.50		
10	Leads, J100 @ £2.75	27.50		
		2498.00	15	355.97
	Delivery (strictly net)	15.00	15	2.25
TERMS: Cash Discount of 5% if paid within 10 days		2513.00		358.22
	VAT	358.22		
	TOTAL	£2871.22		

Tax Point 31/3/81

Figure 17.3 *An example of a detailed VAT invoice*

Fig. 17.3 shows a detailed VAT invoice issued by a supplier, in this example, H.V. Thomas Ltd.

Points to note

1. VAT is calculated on the discount price, i.e. £2498 less 5% cash discount. This gives £2373.10 which is then subject to 15% VAT or £2373.10 x $\frac{15}{100}$ = £355.97.

2. VAT of 15% is charged on delivery, since this indicates that it is *strictly net*, i.e. no cash discount is allowable, therefore the amount of VAT payable is £15 x $\frac{15}{100}$ = £2.25.

3. The total of £2871.22 is inclusive of VAT and delivery. J.H. Dumbarton can deduct £124.90 from this total if he settles with H.V. Thomas Ltd within 10 days, i.e. his cash discount of 5% is worth £124.90 or £2498 x $\frac{5}{100}$.

17.2 Statements

The supplier will send to all of his customers a statement of account. This will be a summary of all the invoices sent to the customer in the last month. It may well indicate any credit allowed or previous payments that have been made. The net total to be paid is clearly shown. (See Fig. 17.4.)

17.3 Credit Notes

In any transaction of goods it is likely that errors or accidents will occur. Goods may simply be damaged in transit, or not enough, or the wrong type or design may be sent. There must, therefore, be a provision for returning goods. Normally, this is achieved by the supplier issuing a credit note printed in red to the customer. The supplier keeps a copy of the credit note and records this

A/C No 642

Date: 1 April 19-1

To: J.V. Stores Ltd.,
    Station Road,
    Exeter, Devon.

Galton Industries Ltd,
80 High Street,
Perivale, Middlesex

VAT Regd No 501 68211 14

Date	Order No.	Cost inc. VAT	Dr	Cr	Balance
March 18th	117	GOODS	853.76		853.76 DR

Terms: Strictly net, 14 days

The last figure is the amount due

Figure 17.4 *An example of a statement*

in sales returns (returns inwards book). He must also credit the customer's account in the ledger. The buyer on receipt of the credit note would need to record entries in the purchases returns (returns outwards book) and debit the supplier's account in the ledger. (See Fig. 17.5.)

CREDIT NOTE

To:

J.V. Stores Ltd.,
Station Road,
Exeter, Devon

Date 28 April 19-1

No 74/4/8

Galton Industries Ltd,
Middlesex
VAT Regd No 501 68211 14

By Credit Invoice No 35216

1 Divan XH2J
(Damaged Springs)   350.00

VAT 15%   52.50
                                     ───────
                                      402.50
                                     ═══════

Figure 17.5 *An example of a credit note*

Note that the adjustment of VAT paid and received has to be very carefully recorded. It must be possible for this information to be cross-referenced to filed copies of credit notes; in this way details of the transaction can be found.

18. Accruals and prepayments

As we know in order to calculate as accurately as possible the net profit of a business, we must attempt to match as closely as possible revenue (sales) with costs (expenses). We have until now made the assumption that cash expenditure on items such as rent, insurance, stationery and advertising represents exactly the amount of these items which has been used up; we have accordingly transferred the balances of the relevant accounts to the profit and loss account as they stand. In fact, for a variety of reasons the balance of these accounts may not represent the amount of the item actually expended and used up, and some adjustment to the account may be necessary before recording the expenditure in the profit and loss account. For example:

1. If we pay £10 per month rent, we may find that at the end of our financial year on 31 December one month's rent has not been paid. We will find that the balance on our rent account is £110 as against the £120 which should have been paid.

2. We may during the year have bought stationery amounting to £200 but an examination of our stationery cupboard may reveal that we have on hand stationery which has not been used worth £50. From this we can deduce that stationery used up or expended is only £150 (£200 − £50).

18.1 Making Adjustments for Accruals

In the first example above it is evident that the charge against gross profit for rent is £120 which is made up of £110 which has been paid, plus £10 which is due but not paid – *accrued*. The rent account prior to the production of the profit and loss account would therefore appear:

RENT

Balance	110	

Rent should be shown in the profit and loss account as follows:

PROFIT AND LOSS ACCOUNT FOR THE YEAR ENDED 19–2
(EXTRACT)

Rent	110		
Add Accrued Rent	10	120	

In other words, the profit and loss account is debited with the amount of rent actually 'used' whether or not it has been paid for in cash £120. If the profit and loss account is debited with £120 then the rent account itself must be credited with a like amount. The result is shown below:

RENT

Balance	110	Profit and Loss	120
Balance b/f	10		
	120		120
		Balance b/f	10

As can be seen, the effect of crediting the rent account with rent used is to leave a credit balance on the rent account equal to the accrued account after production of the profit and loss account. This balance, and any similar balances, should appear on the liabilities side of the balance sheet. Where there is more than one item of accrual there is no need to itemize them separately in the balance sheet. They should be shown together as one item 'accruals' just below creditors. Other items which frequently give rise to accruals are rates, electricity, wages, interest on loans.

18.2 Making Adjustments for Prepayments

In the second example we are dealing with the opposite effects to accruals. These are normally referred to as *prepayments*. Again, the important point to remember is to debit the profit and loss account with the amount of an expense actually used rather than the amount paid for or bought.

In the second example, involving stationery, £150 must be debited to the profit and loss account rather than £200 and the relevant accounts will appear:

STATIONERY

Cash Balance	200	Profit and Loss	150
		Balance	50
	200		200
Balance	50		

PROFIT AND LOSS ACCOUNT (EXTRACT)

Stationery	200		
Less Stationery			
on Hand	50	150	

The remaining debit balances on expense accounts in respect of prepayments should be entered together under the heading 'prepayments' in the balance sheet on the asset side. Prepayments should appear in the balance sheet above bank accounts but below debtors.

Items of expenditure frequently giving rise to prepayments include advertising, insurance, rent and rates.

ASSIGNMENTS

A18.1 A. Dore's financial year ends on 31 December 19—1 and on that date his rent account and stationery account appear as shown below:

RENT ACCOUNT		STATIONERY ACCOUNT	
Dec 31		Dec 31	
Balance 150		Balance 230	

When he produces his profit and loss account for the year he discovers that rent £15 for December is due but not paid and that stationery unused is worth £120.

(a) Show how the double entries to the profit and loss account would appear (using the above outlines). Balance the accounts and bring down any balance which remains to 1 Jan 1981.

(b) Show how rent and stationery would appear in his profit and loss account.

A18.2 The following trial balance was extracted from the books of A. Tring at the end of his financial year on 31 December 1985.

Sales		11 350
Purchases	4320	
Sales Returns	15	
Purchases Returns		25
Stock (1 Jan 1980)	560	
Rent	110	
Rates	50	
Insurance	30	
Advertising	150	
Wages	900	
Postage and Telephone	120	
Discount Allowed	50	
Discount Received		35

Bank Charges	10	
Interest Receivable		15
Bad Debts	25	
Premises	10 000	
Motor Vehicles	1 300	
Furniture and Fittings	2 000	
Debtors	750	
Creditors		120
Deposit Account at Bank	3 000	
Current Account at Bank	1 500	
Cash in Hand	500	
Capital		?
	25,390.	11 548

He has in addition to the above the following information:
1. Stock on 31 December 19–1 valued at cost £750.00
2. Rent for December £10.00 is due but not paid
3. Rates include £15.00 in advance
4. One-third of advertising expenditure refers to next year
5. Wages £20.00 are due but not paid

Taking into account the information above:

(a) Produce A. Tring's trading and profit and loss accounts for the year ended 31 December 19–1.
(b) Show a balance sheet at that date.
(c) Show how the rent account, advertising account and rates account would appear on 1 January 1986.

19. Depreciation

In Chapter 9 we examined how to record fixed assets in our ledger and we saw that since fixed assets are not 'used up' or expended in the same way as items such as stationery, wages, electricity, etc., it would be incorrect to transfer their cost to the profit and loss account in the usual way, so they appear in the balance sheet at cost. We know, however, that most fixed assets will lose some value over a period of time and this loss in value of fixed assets is called depreciation.

19.1 How Depreciation Occurs

Depreciation usually occurs in one of the following ways:

1. *Wear and tear*. As an asset is used it may become more and more worn out and will lose value because it requires more repairs. The value of motor vehicles is an example of this kind of depreciation.
2. *Passage of time*. Occasionally, a fixed asset will lose value merely because time has passed. This kind of depreciation occurs with leasehold property where a lease is purchased for a building costing, for example, £10 000 for a period of 20 years. At the end of the 20-year period the property reverts to its original owner and will therefore have no value to the business. The 20-year lease will lose 1/20 of its value each year.

3. *Changes in fashion.* We may occasionally find that a fixed asset's value changes because there has been a change in fashion which may make the asset obsolete. For example, a business may own a machine which produces a particular piece of machinery that becomes obsolete and so has little or no value. Similarly, the machine itself may be superseded by a more reliable and cheaper model.

19.2 Calculating the Amount of Depreciation

There are a great variety of different methods of calculating depreciation; some of the main ones are as follows.

The revaluation method

The asset is revalued at the end of each financial period and any difference between the valuation and the 'book value' is 'written off' to the depreciation account. E.g. freehold premises have a book value of £20 000, the valuation carried out by a local surveyor reveals a market value of £18 000, therefore depreciation is £2000.

The fixed instalment method

The value of the asset is reduced by the same amount each year, e.g. a firm purchases a machine at a cost of £10 750 and the estimated life of this machine is 20 years. It is therefore calculated that the loss in its value is:

$$\frac{\text{cost} - \text{scrap value}}{\text{life in years}} = \frac{10\,750 - 750}{20}$$

$$= £500 \text{ per year}$$

This is sometimes called the *straight line method.*

Diminishing balance method

The same percentage of book value is written off each year, e.g.
a firm buys a motor van which it decides to depreciate by 25% of
book value. Cost £10 000.

Year 1	Jan 1	Cost	£10 000
	Dec 31	Depreciation 25%	£2 500
Year 2	Jan 1	Book Value	£7 500
	Dec 31	DEP 25%	£1 875
Year 3	Jan 1	Book Value	£5 625
	Dec 31	DEP 25%	£1 406
			£4 219

The method chosen to calculate depreciation should be the one
which most accurately shows the depreciation. Therefore the
straight line method should be used where the life of the asset
can be accurately gauged and the diminishing balance method
for items which tend to lose more value in early years than later
years.

19.3 The Implications of Depreciation

Before we examine the ledger entries involved in depreciation we
may find it useful to review our knowledge of fixed assets and the
effect of depreciation on them.

Firstly, we know that fixed assets lose value as they get older
and that the cost of the fixed asset figure shown in the balance
sheet will usually be an overstatement of a fixed asset's real value.
This will lead to our balance sheet not giving a true and fair view
of the business.

Secondly, we know that as depreciation occurs our fixed assets
are 'used up' or expended. Depreciation is therefore an expense
chargeable against gross profit just like rent, rates and electricity.
Whichever method of book-keeping for depreciation we adopt, it
must simultaneously:

1. Show depreciation as an expense in the profit and loss account.
2. Give a realistic value to fixed assets in the balance sheet.

Book-keeping entries

Method 1. Under this method depreciation is written off directly against the fixed assets.

Example. On 1 Jan Year 1 J. Smith bought for cash: motor van £3000; leasehold premises £12 000. Depreciation is to be: motor van 10% p.a., diminishing balance method; leasehold premises 10% p.a., fixed instalment method. The relevant ledger accounts for the first 3 years would therefore appear as follows:

MOTOR VAN

Cash	3000	Depreciation	300
		Balance	2700
	3000		3000
Balance	2700	Depreciation	270
		Balance	2430
	2700		2700
Balance	2430	Depreciation	243
		Balance	2187
	2430		2430
Balance	2187		

LEASEHOLD PREMISES

Cash	12 000	Depreciation	1 200
		Balance	10 800
	12 000		12 000
Balance	10 800	Depreciation	1 200
		Balance	9 600
	10 800		10 800
Balance	9600	Depreciation	1 200
		Balance	8 400
	9 600		9 600
Balance	8 400		

DEPRECIATION ACCOUNT

Lease	1200	Profit and Loss	1500
Motor Van	300		
	1500		1500
Lease	1200	Profit and Loss	1470
Motor Van	270		
	1470		1470
Lease	1200	Profit and Loss	1443
Motor Van	243		
	1443		1443

PROFIT AND LOSS ACCOUNT (EXTRACT) YEAR 1

Depreciation:			Gross Profit
Lease	1200		
Motor Van	300	1500	

PROFIT AND LOSS ACCOUNT (EXTRACT) YEAR 2

Depreciation:			Gross Profit
Lease	1200		
Motor Van	270	1470	

PROFIT AND LOSS ACCOUNT (EXTRACT) YEAR 3

Depreciation:			Gross Profit
Lease	1200		
Motor Van	243	1443	

BALANCE SHEET AT THE END
OF YEAR 3 (EXTRACT)

Fixed Assets		
Lease	9600	
Less Depreciation	1200	8400
Motor Van	2430	
Less Depreciation	243	2187

Method 2. With Method 2, depreciation is entered to the credit side of a 'provision for depreciation of (name of asset) account' and to the debit side of the profit and loss account only. No other entries are necessary. We will find that over a period of years the value in the 'provision for depreciation account' accumulates as the assets lose value. Note the following points:

1. No entry is made in the account of the asset itself.
2. In order to find the book value of an asset we will need to refer to the asset account itself (with its debit balance) and the provision for depreciation account (with its credit balance).
3. When the assets are eventually disposed of the balance of the asset account is written off against the provision for depreciation.
4. The method of calculating the amount of depreciation remains the same.

Example. The figures in the above example are used below to illustrate the alternative approach to the book-keeping.

LEASEHOLD		PROVISION FOR DEPRECIATION LEASEHOLD	
1 Jan Year 1		Year 1 Profit	
Cash 12 000		and Loss 1200	
		Year 2 Profit	
		and Loss 1200	

MOTOR VAN		PROVISION FOR DEPRECIATION MOTOR VAN	
1 Jan Year 1		Year 1 Profit	
Cash 3 000		and Loss 300	
		Year 2 Profit	
		and Loss 270	

FIXED ASSETS AT THE END OF YEAR 2

Leasehold at Cost	12 000		
Less Provision for Depreciation	2 400	9 600	
Motor Van at Cost	3 000		
Less Provision for Depreciation	570	2 430	12 030

Note. In an examination where a question involves depreciation you should ensure that a full year's depreciation is chargeable. There are two circumstances where a full year's depreciation is not chargeable.

1. Where the accounting period is less than a year.
2. Where the asset or part of the asset is held for less than a year.

The question should be read very carefully so that you understand the examiners' intentions.

19.4 Provisions for Bad Debts

It may be that at the end of our accounting period our balance sheet appears with an item, e.g. debtors, £5000. We may also know from our past experience that some portion of the debtors will not pay, i.e. they will become bad debts. Obviously, if we knew the individuals, we would not have sold to them on credit in the first place. However, we will know from past experience what proportion (percentage) will never pay. If we proceed to produce a balance sheet showing the value of our debtors at £5000, we are in conflict with one of our accounting principles – a true and fair view. In the same way that we adjust our balance sheet value for fixed assets by providing for depreciation, we should now adjust our balance sheet valuation of debtors to allow for bad debts.

Creating a provision for bad debt

The proportion of our debtors that we know will be bad debts may be, for example, 2%. On debtors valued at £5000 our provision for bad debts should be 2% of £5000 = £100. The book-keeping entries for the initial creation of provision for bad debts are debit the profit and loss account (£100), credit provision for bad debts account (£100).

In the above example we may find that by the time we come to the end of the following year the volume of our debtors has increased to £6000; our provision for bad debts must therefore also increase to 2% of £6000 = £120. The entry this year will debit the profit and loss account (£20) and credit provision for bad debts (£20).

What will be the book-keeping entries in the above example if at the end of the third year debtors stood at £4000? Allow a 2% provision.

PROVISION FOR BAD DEBTS				PROFIT AND LOSS ACCOUNT GROSS PROFIT	
Profit and Loss	40	Balance	120	Provision for	
Balance	80			Bad Debts	40
	120		120		
	80		80		

Provisions for bad debts and the treatment of bad debts

In the above example we noticed that bad debts were provided for, although we had no note of any bad debts actually occurring. In the event of a bad debt occurring we have the option of one of the following methods.

Method 1. Actual bad debts, when they occur, are kept quite separate from the provision for bad debts as if the two things are quite unrelated.

Method 2. We keep a separate bad debts account, the balance of which is transferred to the provision for bad debts account at the end of the year, prior to adjusting the provision for bad debts to the new level of debtors.

Method 3. No separate bad debts account is kept at all. When bad debts actually occur they are written off directly to the provision for bad debts account.

Provision for discount allowed

When we make provision for bad debts we are really saying our debtors are worth, for example, £4000 but that some of them, say 2% or £80, will not pay and thus our net balance sheet totals the debts £3920, providing an accurate estimation of the true value of debtors. However, if we are in the habit of allowing cash discount for prompt payment we will be aware that of these debtors £3920 some will pay promptly, being entitled to cash discount, and will pay less. Unless we make allowance for this, our balance sheet statement of debtors will once again be an overstatement of the true position, in other words we must make provision for discount allowed in the same way that we make provision for bad debts. Again we will know from past experience what proportion of debtors is to be represented by a provision for cash discount.

Note. The amount of provision for discount allowed should be calculated on the figure of debtors which is net of provision for bad debts.

ASSIGNMENTS

A19.1   On 1 January 19–1 a trader buys the following assets:

Leasehold premises £10 000, 8-year lease
Motor van £5000
Furniture and fittings £500

He decides to provide for depreciation for these assets on the following basis:

Leasehold premises – straight line method – an appropriate amount each year over the life of the asset.

Motor vans – diminishing balance method – 20% of remaining book value each year.

Furniture and fittings – straight line method – the furniture and fittings have an estimated life of 10 years at the end of which time they will have a scrap value of £100.

Show how the assets would appear in his ledger and show how the related provision for depreciation accounts would appear for the first three years. Show how the assets would appear in his balance sheet at 31 December 1987.

A19.2   On 31 December 19–1 the following balances were extracted from the books of T. Shoesmith.

Purchases	£3892.00
Sales	£6328.00
Returns in	£23.00
Returns out	£42.00
Stock (1 Jan 19–1)	£890.00
Telephone	£60.00
Rates	£144.00
Rent	£110.00
Stationery	£50.00
Advertising	£80.00
Wages	£500.00

Premises	£10 000.00
Motor Vehicles	£2500.00
Furniture and Fittings	£100.00
Debtors	£300.00
Creditors	£500.00
Cash in Hand	£800.00
Bank Overdraft	£2000.00

(a) From the above list of balances calculate capital.

(b) Produce a trading and profit account and balance sheet taking into account the following matters:

A telephone bill of £40.00 has just been received but not paid.

Rates include an item £100.00 for rates for the 6 months ending 31 March 19–2.

Stationery in hand is valued at £10.00.

Rent for December is due but not paid.

Stock at close valued at cost is £750.00.

One quarter of advertising is to be considered prepaid.

Accrued wages amount to £40.00.

Premises are now valued at £9500.00.

Motor vehicles are to be depreciated by 10% of their book value.

Furniture and fittings were bought for £500.00 in 1967. They should be depreciated by 10% of cost.

A19.3 Debtors at the end of S. Peters' financial year on 31 December 19–1 amounted to £75000.00. He decided at this time to create a provision for bad debts at 2½% of debtors.

During the following three years his debtors at year end amounted to

31 December 19–2	£7700.00
19–3	£8000.00
19–4	£7500.00

(a) Show the provision for bad debts account for the four-year period above.

(b)   If S. Peters decided to keep in addition a provision for discount allowed account on 31 December 19–4 at 1% of debtors, show how debtors would appear in his balance sheet at that date.

20. Petty cash

20.1 Analysed Petty Cash Book

The chief cashier of many firms will deal with cash receipts and payments which will amount to hundreds of pounds each day. Because of this heavy responsibility for large payments, they will delegate the responsibility for small day-to-day transactions such as bus fares, office teas, window cleaning, etc., to some junior member of staff. The person responsible for these small or petty payments will record such transactions in analysed petty cash book, a sample of which is shown below.

ANALYSED PETTY CASH BOOK												
£	p	Date	Particulars	Vch No.	£	p	£	p	£	p	£	p
money received												
money paid												
analysis columns												

Any cash which the petty cashier receives will be recorded in the left-hand cash column (debit column) and any cash which he pays out will appear in the right-hand cash column. The date and particulars of every transaction will be recorded in the same date and particulars column.

The operation of these columns in the analysed petty cash book is illustrated in the following example.

Jan 1	Received £20.00 from chief cashier for petty cash
Jan 2	Paid for bus fare to bank £0.40
Jan 3	Bought pens £2.30
Jan 4	Paid window cleaner £2.00
Jan 5	Paid for milk for office teas £0.80
Jan 6	Bought wrapping paper £0.35
Jan 7	Bought postage stamps £3.00

£	p	Date	Particulars	Vch No.	£	p	£	p	£	p
20	–	Jan 1	Chief Cashier							
		Jan 2	Bus Fare			40				
		Jan 3	Pens		2	30				
		Jan 4	Window Cleaner		2	00				
		Jan 5	Milk			80				
		Jan 6	Wrapping Paper			35				
		Jan 7	Stamps		3	00				

All the cash received is recorded in the left-hand cash column and that paid out in the right-hand cash column. To find out how much cash is left, balance the petty cash book in the following way:

Step 1. Total the right-hand column and enter the total.

Step 2. Deduct cash spent from cash received and enter this balance.

Step 3. Total and rule off cash columns bringing down balance on the opposite side as shown below.

£	p	Date	Particulars	Vch No.	£	p	£	p	£	p
20	–	Jan 1	Chief Cashier							
		Jan 2	Bus Fare			40				
		Jan 3	Pens		2	30				
		Jan 4	Window Cleaner		2	–				
		Jan 5	Milk			80				
		Jan 6	Wrapping Paper			35				
		Jan 7	Stamps		3	–				
					8	85				
		Jan 7	Balance		11	15				
20	–				20	–				
11	15	Jan 8	Balance							

20.2   Analysis Columns

You will have noticed that there are many more cash columns on the right-hand side of the page. The petty cashier will use these to analyse the payments as they occur. He will use a separate column for each commonly occurring item of expenditure such as fares and travelling, stationery, postage, sundries, and as he records the amounts paid out in the right-hand cash column he will repeat this amount in the appropriate analysis column. At the end of each week he will total each analysis column and the corresponding expense account in the ledger will be debited. The completed petty cash book in the above example will then appear as shown in Example 20.1.

Under the imprest system of petty cash at the end of each week or other convenient period, the petty cashier will be reimbursed with the exact amount he has paid out so that he begins each new period with the same amount of money – the imprest amount.

£	p	Date	Particulars	Vch No.	£	p	Travelling £ p	Stationery £	p	Postage £	p	Sundries £	p
20	00	Jan 1	Chief Cashier										
		Jan 2	Bus Fare		2	40	40						
		Jan 3	Pens		2	30		2	30				
		Jan 4	Window Cleaner		2	00						2	00
		Jan 5	Milk			80							80
		Jan 6	Wrapping Paper			35			35				
		Jan 7	Stamps		3	00				3	00		
					8	85	40	2	65	3	00	2	80
		Jan 7	Balance		11	15							
20	00				20	00							
11	15	Jan 8	Balance										

Amounts posted to debit side
of ledger accounts

Example 20.1

20.3   Vouchers

In order that the petty cashier has evidence that the payments recorded have actually been made, he will each time he makes a payment demand a petty cash voucher from the person who has made the expenditure. Usually this voucher must be counter-signed by some person in authority. See the example illustrated in Fig. 20.1.

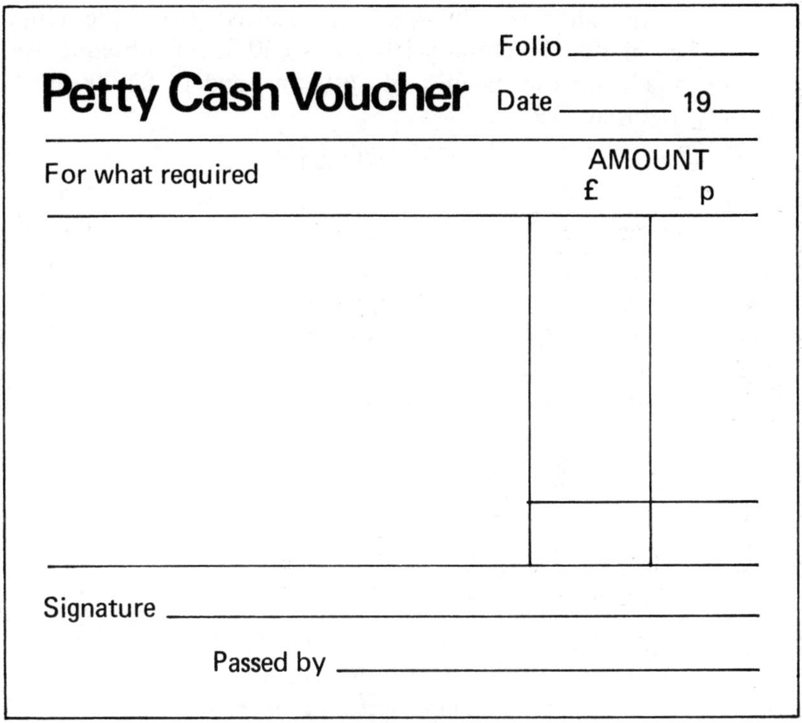

Petty Cash Voucher

Folio _____

Date _____ 19___

For what required	AMOUNT	
	£	p

Signature _____

Passed by _____

Figure 20.1   *An example of a petty cash voucher*

ASSIGNMENTS

A20.1   From the information below enter the relevant details on to analysed petty cash paper. You should use separate analysis columns for stationery, postage, travel and sundries. Balance the petty cash account and carry down the balance on 6 February 19–1 and 12 February 19–1.

In addition, the amount received from the chief cashier on 1 February 19–1 was £20.00; he subsequently made up the balance of cash on hand to £20.00 on 6 February 19–1.

WEEK 1

Name	Date	Purpose	Amount in Total
Johnson	1/2/–1	Bus fare to bank	.20
Smith	1/2/–1	Envelopes	.45
Johnson	2/2/–1	Window cleaner	.85
Patel	3/2/–1	10 stamps @ 12p	1.20
Smith	4/2/–1	10 ball pens/fare to bank (0.20)	1.88
Brown	6/2/–1	Stapler @ £1.50	
		Packet of staples @ 40p	1.90

WEEK 2

Name	Date	Purpose	Amount in Total
Bell	8/2/–1	Bell for enquiries office/ fare to shops (0.20)	2.42
Johnson	9/2/–1	Envelopes/milk for tea (0.40) fare to shops (0.20)	1.40
Patel	9/2/–1	Fare to bank	.20
Brown	11/2/–1	10 stamps @ 12p/ wrapping paper	1.50
Smith	12/2/–1	Window cleaner	.85
Brown	12/2/–1	Taxi fare to station	1.85

A20.2   Record the following transactions on analysed petty cash paper:

Jan 1   Received £20.00 from chief cashier as imprest amount

Jan 2   Paid for bus fare to bank £0.50

Jan 3   Paid window cleaner £1.20

Jan 4   Bought 10 @ 12p stamps

Jan 5   Bought envelopes £0.75

Jan 5   Paid for milk for office teas £3.20

Jan 6   Taxi fare to station £3.00

Balance petty cash book. Continue for second week:

Jan 8   Received cash from chief cashier to make up imprest amount

Jan 8   Bus fare to bank £0.50

Jan 8   Bought string £0.35

Jan 9   Paid window cleaner £1.20

Jan 10   Bought sugar for office teas £0.38

Jan 10   Took bus to stationer's (£0.20) and bought ball pens (£3.00)

Jan 11   Bought envelopes £0.85

Jan 12   Bought 10 @ 12p stamps

Jan 13   Paid for lunch for client £3.20

Balance and rule off petty cash book.

21. Interpretation of accounts

The balance sheet and profit statement for Fine Royal Co. Ltd are shown below. You should examine them carefully and then read the section on the interpretation of accounts. All references to figures used in this section are based on Fine Royal Co. Ltd accounts.

FINE ROYAL CO. LTD BALANCE SHEET AT 31 DECEMBER 19–1

	£	£	£
Fixed Assets			
Machinery at Cost		5000	
Less: Depreciation		500	4500
Current Assets	£		
Stock	2000		
Debtors	150		
Prepayments	256		
Cash in Hand	20		
in Bank	300	2726	
Current Liabilities			
Creditors		900	1826
			£6326
Financed by Owners' Interests			
Capital		5000	
Retained Profit		1326	
			£6326

(For calculation of *working capital* and *acid test ratio* see Section 21.2.)

224

FINE ROYAL CO. LTD
PROFIT STATEMENT FOR THE YEAR ENDED 31 DECEMBER 19—1

		£	
Sales Revenue		12 000	(For reference for calculation of *profitability* see Section 21.3.)
l ess			
Cost of Goods Sold		6 800	
	Gross Profit	5 200	(For reference for calculation of *profitability* see Section 21.3.)
Less			
Other Expenses			
Wages	1800		
Rent	974		
Depreciation	500		
General	600	3 874	
	Net Profit	£1 326	(For reference for calculation of *profitability* see Section 21.3.)

21.1 Interpretation of Accounts

There are a number of very useful calculations a businessman may perform given the information contained in a balance sheet and the trading and profit and loss account. These calculations may help to interpret or identify trends or patterns that are occurring in his firm and may indicate that he should pay special attention to them. Many of the calculations will be concerned with the profitability and liquidity of the business. For the purpose of this book and your course it is necessary to concentrate on the following key areas:

A. Liquidity:
   1. Working Capital
   2. 'Acid Test' Ratio or Liquid Capital Ratio
   3. Stock Turnover

B. Profitability:
   1. Gross Profit as a % of Turnover
   2. Net Profit as a % of Turnover

21.2 Liquidity

1. Working capital

One of the most common reasons for failure in business is that a firm has run short of working capital. Obviously, therefore, any business needs to pay attention to its working capital to ensure that it remains solvent. Working capital is the capital that is required to run the business once the fixed assets such as plant, machinery, etc., have been purchased. It can be calculated by determining how much current assets exceed current liabilities:

Working Capital = Current Assets − Current Liabilities.

The following example is taken from the balance sheet of Fine Royal Co. Ltd, see page 224.

Working Capital of Fine Royal Co. Ltd at 31 December 19–1

Current Assets   −   Current Liabilities   = Working Capital
  (£2726)   (£900)   (£1826)

It is clear from this example that Fine Royal's current assets safely exceed its current liabilities. This may also be expressed as a ratio,

$$\frac{\text{Current Assets}}{\text{Current Liabilities}} = \frac{£2726}{£\ 900} = 3 \text{ times}$$

Relating working capital to sales produced it can be seen that for every £1 of working capital used £6.57 of sales have resulted. This figure does not mean very much on its own; the company would need to compare it with the previous years' figures and with figures produced by other firms who deal in a similar trade.

2. 'Acid test' or liquid capital ratio

The purpose of this ratio is to discover quickly whether the firm can meet its current liabilities. Stock is not included in current assets, since it may be some time before it is possible to sell it. Similarly, prepayments are excluded, because they cannot be quickly converted into cash to meet immediate liabilities.

The acid test ratio is calculated:

$$\frac{\text{Current Assets} - \text{Stock}}{\text{Current Liabilities}}$$

For Fine Royal Co. this is calculated:

$$\frac{£2726 - 2256}{£900}$$

$$= \frac{£470}{£900} = 0.52 \text{ times}$$

This indicates that Fine Royal is weak regarding its liquid assets, i.e. too much of its current assets is stock.

3. Stock turnover

Many traders will attempt to sell their stock as quickly as possible, especially if their trade is one where the risks of holding large quantities of stock are great. The trader calculates the average stocks that are held and values them at cost; this figure is then divided into the year's turnover at cost, i.e. cost of sales, thus:

$$\frac{\text{Year's Turnover at Cost}}{\text{Average Stock at Cost}} = \text{Rate of Turnover}$$

If the Year's Cost of Sales = £6800 and Average Stock = £2000 the Rate of Turnover = $\frac{6800}{2000}$ or 3.4.

This means that the trader turns his stock over 3.4 times a year, or expressed another way, the trader keeps goods in stock for about 15 weeks (i.e. 52 weeks divided by 3.4) before they are replaced. Of course, for this to have any meaning it must be set in the context of the businessman's particular trade or industry, e.g. it would be usual to expect perishable goods such as flowers or strawberries to turn over quicker than this.

21.3 Profitability

1. Gross profit as a percentage of turnover

Every trader has a reasonable idea of what his gross profit is likely to be. In fixing the price of the article he sells he has already added on to the cost price a certain percentage (known as 'mark up'). Thus if his 'mark up' is 35% on the cost price of an article that costs £5 the selling price will be £6.75, i.e. $5 \times \dfrac{135}{100}$

The gross profit as a percentage of turnover of Fine Royal Co. Ltd can be calculated (refer back to the profit statement, page 225).

$$\text{Percentage of Gross Profit} = \frac{\text{Gross Profit}}{\text{Turnover}} \times 100 = \frac{£5200}{£12\,000} \times \frac{100}{1} = 43.3\%$$

2. Net profit as a percentage of turnover

Net profit is the profit that remains after costs and expenses have been deducted from gross profit. Should the trader notice a significant change in his net profit percentage he may wish to investigate further to determine the reason.

The net profit as a percentage of turnover of Fine Royal Co. Ltd can be calculated (refer to profit statement, page 225):

$$\text{Percentage of Net Profit} = \frac{\text{Net Profit}}{\text{Turnover}} \times 100 = \frac{1326}{12\,000} = 11\%$$

If net profit has fallen look, for example, at expenses to see if this has risen compared to previous years:

$$\text{e.g. Wages } \frac{1800}{12\,000} \times 100 = 15\%$$

In this way a quick check may be made to identify those expenses that contribute to a fall in net profit.

ASSIGNMENTS

A21.1   Calculate the working capital of Regal Industries when current liabilities total £3600 and current assets £5870. Express this as a ratio.

A21.2   From the details given in Frome Knight Ltd balance sheet calculate:

(a)   Working capital.
(b)   Liquid capital ratio or 'acid test'.

FROME KNIGHT LTD BALANCE SHEET
AT 1 JANUARY 19--1

	£	£	£
Fixed Assets			
Premises		3000	
Plant		5300	
Motor Vans		1800	10 100
Current Assets	£		
Cash	60		
Bank	575		
Debtors	1360		
Stock	3600	5595	
Current Liabilities			
Creditors		3108	
			2 487
			£12 587
Financed by:			
Owners' Interests			
Capital		9297	
Retained Profit		3290	
			£12 587

A21.3   Hine Brothers' turnover and profit figures for two years are:

	Year 1	*Year 2*
Turnover	£44 000	£52 000
Gross Profit	£13 200	£14 040
Net Profit	£4 840	£6 110

Calculate:

(a)   Gross profit as a percentage of turnover for years 1 and 2.

(b)   Net profit as a percentage of turnover for years 1 and 2.

A21.4   Hypermarket have two branches in Liverpool and Leeds selling the same goods. The turnover and profit figures are:

	Turnover	*Gross Profit*	*Net Profit*
Liverpool	£400 000	£110 000	£60 000
Leeds	£62 000	£18 600	?

(a)   Leeds Branch has the same net profit percentage as Liverpool. What is this percentage?

(b)   Calculate the net profit for Leeds.

(c)   What is the gross profit percentage for both branches?

22.   The business entity

For the purposes of book-keeping and accounts we make the assumption that the business and the owner of the business have quite separate identities. Therefore, if C. Fiddler happens to own a business which buys and sells violins, we confine our accounting records to those transactions which relate to the business of C. Fiddler and exclude all transactions which relate to his personal life. This separation of the owner and the business is called the *entity concept*.

In the case of sole traders and partnerships the distinction between the owner and his business is in the eyes of the law an artificial one, but in the case of a joint stock company (for example, a limited company) the law recognizes the company as a separate entity or person.

From the point of view of keeping accounting records this separation of the proprietor from his business means that we must be careful to decide what is a business transaction and what is a personal transaction. Using the example of C. Fiddler above, if he buys stationery to use at work, we should enter the transaction in the accounting record of the firm, but if he buys stationery to use at home, we will regard this as a personal transaction and exclude it from our accounting records. We must at all times bear in mind that we are keeping the books of the firm, not the owner of the firm.

22.1   The Reason for Double Entries

The method of book-keeping that is most widely used in business throughout the world is the double-entry system. With this system every transaction is entered into our ledger twice. The reason for this double entering is so that we are able to record transactions from two points of view.

Example. If we buy goods for cash £50 two things are happening:

1.   Cash — £50 will flow out of the firm.
2.   Goods — £50 will come into the firm.

We are exchanging one asset for another. See Section 1.7.

Example. If we sell goods for cash £75 two things are happening:

1.   Goods — £75 will flow out of the firm.
2.   Cash — £75 will flow into the firm.

Again we are exchanging one asset for another.

Example. If we buy goods on credit £80, that is to say we take the goods and promise to pay for them at a later date, two things are happening:

1.   Goods £80 are coming into the firm.
2.   We are incurring a debt £80 which must be paid later.

This idea of two points of view of each transaction is called the duality concept.

22.2   The Balance Sheet

We describe the items that the firm owns, i.e. the stock, cash, debts receivable, premises, motor vans, furniture, etc., as *assets*. In Section 1.6 we saw how assets can be divided into:

1.   Fixed assets — assets of a permanent nature to be held for use in the firm, year after year: premises, motor vehicles, office machinery, etc.
2.   Current assets — assets which move fluidly through the firm: stock, debts receivable, cash, etc.

We describe the items which the firm owes as *liabilities* and liabilities can be classified into categories in a similar way to assets. We have examined the idea of debts which the firm must repay to its suppliers. The firm may also make short-term loans, i.e. borrow from other people such as the bank or finance companies. These debts which must be met in a fairly short period of time are called current liabilities. The other sub-division of liabilities is capital. You may at first find that the idea of capital being a liability is a strange one but you must remember what we have said about the business entity, i.e. the business and the owner of the business are kept separate. This means that when C. Fiddler starts business with capital in cash of £10 000, C. Fiddler (*the person*) is lending C. Fiddler (*the business*) £10 000 in cash.

A businessman may wish to draw up lists of what his business owns and what his business owes. He may call one of these lists assets and the other liabilities. Let us take the simple example of a new business, e.g. C. Fiddler, who starts business with capital in cash £10 000 on 1 January 19−1. As we know from our study of the duality concept and our study of the entity concept this means that C. Fiddler lends the business £10 000 in cash. The business therefore has one asset − cash £10 000 − and one liability − capital (a debt payable to C. Fiddler) £10 000. The lists of assets and liabilities would therefore appear:

Assets		*Liabilities*	
Cash	10 000	Capital	10 000

When we make a list of assets and liabilities we call the list a *balance sheet*. We can therefore define a balance sheet as a statement showing all assets and liabilities of a firm at a particular moment in time. We say at a particular moment in time since, as we shall see, as soon as Fiddler commences to trade the balance sheet above will no longer show the true position. Therefore, an accepted layout and heading of the above balance sheet is as follows:

C. FIDDLER
BALANCE SHEET AS AT 1 JANUARY 19−1

Assets		*Liabilities*	
Cash	10 000	Capital	10 000
	10 000		10 000

Suppose now that on 2 January C. Fiddler bought goods to form his stock £2000 and a motor van for deliveries £3000. He is exchanging the asset cash £2000 for stock and exchanging more of the asset cash £3000 for a motor vehicle. His balance sheet at the end of the day therefore appears as follows:

C. FIDDLER
BALANCE SHEET AS AT 2 JANUARY 19–1

Assets			*Liabilities*	
Fixed Assets				
Motor Vehicle		3 000	Capital	10 000
Current Assets				
Stock	2000			
Cash	5000	7 000		
		10 000		10 000

Notice that at this point his capital is unaltered; it is just represented by a different mix of assets. Notice also the sub-division between fixed assets and current assets.

Suppose now that on 3 January 19–1 C. Fiddler sells half his stock for £1500 on credit, bearing in mind that half his stock cost him £1000 this means that:

1. The business has made a profit of £500.
2. He has exchanged one asset (stock) valued at £1000 for another asset, a debtor for £1500.

Before we draw up the new balance sheet we should ask ourselves who this profit belongs to. It does, of course, belong to the owner of the business, C. Fiddler. His new balance sheet therefore appears:

C. FIDDLER
BALANCE SHEET AS AT 3 JANUARY 19–1

Assets			*Liabilities*		
Fixed Assets					
Motor Vehicle		3 000	Capital	10 000	
Current Assets			Add net profit	500	10 500
Stock	1000				
Debtors	1500				
Cash	5000	7 500			
		10 500			10 500

We could continue recording the effect of individual transactions on C. Fiddler's balance sheet and eventually build up a picture of his trading activity. You may like to write in your notebook how his balance sheet would appear if on the next day the transactions listed in A22.1 occurred.

Rewriting the balance after each transaction is a very inefficient way of recording transactions. In the double-entry system of book-keeping each class of asset and liability has a separate account so that after each transaction we merely adjust the balance of the two accounts which are affected. We can then, whenever we wish, produce a balance sheet merely by listing the balances of each account.

ASSIGNMENT

A22.1   Show how C. Fiddler's balance sheet would appear if
on 4 January the following transactions occurred.

   (a)   The customer who owed him £1500 cash paid
          him in full
   (b)   He bought goods for £250 on credit
   (c)   He paid cash £10 for travelling expenses

SOLUTIONS

Chapter 1

A1.1   (a)

	£	£
SALES		650
Less Cost of Sales		490
GROSS PROFIT		160
Less Expenses		
Advertising	25	
Postage	5	30
NET PROFIT		130

(b)

	£	£
SALES		1500
Less Cost of Sales		800
GROSS PROFIT		700
Less Expenses		
Wages	150	
Telephone	5	
Stationery	6	
Advertising	35	196
NET PROFIT		504

(c)

	£	£
SALES		3500
Less Cost of Sales		2430
GROSS PROFIT		1070
Less Expenses		
Wages	185	
Delivery Expenses	35	
Postage	50	
Stationery	35	
Advertising	30	335
NET PROFIT		735

A1.2 (a) (i) Current Assets   £
                    Stock   3 000
                    Cash   1 500
                                                      4 500

          (ii) Fixed Assets
                    Premises   10 000
                    Motor Vans   5 000
                    Machinery   1 000
                    Furniture   500
                                                     16 500

(b) Net worth of firm = total of assets (£16 500 + £4500) less
     current liabilities (£1750).
     Net worth = £21 000 – £1750 = £19 250

(c) Capital = net worth = £19 250

Chapter 2

A2.1

					CASH				
June 1	Balance		12	80	June 4	Purchases		5	60
June 3	Sales		48	25	June 10	Purchases		4	00
June 12	Sales		63	28	June 10	Wages		10	00
June 25	Sales		104	36	June 12	Electricity		4	00
					June 13	Telephone		8	00
					June 25	Travelling		2	00
					June 30	Purchases		5	40
					June 30	Balance	c/d	189	69
			228	69				228	69
Jul 1	Balance	b/d	189	69	Jul 5	Purchases		9	20
Jul 1	Sales		23	30	Jul 14	Travelling		3	52
Jul 17	Sales		35	90	Jul 18	Wages		10	00
Jul 31	Sales		39	20	Jul 20	Stationery		7	28
					Jul 25	Purchases		4	50
					Jul 31	Balance	c/d	253	59
			288	09				288	09
Aug 1	Balance	b/d	253	59					

A2.2   A. Swindle

Feb 1	Sales		350	00	Feb 4	Purchases		130	00
Feb 12	Sales		390	00	Feb 7	Stationery		3	20
Feb 25	Sales		350	00	Feb 10	Purchases		120	00
					Feb 15	Insurance		8	00
					Feb 18	Purchases		90	00
					Feb 28	Wages		50	00
					Feb 28	Balance		688	80
			1090	00				1090	00
Mar 1	Balance		688	80	Mar 7	Purchases		85	00
Mar 4	Sales		150	00	Mar 10	Electricity		8	20
Mar 16	Sales		230	00	Mar 25	Stationery		5	20
Mar 31	Sales		400	00	Mar 28	Cleaning		3	50
					Mar 31	Balance		1366	90
			1468	80				1468	80
Apr 1	Balance		1366	90					

A.2.3   B. Shifty

Cash book total shows	£454.19
Less items shown total	£440.93
Missing Entry is: Tea, etc.	13.26

Chapter 3

A3.1

Q	ACCOUNT TO BE DEBITED	ACCOUNT TO BE CREDITED
(a)	Cash	Sales
(b)	Stationery	Cash
(c)	Purchases	Cash
(d)	Wages	Cash
(e)	Telephone	Cash
(f)	Gas	Cash
(g)	Cash	Sales
(h)	Cash	Electricity
(i)	Sales or sales returns	Cash

A3.2

CASH

June 1	Sales	33	90	June 4	Purchases		12	90
June 6	Sales	33	28	June 5	Wages		15	–
June 7	Sales	28	90	June 8	Wages		15	–
June 10	Sales	23	40	June 9	Purchases		4	90
				June 10	Balance		71	68
		119	48				119	48
June 10	Balance	71	68					

SALES

				June 1	Cash		33	90
				June 6	Cash		33	28
				June 7	Cash		28	90
				June 10	Cash		23	40

PURCHASES

June 4	Cash	12	90
June 9	Cash	4	90

WAGES

June 5	Cash	15	–
June 8	Cash	15	–

A3.3

CASH

Feb 1	Sales	75	28	Feb 2	Purchases		22	98
Feb 4	Sales	35	98	Feb 5	Stationery		23	98
Feb 9	Sales	83	20	Feb 9	Wages		33	90
Feb 13	Sales	130	90	Feb 10	Electricity		12	90
Feb 14	Sales	120	90	Feb 11	Rent		14	20
				Feb 12	Purchases		10	30
				Feb 14	Balance		328	00
		446	26				444	26

Feb 14	Balance		328	—					
				SALES					
					Feb 1	Cash		75	28
					Feb 4	Cash		35	98
					Feb 9	Cash		83	20
					Feb 13	Cash		130	90
					Feb 14	Cash		120	90
				PURCHASES					
Feb 2	Cash		22	98					
Feb 12	Cash		10	30					
				STATIONERY					
Feb 5	Cash		23	98					
				WAGES					
Feb 9	Cash		33	90					
				ELECTRICITY					
Feb 10	Cash		12	90					
				RENT					
Feb 11	Cash		14	20					

A3.4

				CASH					
Aug 1	Sales		55	—	Aug 2	Purchases		35	—
Aug 3	Sales		75	—	Aug 4	Stationery		7	—
Aug 6	Sales		70	—	Aug 5	Wages		20	—
Aug 12	Sales		80	—	Aug 8	Electricity		10	—
Aug 16	Sales		50	—	Aug 9	Purchases		35	—
Aug 21	Sales		80	—	Aug 10	Haulage		5	—
					Aug 11	Wages		20	—

				Aug 13	Stationery	8	–
				Aug 17	Postage	5	–
				Aug 18	Rates	30	–
				Aug 19	Wages	20	–
				Aug 21	Balance	215	–
		410	–			410	–
Aug 22	Balance	215	–				

SALES

Aug 22				Aug 1	Cash	55	–
				Aug 3	Cash	75	–
				Aug 6	Cash	70	–
				Aug 12	Cash	80	–
				Aug 16	Cash	50	–
				Aug 21	Cash	80	–

PURCHASES

Aug 2	Cash	35	–
Aug 9	Cash	35	–

STATIONERY

Aug 4	Cash	7	–
Aug 13	Cash	8	–

WAGES

Aug 5	Cash	20	–
Aug 11	Cash	20	–
Aug 19	Cash	20	–

ELECTRICITY

Aug 8	Cash	10	–

HAULAGE

Aug 10	Cash	5	–

POSTAGE

Aug 17	Cash	5	–

RATES

Aug 18	Cash	30	—			

Chapter 4

A4.1   D. Cole

CASH

Jan 1	Capital	300	—	Jan 2	Purchases	60	—
Jan 3	Sales	40	—	Jan 4	Drawings	30	—
Jan 5	Sales	70	—	Jan 6	Stationery	5	—
				Jan 7	Wages	10	—
				Jan 7	Balance	305	—
		410	—			410	—
Jan 7	Balance	305	—				

CAPITAL

				Jan 7	Cash	300	—

PURCHASES

Jan 2	Cash	60	—				

SALES

				Jan 3	Cash	40	—
				Jan 5	Cash	70	—

DRAWINGS

Jan 4	Cash	30	—				
Jan 8	Stationery	3	—				

STATIONERY

Jan 6	Cash	5	—	Jan 8	Drawings	3	—

A.4.2   D. Dave

CASH

Jan 1	Capital	400	–	Jan 4	Purchases	80	–
Jan 5	Sales	30	–	Jan 7	Wages	15	–
Jan 8	Sales	90	–	Jan 9	Stationery	6	–
Jan 12	Sales	90	–	Jan 10	Drawings	25	–
Jan 13	Capital	350	–	Jan 11	Purchases	20	–
Jan 14	Sales	120	–	Jan 15	Shop Equipment	30	–
				Jan 16	Wages	15	–
				Jan 17	Purchases	10	–

CAPITAL

Jan 1	Cash	400	–
Jan 13	Cash	350	–
Jan 18	Motor Car	500	–

PURCHASES

Jan 4	Cash	80	–
Jan 11	Cash	20	–
Jan 17	Cash	10	–

SALES

Jan 5	Cash	30	–
Jan 8	Cash	90	–
Jan 12	Cash	90	–
Jan 14	Cash	120	–

WAGES

Jan 7	Cash	15	–
Jan 16	Cash	15	–

STATIONERY

Jan 9	Cash	6	–

DRAWINGS

Jan 10	Cash	25	–

SHOP EQUIPMENT

| Jan 15 | Cash | | 30 | — | | | | | |

MOTOR CAR

| Jan 18 | Capital | | 500 | — | | | | | |

Chapter 5

A5.1   A. Johnson

CASH (1)

Jan 1	Capital	2	100	—	Jan 2	Purchases	4	60	—
Jan 4	Sales	6	90	—	Jan 3	Haulage	5	10	—
Jan 6	Sales	6	100	—	Jan 5	Advertising	7	3	—
Jan 7	Sales	6	60	—	Jan 5	Wages	8	15	—
					Jan 7	Drawings	9	20	—
					Jan 7	Advertising	7	2	—
					Jan 7	Haulage	5	15	—
					Jan 7	Balance		225	—
			350	—				350	—
Jan 8	Balance		225	—					

CAPITAL (2)

| | | | | | Jan 1 | Cash | 1 | 100 | — |
| | | | | | Jan 1 | Stock | 3 | 45 | — |

STOCK (3)

| Jan 1 | Capital | 2 | 45 | — | | | | | |

PURCHASES (4)

| Jan 2 | Cash | 1 | 60 | — | | | | | |

HAULAGE (5)

| Jan | 3 | Cash | 1 | 10 | – |
| Jan | 7 | Cash | 1 | 15 | – |

SALES (6)

						Jan	4	Cash	1	90	–
						Jan	6	Cash	1	100	–
						Jan	7	Cash	1	60	–

ADVERTISING (7)

| Jan | 5 | Cash | 1 | 3 | – |
| Jan | 7 | Cash | 1 | 2 | – |

WAGES (8)

| Jan | 6 | Cash | 1 | 15 | – |

DRAWINGS (9)

| Jan | 7 | Cash | 1 | 20 | – |

A. JOHNSON
TRIAL BALANCE 7 JANUARY 19–1

			Dr		Cr	
	Cash		225	–		
	Capital				145	–
	Stock		45	–		
	Purchases		60	–		
	Haulage		25	–		
	Sales				250	–
	Advertising		5	–		
	Wages		15	–		
	Drawings		20	–		
			395	–	395	–

A5.2   A. Patel

CASH

Capital	200.00	Purchases	80.00
Sales	166.00	Shop	
Sales	90.00	Equipment	23.00
Sales	24.00	Advertising	3.00
Sales	92.00	Purchases	64.00
		Postage	00.90
		Shop	
		Equipment	6.00
		Purchases	3.00
		Haulage	43.00
		Tea	17.10
		Balance	332.00
	572.00		572.00
Balance	332.00		

SALES

		Cash	166.00
		Cash	90.00
		Cash	24.00
		Cash	92.00

HAULAGE

Cash	43.00		

TEA

Cash	17.10		

CAPITAL

		Cash	200.00

PURCHASES

Cash	80.00		
Cash	64.00		
Cash	3.00		

SHOP EQUIPMENT

Cash	23.00		
Cash	6.00		

ADVERTISING

Cash	3.00		

POSTAGE

Cash	00.90		

TRIAL BALANCE

Cash	332.00	
Capital		200.00
Purchases	147.00	
Shop		
Equipment	29.00	
Advertising	3.00	
Postage	00.90	
Sales		372.00
Haulage	43.00	
Tea	17.10	
	572.00	572.00

Chapter 6

A6.1   B. Good

CASH

Capital	500.00	Purchases	30.00
Sales	25.00	Drawings	5.00
Sales	15.00	Stationery	6.00
Sales	35.00	Wages	15.00
Sales	45.00	Motor	
Sales	55.00	Van	150.00
		Drawings	5.00
		Purchases	35.00
		Balance	429.00
	675.00		675.00
Balance	429.00		

CAPITAL

Drawings	10.00	Cash	500.00
Balance	579.00	Net Profit	89.00
	589.00		589.00
		Balance	579.00

PURCHASES

Cash	30.00	Trading	
Cash	35.00	Account	65.00
	65.00		65.00

SALES

		Cash	25.00
		Cash	15.00
		Cash	35.00
		Cash	45.00
		Cash	55.00
Trading			
Account	175.00		175.00

DRAWINGS

Cash	5.00	Capital	
Cash	5.00	Account	10.00
	10.00		10.00

STATIONERY

Cash	6.00	Profit	
		and Loss	6.00

WAGES

Cash	15.00	Profit	
		and Loss	15.00

MOTOR VAN

Cash	150.00		

TRADING AND PROFIT AND LOSS ACCOUNT

Purchases	65.00	Sales	175.00
Gross			
Profit	110.00		
	175.00		175.00
Stationery	6.00	Gross	
Wages	15.00	Profit	110.00
Net Profit	89.00		
	110.00		110.00

A6.2   D. Layham

CASH

July 1	Capital	2 000	—	July 2	Purchases	90	—
July 7	Sales	120	—	July 3	Purchases	80	—
July 12	Sales	90	—	July 5	Advertising	15	—
July 17	Sales	65	—	July 15	Wages	35	—
July 22	Sales	150	—	July 20	Stationery	5	—
July 30	Sales	90	—	July 28	Wages	35	—
				July 30	Balance	2 255	—
		2 515	—			2 515	—
Aug 1	Balance	2 255	—				

CAPITAL

				July 1	Cash	2 000	—
				July 1	Stock	150	—
				July 1	Premises	10 000	—
July 30	Balance	12 255	—	July 30	Net Profit	105	—
		12 255	—			12 255	—
				Aug 1	Balance	12 255	—

STOCK

July 1	Capital	150	—	July 30	Trading Account	150	—

PREMISES

July 1	Capital	10 000	—				

PURCHASES

July 2	Cash	90	—		Trading Account	170	—
July 3	Cash	80	—				
		170	—			170	—

ADVERTISING

July 5	Cash	15	—	July 30	Profit and Loss	15	—

SALES

			July 7	Cash	120	–
			July 12	Cash	90	–
			July 17	Cash	65	–
July 30	Trading		July 22	Cash	150	–
	Account	515 –	July 30	Cash	90	–
		515 –			515	–

WAGES

July 15	Cash	35 –	July 30	Profit		
July 28	Cash	35 –		and Loss	70	–
		70 –			70	–

STATIONERY

July 20	Cash	5 –	July 30	Profit		
				and Loss	5	–

D. LAYHAM
TRADING AND PROFIT AND LOSS ACCOUNT FOR THE MONTH ENDED 31 JULY 1980

July 30	Stock	150 –	July 30	Sales	515	–
	Add Purchases	170 –				
		320 –				
	Gross Profit	195 –				
		515 –			515	–
July 30	Advertising	15 –	July 30	Gross		
	Wages	70 –		Profit	195	–
	Stationery	5 –				
	Net Profit	105 –				
		195 –			195	–

TRIAL BALANCE

Cash	2 255	−		
Capital			12 150	−
Stock	150	−		
Premises	10 000	−		
Purchases	170	−		
Advertising	15	−		
Sales			515	−
Wages	70	−		
Stationery	5	−		
	12 665	−	12 665	−

A6.3

D. CARR
TRADING AND PROFIT AND LOSS ACCOUNT
FOR THE YEAR ENDED 31 DECEMBER 19−1

	£	£
SALES		14 350
Less		
Stock (1 Jan 19−1)	1 500	
Add Purchases	7 300	
		8 800
GROSS PROFIT		5 550
Less		
Wages	1 500	
Rent	800	
Electricity	50	
Advertising	120	
Telephone	80	
Stationery	20	
		2 570
NET PROFIT		2 980

Chapter 7

A7.1

B. GOOD
BALANCE SHEET AS AT
15 JANUARY 19- -

Fixed Assets		CAPITAL	500	
Motor Van	150	Add Net Profit	89	
			589	
Current Assets				
Cash	429	Less Drawings	10	
	579			579
				579

A7.2   A. Salter

(a)			CASH			
June 1	Capital	500 —	June 2	Purchases	50 —
June 8	Sales	30 —	June 4	Rent	10 —
June 12	Sales	40 —	June 6	Wages	15 —
June 14	Sales	60 —	June 9	Purchases	20 —
June 23	Sales	80 —	June 18	Wages	15 —
June 25	Sales	70 —	June 19	Rent	10 —
June 28	Sales	85 —	June 20	Stationery	5 —
June 30	Sales	95 —	June 22	Advertising	5 —
			June 26	Rent	10 —
			June 27	Wages	15 —
			June 30	Balance	805 —
		960 —			960 —
July 1	Balance	805 —			
			CAPITAL		
			June 1	Cash	500 —
June 30	Balance	805 —	June 30	Net Profit	305 —
		805 —			805 —
			Aug 1	Balance	805 —

RENT

June 4	Cash	10	–				
June 19	Cash	10	–	June 30	Profit		
June 26	Cash	10	–		and Loss	30	–
		30	–			30	–

WAGES

June 6	Cash	15	–				
June 18	Cash	15	–	June 30	Profit		
June 27	Cash	15	–		and Loss	45	–
		45	–			45	–

SALES

				June 8	Cash	30	–
				June 12	Cash	40	–
				June 14	Cash	60	–
				June 23	Cash	80	–
				June 25	Cash	70	–
June 30	Trading			June 28	Cash	85	–
	Account	460	–	June 30	Cash	95	–
		460	–			460	–

PURCHASES

June 2	Cash	50	–	June 30	Trading		
June 9	Cash	20	–		Account	70	–
		70	–			70	–

STATIONERY

June 20	Stationery	5	–	June 30	Profit		
					and Loss	5	–

ADVERTISING

June 22	Cash	5	–	June 30	Profit		
					and Loss	5	–

254—*An introduction to book-keeping*

(b)   TRIAL BALANCE

	Dr	Cr
Cash	805 —	
Capital		500 —
Rent	30 —	
Wages	45 —	
Sales		460 —
Purchases	70 —	
Stationery	5 —	
Advertising	5 —	
	960 —	960 —

(c)   A. SALTER
TRADING AND PROFIT AND LOSS ACCOUNT
FOR THE MONTH ENDED 30 JUNE 19—1

June 30	Purchases	70 —	June 30	Sales	460	—
	Gross Profit	390 —				
		460 —			460	—
June 30	Rent	30 —	June 30	Gross Profit	390	—
	Wages	45 —				
	Stationery	5 —				
	Advertising	5 —				
	Net Profit	305 —				
		390 —			390	—

(d)   A. SALTER
BALANCE SHEET AS AT
30 JUNE 19—1

Assets		Capital	500	
Cash	805	Add Net Profit	305	
				805
	805			805

Chapter 8

A8.1

(a) TRADING ACCOUNT

Stock at Start	50	—	Sales	550 —
Add Purchases	450	—		
	500	—		
Less Stock at Close	150	—		
Cost of Sales	350	—		
Gross Profit	200	—		
	550	—		550 —

(b) TRADING ACCOUNT

Stock at Start	735	—	Sales	8 900 —
Add Purchases	7 250	—		
	7 985	—		
Less Stock at Close	625	—		
Cost of Sales	7 360	—		
Gross Profit	1 540	—		
	8 900	—		8 900 —

(c) TRADING ACCOUNT

Stock at Start	1 050	—	Sales	34 950 —
Add Purchases	23 480	—		
	24 530	—		
Less Stock at Close	920	—		
Cost of Sales	23 610	—		
Gross Profit	11 340	—		
	34 950	—		34 950 —

(d) TRADING ACCOUNT

Stock at Start	1 095	—	Sales	15 480 —
Add Purchases	14 320	—		
	15 415	—		

Less Stock at Close	2 395	–						
Cost of Sales	13 020	–						
Gross Profit	2 460	–						
	15 480	–				15 480	–	

A8.2 G. Tar

(a) CASH

Jan 1	G. Tar	500	–	Jan 2	Purchases	200	–	
Jan 16	Sales	150	–	Jan 3	Advertising	12	–	
Jan 18	Sales	70	–	Jan 8	Purchases	50	–	
Jan 31	Sales	20	–	Jan 12	Delivery			
					Expenses	5	–	
				Jan 25	Stationery	5	–	
				Jan 26	Advertising	15	–	
				Jan 31	Balance	453	–	
		740	–			740	–	
Feb 1	Balance	453	–					

CAPITAL

				Jan 1	Cash	500	–	
Jan 31	Balance	528	–	Jan 31	Net Profit	28	–	
		528	–			528	–	
				Feb 1	Balance	528	–	

PURCHASES

Jan 2	Cash	200	–	Jan 31	Trading			
Jan 4	Cash	50	–		Account	250	–	
		250	–			250	–	

ADVERTISING

Jan 3	Cash	12	–	Jan 31	Profit			
Jan 26	Cash	15	–		and Loss	27	–	
		27	–			27	–	

DELIVERY EXPENSES

Jan 12	Cash	5	–	Jan 31	Profit and Loss	5	–

SALES

				Jan 16	Cash	150	–
				Jan 18	Cash	70	–
Jan 31	Trading	240	–	Jan 31	Cash	20	–
		240	–			240	–

STATIONERY

Jan 25	Cash	5	–	Jan 31	Profit and Loss	5	–

STOCK

Jan 31	Trading Account	75	–

(b)

TRIAL BALANCE

	Cash	453	–		
	Capital			500	–
	Purchases	250	–		
	Advertising	27	–		
	Delivery Expenses	5	–		
	Sales			240	–
	Stationery	5	–		
		740	–	740	–

(c)

G. TAR
TRADING AND PROFIT AND LOSS ACCOUNT
FOR THE MONTH ENDED 31 JANUARY 19–1

Jan 31	Purchases	250	–	Jan 31	Sales	240	–
	Less Stock at Close	75	–				
	Cost of Sales	175	–				

	Gross Profit	65	–						
		240	–					240	–
	Advertising	27	–	Jan 31	Gross				
	Delivery				Profit			65	–
	Expenses	5	–						
	Stationery	5	–						
	Net Profit	28	–						
		65	–					65	–

(d)

G. TAR
BALANCE SHEET AS AT
31 JANUARY 19–1

Assets					
Stock	75	*Capital*	500		
Cash	453	Add Net Profit	28	528	
	528			528	

A8.3 (a) Rate of Stock Turnover = $\dfrac{\text{Cost of Sales}}{\text{Average Stock}}$

Average Stock = $\dfrac{\text{Stock at Start + Stock at Close}}{2}$

Stock at Start	4 350
Add Purchases	12 300
	16 650
Less Stock at Close	5 380
Cost of Sales	11 270

Rate of Stock Turnover = $\dfrac{11\ 270}{\frac{1}{2}\ (4350 + 5380)}$

$= \dfrac{11\ 270}{4865} = \underline{\underline{2.3}}$

(b)   Rate of turnover is too low since on average stock will only be renewed after 5–6 months. Green vegetables will perish in less than one week.

Chapter 9

A9.1   E. Earlson

CASH

Jan	1	Capital	350	–	Jan	2	Purchases	50	–
Jan	5	Sales	90	–	Jan	3	Stationery	10	–
Jan	6	Sales	30	–	Jan	4	Shop		
Jan	9	Sales	30	–			Equipment	20	–
					Jan	7	Shop		
							Equipment	15	–
					Jan	8	Wages	10	–
					Jan	9	Balance	395	–
			500	–				500	–
Jan	10	Balance	395	–					

CAPITAL

					Jan	1	Cash	350	–
Jan	9	Balance	450	–	Jan	9	Net Profit	100	–
			450	–				450	–
					Jan	10	Balance	450	–

PURCHASES

Jan	2	Cash	50	–	Jan	8	Trading		
							Account	50	–

STATIONERY

Jan	3	Cash	10	–	Jan	8	Profit		
							and Loss	10	–

		SHOP EQUIPMENT				
Jan 4	Cash	20 –				
Jan 7	Cash	15 –				

		SALES				
			Jan 5	Cash	90 –	
			Jan 6	Cash	30 –	
Jan 8	Trading Account	150 –	Jan 9	Cash	30 –	
		150 –			150 –	

		WAGES				
Jan 8	Cash	10 –	Jan 8	Profit and Loss	10 –	

(a) TRIAL BALANCE

Cash	395 –		
Capital		350 –	
Purchases	50 –		
Stationery	10 –		
Shop Equipment	35 –		
Sales		150 –	
Wages	10 –		
	500 –	500 –	

(b) E. EARLSON
TRADING AND PROFIT AND LOSS ACCOUNT
FOR THE EIGHT DAYS ENDED 8 JANUARY 19–1

Jan 8	Purchases	50 –	Jan 8	Sales	150 –	
	Less Stock	20 –				
	Cost of Sales	30 –				
	Gross Profit	120 –				
		150 –			150 –	

Jan 8	Stationery	10	–	Jan 8	Gross		
	Wages	10	–		Profit	120	–
	Net Profit	100	–				
		120	–			120	–

(c)

E. EARLSON
BALANCE SHEET AS AT
8 JANUARY 19–1

Fixed Assets			*Capital*	350	
Shop Equipment	35		Add Net Profit	100	
					450
Current Assets					
Stock	20				
Cash	395	415			
		450			450

A9.2   F. Clark

CASH

Jan 1	Capital	500	–	Jan 2	Purchases	90	–
Jan 3	Sales	70	–	Jan 4	Stationery	10	–
Jan 5	Sales	30	–	Jan 6	Shop		
Jan 9	Sales	50	–		Equipment	30	–
Jan 11	Sales	100	–	Jan 7	Wages	15	–
				Jan 8	Delivery		
					Van	120	–
				Jan 10	Stationery	15	–
				Jan 11	Balance	470	–
		750	–			750	–
Jan 12	Balance	470	–				

CAPITAL

				Jan 1	Cash	500	–
				Jan 1	Stock	50	–
Jan 11	Balance	685	–	Jan 11	Net Profit	135	–

		685	—		685	—
				Jan 12	Balance	685	—

STOCK

Jan 1	Capital	50	—	Jan 11	Trading Account	50	—
Jan 11	Trading Account	65	—				

PURCHASES

Jan 2	Cash	90	—	Jan 11	Trading Account	90	—

SALES

				Jan 3	Cash	70	—
				Jan 5	Cash	30	—
				Jan 9	Cash	50	—
Jan 11	Trading Account	250	—	Jan 11	Cash	100	—
		250	—			250	—

STATIONERY

Jan 4	Cash	10	—				
Jan 10	Cash	15	—	Jan 11	Profit and Loss	25	—
		25	—			25	—

SHOP EQUIPMENT

Jan 6	Cash	30	—				

WAGES

Jan 7	Cash	15	—	Jan 11	Profit and Loss	15	—

DELIVERY VAN

Jan 8	Cash	120	—

(a)   TRIAL BALANCE

Cash	470	—		
Capital			550	—
Stock	50	—		
Purchases	90	—		
Sales			250	—
Stationery	25	—		
Shop Equipment	30	—		
Wages	15	—		
Delivery Van	120	—		
	800	—	800	—

(b)   **F. CLARK**
TRADING AND PROFIT AND LOSS ACCOUNT
FOR THE ELEVEN DAYS ENDED 11 JANUARY 19—1

Jan 11	Stock at Start	50	—	Jan 11	Sales		250	—
	Add Purchases	90	—					
		140	—					
	Less Stock at Close	65	—					
	Cost of Sales	75	—					
	Gross Profit	175	—					
		250	—				250	—
Jan 11	Stationery	25	—	Jan 11	Gross Profit		175	—
	Wages	15	—					
	Net Profit	135	—					
		175	—				175	—

(c)

F. CLARK
BALANCE SHEET
AS AT 11 JANUARY 19–1

Fixed Assets				Capital	550 –	
Delivery				Add		
Van	120 –			Net Profit	135 –	
Shop						685 –
Equipment	30 –					
		150 –				
Current Assets						
Stock	65 –					
Cash	470 –					
		535 –				
		685 –				685 –

A9.3   E. Smith

CASH

Capital	700	Purchases	30
Sales	45	Purchases	35
Sales	35	Stationery	5
Sales	25	Wages	15
Sales	38	Shop	
		Equipment	25
		Shop	
		Equipment	20
		Delivery	
		Van	150
		Wages	15
		Balance	548
	843		843

CAPITAL

Net loss	12	Cash	700
Balance	753	Stock	65
	765		765
		Balance	753

SHOP EQUIPMENT

Cash	25	
Cash	20	

DELIVERY VAN

Cash	150	

PURCHASES

Cash	30		
Cash	35	Trading	
		Account	65
	65		65

SALES			STATIONERY		WAGES		
	Cash	45	Cash	5	Profit and	Cash	15
	Cash	35		=	Loss 5	Cash	15	Profit and
	Cash	25			=			Loss 30
Sales 143	Cash	38					30	30
143		143						

(a)   TRIAL BALANCE

Cash	548	
Capital		700
Purchases	65	
Sales		143
Stationery	5	
Wages	30	
Shop Equipment	45	
Delivery Van	150	
	843	843

(b)   TRADING AND PROFIT AND LOSS ACCOUNT

Opening Stock	65	Sales	143
Purchases	65		
	130		
Less Stock at Close	10		
Cost of Sales	120		
Gross Profit	23		
	143		143
Stationery	5	Gross Profit	23
Wages	30	Net Loss	12
	35		35

(c)   BALANCE SHEET

Delivery Van	150	Capital	765
Shop Equipment	45	Less Net Loss	12
Stock	10		
Cash	548		
	753		753

Chapter 10

A10.1   J. Bloggs

CASH

Jan 1	Capital	300	–	Jan 2	Purchases	30	–
Jan 6	Sales	30	–	Jan 3	Stationery	10	–
Jan 10	A. Red	35	–	Jan 4	Wages	15	–
Jan 12	B. Blue	5	–	Jan 5	Shop Equipment	70	–
				Jan 14	Purchases	30	–
				Jan 14	Balance	215	–
		370	–			370	–
Jan 15	Balance	215	–				

CAPITAL

				Jan 1	Cash	300	–
Jan 14	Balance	370	–	Jan 14	Net Profit	70	–
		370	–			370	–
				Jan 15	Balance	370	–

PURCHASES

Jan 2	Cash	30	–	Jan 14	Trading Account	60	–
Jan 14	Cash	30	–				
		60	–			60	–

STATIONERY

Jan 3	Cash	10	–	Jan 14	Profit and Loss	10	–

WAGES

Jan 4	Cash	15	–	Jan 14	Profit and Loss	15	–

		SHOP EQUIPMENT							
Jan 5	Cash	70	–						

		SALES							
				Jan 6	Cash	30	–		
				Jan 7	A. Red	15	–		
				Jan 8	B. Blue	10	–		
				Jan 9	A. Red	20	–		
Jan 14	Trading			Jan 11	B. Blue	25	–		
	Account	120	–	Jan 13	A. White	20	–		
		120	–			120	–		

		A. RED							
Jan 7	Sales	15	–						
Jan 9	Sales	20	–	Jan 10	Cash	35	–		
		35	–			35	–		

		B. BLUE							
Jan 8	Sales	10	–	Jan 12	Cash	5	–		
Jan 11	Sales	25	–	Jan 14	Balance	30	–		
Jan 14	Balance	30	–						
		35	–			35	–		
Jan 15	Balance	30	–						

		A. WHITE							
Jan 13	Sales	20	–						

(a)   **TRIAL BALANCE**

Cash	215	–		
Capital			300	–
Purchases	60	–		
Stationery	10	–		
Wages	15	–		
Shop				
Equipment	70	–		
Sales			120	–
Debtors	50	–		
	420	–	420	–

(b)
J. BLOGGS
TRADING AND PROFIT AND LOSS ACCOUNT
FOR THE WEEK ENDED 14 JANUARY

Jan 14	Purchases	60	–	Jan 14	Sales	120	–
	Less Stock at Close	35	–				
	Cost of Sales	25	–				
	Gross Profit	95	–				
		120	–			120	–
Jan 14	Stationery	10	–	Jan 14	Gross Profit	95	–
	Wages	15	–				
	Net Profit	70	–				
		95	–			95	–

STOCK

Jan 14	Trading Account	35	–

(c)
J. BLOGGS
BALANCE SHEET AS AT
14 JANUARY 19–1

Fixed Assets				Capital	300	–
Shop Equipment		70	–	Add		
				Net Profit	70	–
					370	–
Current Assets						
Stock	35	–				
Debtors	50	–				
Cash	215	–	300	–		
			370	–	370	–

A10.2   T. Smith

CASH

Jan 1	Capital	300	–	Jan 2	Purchases	50	–
Jan 3	Sales	60	–	Jan 4	Wages	16	–

Jan 8	Sales		30	–	Jan 5	Telephone		16	–
Jan 11	B. Black		20	–	Jan 9	Purchases		35	–
					Jan 13	Wages		16	–
					Jan 13	Balance		277	–
			410	–				410	–
Jan 14	Balance		277	–					

CAPITAL

					Jan 1	Cash		300	–
Jan 13	Balance		387	–	Jan 13	Net Profit		87	–
			387	–				387	–
					Jan 15	Balance		387	–

PURCHASES

Jan 2	Cash		50	–					
Jan 9	Cash		35	–	Jan 13	Trading Account		85	–
			85	–				85	–

SALES

					Jan 3	Cash		60	–
					Jan 6	B. Black		30	–
					Jan 7	W. White		15	–
					Jan 8	Cash		30	–
					Jan 10	W. White		10	–
Jan 13	Trading Account		175	–	Jan 12	B. Black		30	–
			175	–				175	–

B. BLACK

Jan 6	Sales		30	–	Jan 11	Cash		20	–
Jan 12	Sales		30	–	Jan 13	Balance		40	–
			60	–				60	–
Jan 14	Balance		40	–					

W. WHITE

Jan 7	Sales	15	–					
Jan 10	Sales	10	–	Jan 13	Balance		25	–
		25	–				25	–
Jan 14	Balance	25	–					

WAGES

Jan 4	Cash	16	–					
Jan 13	Cash	16	–	Jan 13	Profit and Loss		32	–
		32	–				32	–

TELEPHONE

Jan 5	Cash	16	–	Jan 13	Profit and Loss		16	–

(a)

TRIAL BALANCE

Cash	277	–		
Capital			300	–
Purchases	85	–		
Sales			175	–
Debtors	65	–		
Wages	32	–		
Telephone	16	–		
	475	–	475	–

(b)

T. SMITH
TRADING AND PROFIT AND LOSS ACCOUNT
FOR THE THIRTEEN DAYS ENDED 31 JANUARY 19–1

Jan 13	Purchases	85	–	Jan 13	Sales	175	–
	Less Stock at Close	45	–				
	Cost of Sales	40	–				
	Gross Profit	135	–				
		175	–			175	–

Jan 13	Wages	32	–	Jan 13	Gross Profit	135	–
	Telephone	16	–				
	Net Profit	87	–				
		135	–			135	–

STOCK

| Jan 14 | Trading Account | 45 | – | | | | |

(c)

T. SMITH
BALANCE SHEET
AS AT 13 JANUARY

Fixed Assets				*Capital*	300	–		
				Add				
				Net Profit	87	–	387	–
Current Assets								
Stock								
at Close	45	–						
Debtors	65	–						
Cash	277	–						
			387	–				
			387	–				387 –

A10.3 A. Angler

CASH					PURCHASES				
Balance	900	Motor Van	300	B. Line	65				
Sales	120	Wages	15	C. Float	75				
S. Pike	80	Stationery	5	D. Sinker	55				
U. Rudd	20	B. Line	45	C. Float	35				
		Wages	15	B. Line	20	Trading			
		Drawings	15	Cash	20	Account		270	
		Purchases	20		270			270	
		Balance	705						
	1 120		1 120						
Balance	705								

PREMISES

Balance	11 000		

MOTOR VAN

Balance	600		
Cash	300	Balance	900
	900		900
Balance	900		

STOCK

Balance	200	Trading Account	200
Trading Account	270		

SHOP EQUIPMENT

Balance	300		

CAPITAL

Drawings	15	Balance	13 000
Balance	13 090	Net Profit	105
	13 105		13 105
		Balance	13 090

WAGES

Cash	15	Profit and Loss	
Cash	15		30
	30		30

STATIONERY

Cash	5	Profit and Loss	5

DRAWINGS

Cash	15	Capital	15

B. LINE

Cash	45	Purchases	65
Balance	40	Purchases	20
	85		85
		Balance	40

C. FLOAT

Balance	110	Purchases	75
		Purchases	35
	110		110
		Balance	110

D. SINKER

		Purchases	55

SALES

		S. Pike	80
		T. Bream	95
		U. Rudd	45
Trading		Cash	120
Account	365	V. Salmon	25
	365		365

S. PIKE

Sales	80	Cash	80

T. BREAM

Sales	95		

U. RUDD

Sales	45	Cash	20
		Balance	25
	45		45
Balance	25		

V. SALMON				BAD DEBTS			
Sales	25	Bad Debts	25	V. Salmon	25	Profit and Loss	25

(a) **TRIAL BALANCE**

Cash	705	
Premises	11 000	
Motor Vans	900	
Stock	200	
Shop Equipment	300	
Capital		13 000
Wages	30	
Stationery	5	
Drawings	15	
Purchases	270	
Creditors		205
Sales		365
Debtors	120	
Bad Debts	25	
	13 570	13 570

(b)
A. ANGLER
TRADING AND PROFIT AND LOSS ACCOUNT
FOR THE 21 DAYS ENDED 21 JANUARY 19--

Stock at Start	200	Sales	365
Add Purchases	270		
	470		
Less Stock at Close	270		
Cost of Sales	200		
Gross Profit	165		
	365		365
Wages	30	Gross Profit	165
Stationery	5		
Bad Debts	25		
Net Profit	105		
	165		165

(c)

A. ANGLER
BALANCE SHEET AS AT 21 JANUARY 19‑ ‑

Fixed Assets			*Capital*	13 000	
Premises	11 000		Less Drawings	15	
Motor Van	900				
Shop Equipment	300	12 200		12 985	
Current Assets			Add Net Profit	105	13 090
Stock	270		*Current Liabilities*		
Debtors	120		Creditors		205
Cash	705	1 095			
		13 295			13 295

A10.4 T. Singh

Note: Ledger entries marked * relate to the second accounting period (15–28 January).

CASH ACCOUNT

Capital	300	Purchases	35
Sales	35	Wages	15
A. Red	35	Rent	30
		Purchases	15
		A. Ash	10
		Balance	265
	370		370
Balance	265	E. Elm	30*
*Sales	80	Wages	15*
*P. Pink	60	Rent	30*
		Shop Equipment	70*
		Balance	260*
	*405		405*
*Balance	260		

O. OAK

		Purchases	15

SALES

		A. Red	35
		B. Blue	25
		Cash	35
		P. Pink	40
Trading Account	135		
	135		135
		Cash	80*
		P. Pink	60*
		A. Red	15*
*Trading Account	175	P. Pink	20*
	*175		175*

CAPITAL				A. RED			
		Cash	300	Sales	35	Cash	35
Balance	340	Net Profit	40	*Sales	15		
	340		340				
		Balance	340	**B. BLUE**			
*Balance	380	Net Profit	40*	Sales	25		
	*380		380*				
		Balance	380*	**P. PINK**			
				Sales	40	Cash	60*
PURCHASES				*Sales	60		
Cash	35			*Sales	20	Balance	60*
A. Ash	20				120		120*
E. Elm	30			*Balance	60		
Cash	15						
O. Oak	15	Trading		**WAGES**			
		Account	115	Cash	15	Profit	
	115		115			and Loss	15
*E. Elm	65	Trading		*Cash	15	Profit	
		Account	65*			and Loss	15*
A. ASH				**RENT**			
Cash	10	Purchases	20	Cash	30	Profit	
Balance	10					and Loss	30
	20		20	*Cash	30	Profit	
		Balance	10			and Loss	30*
E. ELM				**STOCK**			
*Cash	30	Purchases	30	Trading	65	Trading	65*
		Purchases	65*	*Trading	40		
				SHOP EQUIPMENT			
				*Cash	70		

(a)   TRIAL BALANCE AS AT 14 JANUARY 19--

Cash	265	
Capital		300
Purchases	115	
Creditors:		
A. Ash		10
E. Elm		30
O. Oak		15
Sales		135
Debtors:		
B. Blue	25	
P. Pink	40	
Wages	15	
Rent	30	
	490	490

(b)   T. SINGH
TRADING AND PROFIT AND LOSS ACCOUNT
TWO WEEKS ENDING 14 JANUARY 19--

Purchases	115		Sales	135
Less Stock at Close	65			
	——			
Cost of Sales	50			
Gross Profit	85			
	——			——
	135			135
	══			══
Wages	15		Gross Profit	85
Rent	30			
Net Profit	40			
	——			——
	85			85
	══			══

(c)   T. SINGH
BALANCE SHEET AS AT 14 JANUARY 19--

Capital	300		*Fixed Assets*	
Add Net Profit	40	340		
Current Liabilities			*Current Assets*	
Creditors		55	Stock	65
			Debtors	65
			Cash	265
		——		——
		395		395
		══		══

(d)

T. SINGH
TRIAL BALANCE AS AT 28 JANUARY 19– –

Cash	260	
Capital		340
Purchases	65	
Creditors:		
A. Ash		10
E. Elm		65
O. Oak		15
Sales		175
Debtors:		
A. Red	15	
B. Blue	25	
P. Pink	60	
Wages	15	
Rent	30	
Stock	65	
Office Equipment	70	
	605	605

(e)

T. SINGH
TRADING AND PROFIT AND LOSS ACCOUNT
TWO WEEKS ENDED 28 JANUARY 19– –

Stock at Start	65	Sales	175
Add Purchases	65		
	130		
Less Stock at Close	70		
Cost of Sales	60		
Gross Profit	115		
	175		175
Wages	15	Gross Profit	115
Rent	30		
Net Profit	70		
	85		85

(f)

T. SINGH
BALANCE SHEET AS AT 28 JANUARY 19--

Capital	340		*Fixed Assets*		
Add Net Profit	70	410	Office Equipment		70
			Current Assets		
Current Liabilities		90	Stock	70	
Creditors			Debtors	100	
			Cash	260	430
		500			500

Chapter 11

A11.1   D. Peters

Date	Detail	Cash	Bank		Date	Detail	Cash	Bank
Jan 1	Capital	2 000	—		Jan 2	Bank	1 900	—
Jan 2	Cash	—	1 900		Jan 3	Purchases	50	—
Jan 5	Sales	200	—		Jan 4	Purchases	—	110
Jan 6	Sales		190		Jan 7	Bank	150	—
Jan 7	Sales		150		Jan 8	Electricity	—	80
Jan 9	Sales	80	—		Jan 11	Wages	—	120
Jan 10	A. Red		120		Jan 12	Drawings	20	—
					Jan 12	Balance	160	2 050
		2 280	2 360				2 280	2 360
Jan 12	Balance b/d	160	2 050					

A11.2 J. Finn

Date	Details	Cash	Bank		Date	Details	Cash	Bank
Jan 1	Capital	12 000	—		Jan 2	Bank	11 500	—
Jan 2	Bank	—	11 500		Jan 3	Premises	—	7 500
Jan 4	Sales	300	—		Jan 4	Purchases	250	—
Jan 6	D. Smith	—	35		Jan 5	Purchases	—	120
Jan 7	Sales	400	—		Jan 8	Bank	620	—
Jan 8	Cash	—	620		Jan 9	Drawings	20	—
Jan 12	Sales	45	—		Jan 10	Purchases	—	10
					Jan 11	Wages	—	150
					Jan 13	J. Johnson	—	15
					Jan 14	Motor Van	—	150
					Jan 14	Balance	355	4 210
		12 745	12 155				12 745	12 155
Jan 15	Balance	355	4 210		Jan 15	Premises	—	5 000
Jan 16	Sales	20	—		Jan 17	Cash	—	30
Jan 17	Bank	30	—		Jan 18	Stationery	—	40
Jan 20	Sales	150	—		Jan 19	Purchases	100	—
Jan 21	D. Finch	—	30		Jan 21	Balance	455	—
Jan 21	Balance	—	830					
		555	5 070				555	5 070
Jan 22	Balance b/d	455	—		Jan 22	Balance	—	830

A11.3   A. Portley

PREMISES

| Jan 1 | Balance | 10 000 | – | | | | | |

MOTOR VAN

| Jan 1 | Balance | 500 | – | | | | | |

EQUIPMENT

| Jan 1 | Balance | 200 | – | | | | | |

STOCK

| Jan 1 | Balance | 50 | – | Jan 14 | Trading Account | 50 | – |
| Jan 14 | Trading Account | 85 | – | | | | |

CAPITAL

				Jan 1	Balance	12 100	–
Jan 14	Balance	12 225	–	Jan 14	Net Profit	125	–
		12 225	–			12 225	–
				Jan 1	Balance	12 225	–

WAGES

| Jan 7 | Bank | 30 | – | Jan 14 | Profit and Loss | 30 | – |

CLEANING

| Jan 12 | Cash | 10 | – | Jan 14 | Profit and Loss | 10 | – |

PURCHASES

Jan 2	B. Elm	80	–	Jan 14	Trading Account	170	–
Jan 3	A. Oak	90	–				
		170	–			170	–

B. ELM

| Jan 6 | Bank | 80 | – | Jan 2 | Purchases | 80 | – |

A. OAK

			Jan 3	Purchases	90	–

SALES

				Jan 4	Cash	60	–
				Jan 5	A. Red	90	–
				Jan 8	Cash	90	–
				Jan 10	Cash	30	–
Jan 14	Trading Account	300	–	Jan 14	Cash	30	–
		300	–			300	–

A. RED

Jan 5	Sales	90	–	Jan 9	Bank	50	–

(a)   CASH BOOK

Jan 1	Balance	250	–	1 100	–	Jan 6	B. Elm			80	–
Jan 4	Sales	60	–			Jan 7	Wages			30	–
Jan 8	Sales	90	–			Jan 12	Cleaning	10	–		
Jan 9	A. Red			50	–						
Jan 10	Sales	30	–								
Jan 14	Sales	30	–			Jan 14	Balance	450	–	1 040	–
		460	–	1 150	–			460	–	1 150	–
Jan 15	Balance	450	–	1 040	–						

(b)   TRIAL BALANCE

Cash	450	–		
Bank	1 040	–		
Premises	10 000	–		
Motor Van	500	–		
Equipment	200	–		
Stock	50	–		
Capital			12 100	–
Wages	30	–		
Cleaning	10	–		
Purchases	170	–		
Creditors			90	–
Sales			300	–
Debtors	40	–		
	12 490	–	12 490	–

(c)   <u>A. PORTLEY</u>
<u>TRADING AND PROFIT AND LOSS ACCOUNT</u>
FOR THE 2 WEEKS ENDED 14 JANUARY 19––

Jan 14	Stock			Jan 14	Sales	300	–
	at Start	50	–				
	Add						
	Purchases	170	–				
		220	–				
	Less Stock						
	at Close	85	–				
	Cost of						
	Sales	135	–				
	Gross Profit	165	–				
		300	–			300	–
				Jan 14	Gross Profit	165	–
Jan 14	Wages	30	–				
	Cleaning	10	–				
	Net Profit	125	–				
		165	–			165	–

284–*An introduction to book-keeping*

(d)

A. PORTLEY
BALANCE SHEET AS AT
14 JANUARY 19––

Capital	12 100 –			*Fixed Assets*		
Add Net Profit	125 –			Premises	10 000 –	
		12 225 –		Motor Van	500 –	
				Equipment	200 –	
						10 700 –
Current Liabilities				*Current Assets*		
Creditors		90 –		Stock	85 –	
				Debtors	40 –	
				Bank	1 040 –	
				Cash	450 –	
						1 615 –
		12 315 –				12 315 –

A11.4   **J. WOOD'S BANK RECONCILIATION STATEMENT**

	£	£
Balance as per Bank Statement		320
Less Cheques not yet presented for payment:		
A. Oak	35	
B. Elm	25	
C. Ash	40	100
		220
Add Cheques not yet cleared:		
A. Red	20	
B. Blue	40	
C. Yellow	25	85
Balance as per Cash Book		305

A11.5   K. Roads

	£
Adjusting Cash Book:	
Cash Book Old Balance	1429
Add	
Interest received on Deposit Account	23
	1452

	£	
Less		
Bank Charges	3	
Standing Order Rent	14	17
Cash Book New Balance		1435

K. ROADS' BANK RECONCILIATION STATEMENT

	£
Balance as per Cash Book	1435
Add Cheques not yet presented	53
	1488
Less Cheques not yet cleared	92
Balance as per Bank Statement	1396

A12.1   A. Bird

	PURCHASES JOURNAL					Page 1	
Jan 1	A. Wren	001	CL 1			23	40
Jan 1	B. Sparrow	002	CL 2			43	90
Jan 1	C. Snipe	003	CL 3			24	30
Jan 2	D. Eagle	004	CL 4			12	30
Jan 2	E. Pigeon	005	CL 5			13	90
Jan 2	F. Crow	006	CL 6			43	90
Jan 3	B. Sparrow	007	CL 2			12	30
Jan 4	D. Eagle	008	CL 4			14	20
Jan 6	A. Wren	009	CL 1			12	30
Jan 6	B. Sparrow	010	CL 2			14	50
			NL 1			215	—
						Page 2	
Jan 8	A. Wren	011	CL 1			12	30

Jan 8	B. Sparrow		012	CL 2					14	90
Jan 8	D. Eagle		013	CL 4					18	20
Jan 10	A. Wren		014	CL 1					25	90
Jan 10	G. Swift		015	CL 7					14	90
Jan 10	C. Snipe		016	CL 3					12	90
Jan 11	D. Eagle		017	CL 4					14	20
Jan 12	E. Pigeon		018	CL 5					28	90
Jan 13	B. Sparrow		019	CL 2					14	20
				NL 1					156	40

CREDITORS LEDGER
A. WREN (1)

			Jan 1	Goods	PJ 1	23	40
			Jan 6	Goods	PJ 1	12	30
			Jan 8	Goods	PJ 2	12	30
			Jan 10	Goods	PJ 2	25	90

B. SPARROW (2)

			Jan 1	Goods	PJ 1	43	90
			Jan 3	Goods	PJ 1	12	30
			Jan 6	Goods	PJ 1	14	50
			Jan 8	Goods	PJ 2	14	90
			Jan 13	Goods	PJ 2	14	20

C. SNIPE (3)

			Jan 1	Goods	PJ 1	24	30
			Jan 10	Goods	PJ 2	12	90

D. EAGLE (4)

			Jan 2	Goods	PJ 1	12	30
			Jan 4	Goods	PJ 1	14	20
			Jan 8	Goods	PJ 2	18	20
			Jan 11	Goods	PJ 2	14	20

E. PIGEON (5)

			Jan 2	Goods	PJ 1	13	90
			Jan 12	Goods	PJ 2	28	90

				F. CROW (6)				
				Jan 2	Goods	PJ 1	43	90
				E. SWIFT (7)				
				Jan 10	Goods	PJ 2	14	90

NOMINAL LEDGER
PURCHASES ACCOUNT (1)

Jan 7	Goods on credit	PJ1	215	−	
Jan 14	Goods on credit	PJ2	156	40	

A12.2 Q. Fish

		SALES JOURNAL				Page 1	
Jan 2	A. Trout		001	DL 1		53	90
Jan 2	B. Bream		002	DL 2		42	80
Jan 2	C. Pike		003	DL 3		63	80
Jan 2	D. Rudd		004	DL 4		75	63
Jan 2	E. Roach		005	DL 5		82	90
Jan 3	B. Bream		006	DL 2		7	−
Jan 3	C. Pike		007	DL 3		12	90
Jan 4	A. Trout		008	DL 1		14	20
Jan 4	D. Rudd		009	DL 4		15	30
Jan 5	E. Roach		010	DL 5		24	30
				NL 1		392	73
						Page 2	
Jan 8	B. Bream		011	DL 2		15	−
Jan 8	C. Pike		012	DL 3		16	20
Jan 8	D. Rudd		013	DL 4		12	30
Jan 8	E. Roach		014	DL 5		14	90
Jan 9	C. Pike		015	DL 3		16	35
Jan 10	B. Bream		016	DL 2		14	35
				NL 1		89	10

					NOMINAL LEDGER SALES ACCOUNT (1)				
					Jan 7	Goods sold on credit	SJ1	392	73
					Jan 14	Goods sold on credit	SJ2	89	10
				DEBTORS LEDGER A. TROUT (1)					
Jan 2	Goods	SJ 1	53	90					
Jan 4	Goods	SJ 1	14	20					
				B. BREAM (2)					
Jan 2	Goods	SJ 1	42	80					
Jan 3	Goods	SJ 1	7	00					
Jan 8	Goods	SJ 2	15	00					
Jan 10	Goods	SJ 2	14	35					
				C. PIKE (3)					
Jan 2	Goods	SJ 1	63	80					
Jan 3	Goods	SJ 1	12	90					
Jan 8	Goods	SJ 2	16	20					
Jan 9	Goods	SJ 2	16	35					
				D. RUDD (4)					
Jan 2	Goods	SJ 1	75	63					
Jan 4	Goods	SJ 1	15	30					
Jan 8	Goods	SJ 2	12	30					
				E. ROACH (5)					
Jan 2	Goods	SJ 1	82	90					
Jan 5	Goods	SJ 1	24	30					
Jan 8	Goods	SJ 2	14	90					

Chapter 14

A14.1   M. Samuel

A. Red	10% of £23.90	=	£2.39

B. Blue	5% of £14.28	=	£0.71
	7½% of £23.90	=	£1.79
			2.50

C. Yellow	5% of £23.90	=	£1.19½

D. Green	0% of £24.90	=	no discount
	5% of £15.20	=	£0.76

A14.2   A. House – Treble-column cash book

Date	Particulars	Discount Allowed	Cash	Bank	Date	Particulars	Discount Received	Cash	Bank
Jan 1	Balance		500 —	3500 —	Jan 1	A. Rose	3 50		31 50
Jan 1	Sales		50 —		Jan 2	Wages		45 —	
Jan 2	J. Slate	1 —		19 —	Jan 3	Electricity			95 —
Jan 3	D. Pebble	5 50		49 50	Jan 4	C. Daisy	2 50	22 50	
Jan 4	A. Rock	1 50	18 50		Jan 7	D. Violet	45		8 55
Jan 7	Sales		35 —		Jan 8	Advertising			15 —
Jan 8	C. Flint	2 25		42 75	Jan 14	Balance		581 00	3500 20
Jan 9	D. Pebble	1 —		19 —					
Jan 13	E. Granite			20 —					
Jan 14	Sales		45 —						
		11 25	648 50	3650 25			6 45	648 50	3650 25
		NL 2					NL 1		
Jan 15	Balance		581 00	3500 20					

NOMINAL LEDGER
DISCOUNT RECEIVED (1)

Jan 14	Discount received these two weeks	CB 1	6 45

DISCOUNT ALLOWED (2)

Jan 14	Discount allowed these two weeks	CB 1	11 25

Chapter 16
A16.1,2 and 3   WEEK 3

Name	Gross Pay £ p	Total Pay to Date £ p	Total Tax Free Pay to Date £ p	Total Taxable Pay to Date £ p	Total Income Tax Due to Date £ p	Tax Code	Employer's & Employee's N.I. Cont. £ p	Employee's N.I. Cont. £ p	Income Tax Due £ p	Trade Union £ p	Pension Scheme £ p	SAYE £ p	Total Deductions £ p	Net Pay £ p	Employer's N.I. £ p
ADAMS	84.00	264.00	118.80	145.20	43.50	205	17.23	7.58	13.50	0.75			21.83	62.17	9.65
PATEL	112.20	308.20	121.68	186.52	55.80	210	22.95	10.10	21.60	0.75			32.45	79.75	12.85
PRINGLE	152.40	392.40	115.92	276.48	82.80	200	31.13	13.70	34.20	0.75			48.65	103.75	17.43
THOMAS	240.00	636.00	144.75	491.25	147.30	250	49.13	21.62	57.60		*9.00		88.22	151.78	27.51
SHARP	254.00	612.00	104.37	507.63	152.10	180	51.12	22.50	65.70		*7.70		95.90	158.10	28.62
MONEYPIECE	100.00	300.00	115.92	184.08	55.20	200	20.50	9.02	18.60				27.72	72.28	11.48
GOLDBERG	210.00	630.00	115.35	514.65	154.20	199	42.99	18.92	51.30		*10.50		80.72	129.28	24.07
	1152.60	3142.60	836.79	2305.81									395.49	757.11	131.61

Chapter 18

A18.1

(a)

A. DORES
TRADING AND PROFIT AND LOSS ACCOUNT
FOR THE YEAR ENDED 31 DECEMBER 19——
(EXTRACT)

	£	£	
Rent	150		Gross Profit
Add Accrued	15		
		165	
Stationery	230		
Less Unused	120		
		110	

(b)
RENT ACCOUNT

Dec 31	Balance	150	—	Dec 31	Profit and		
Dec 31	Balance				Loss	165	—
	c/f	15	—				
		165	—			165	—
				Jan 1	Balance	15	—

STATIONERY ACCOUNT

Dec 31	Balance	230	—	Dec 31	Profit and		
					Loss	110	—
				Dec 31	Balance	120	—
		230	—			230	—
Jan 1	Balance	120	—				

A18.2	Calculation of Capital:		£
	Debit Side of Trial Balance	=	25 390
	Credit Side of Trial Balance	=	11 545
	∴ Capital	=	13 845

A18.2

(a)

A. TRING
TRADING AND PROFIT AND LOSS ACCOUNT
FOR THE YEAR ENDED 31 DECEMBER 19—

Dr					Cr			
Dec 31	Stock 1 Jan 1980			560 —	Dec 31	Sales		11 350 —	11 335 —
	Add Purchases	4 320 —				Less Sales Returns		15 —	
	Less Purchases Returns	25 —		4 295 —					
				4 855 —					
	Less Stock 31 Dec 1980			750 —					
	Cost of Sales			4 105 —					
	Gross Profit			7 230 —					
				11 335 —					11 335 —
Dec 31	Rent	110 —			Dec 31	Gross Profit			7 230 —
	Add Accrued	10 —		120 —					
	Rates	50 —							
	Less Rates in Advance	15 —		35 —					
	Insurance			30 —					
	Advertising	150 —							
	Less Prepaid	50 —		100 —					
	Wages	900 —							
	Add Accrued	20 —		920 —					

Postage and Telephone	120	
Discount Allowed	50	
Bank Charges	10	
Bad Debts	25	
Net Profit	5 870	
		7 280

Discount Received	35	
Interest Receivable	15	
		7 280

(b)

A. TRING
BALANCE SHEET
AS AT 31 DECEMBER 1980

Capital	13 845		
Add Net Profit	5 870	19 715	
Current Liabilities			
Creditors	120		
Accruals	30	150	

Fixed Assets			
Premises		10 000	
Motor Vehicles		1 300	
Furniture and Fittings		2 000	13 300
Current Assets			
Stock 31/12/80		750	
Debtors		750	
Prepayments		65	
Bank Deposit Account		3 000	
Bank Current Account		1 500	
Cash in Hand		500	6 565

(c)

RENT ACCOUNT

Dec 31	Balance	110	–	Dec 31	Profit and Loss		120	–
Dec 31	Balance	10	–					
		120	–				120	–
				Jan 1	Balance		10	–

ADVERTISING

Dec 31	Balance	150	–	Dec 31	Profit and Loss		100	–
				Dec 31	Balance		50	–
		150	–				150	–
Jan 1	Balance	50	–					

RATES

Dec 31	Balance	50	–	Dec 31	Profit and Loss		35	–
				Dec 31	Balance		15	–
		50	–				50	–
Jan 1	Balance	15	–					

Chapter 19

A19.1

LEASEHOLD PREMISES

19–1								
Jan 1	Cash	10 000	–					

PROVISION FOR DEPRECIATION OF LEASEHOLD PREMISES

19–1				1980				
Dec 31	Balance	1250	–	Dec 31	Profit and Loss		1250	–

		Dr				Cr	
19—2 Dec 31	Balance	2500	—	19—2 Jan 1 Dec 31	Balance Profit and Loss	1250 1250	— —
		2500	—			2500	—
19—2 Dec 31	Balance	3750	—	19—3 Jan 1 Dec 31	Balance Profit and Loss	2500 1250	— —
		3750	—			3750	—
				19—3 Jan 1	Balance	3750	—

MOTOR VANS

		Dr				Cr	
19—1 Jan 1	Cash	5000	—				

PROVISION FOR DEPRECIATION OF MOTOR VANS

		Dr				Cr	
19—1 Dec 31	Balance	1000	—	19—1 Dec 31	Profit and Loss	1000	—
19—2 Dec 31	Balance	1800	—	19—2 Jan 1 Dec 31	Balance Profit and Loss	1000 800	— —
		1800	—			1800	—
19—3 Dec 31	Balance	2440	—	19—3 Jan 1 Dec 31	Balance Profit and Loss	1800 640	— —
		2440	—			2440	—
				19—3 Jan 1	Balance	2440	—

FURNITURE AND FITTINGS

Date	Particulars	Amount		Date	Particulars	Amount	
19—1							
Jan 1	Cash	500	—				

PROVISION FOR DEPRECIATION OF FURNITURE AND FITTINGS

Date	Particulars	Amount		Date	Particulars	Amount	
19—1				19—1			
Dec 31	Balance	40	—	Dec 31	Profit and Loss	40	—
19—3				19—2			
Dec 31	Balance	80	—	Jan 1	Balance	40	—
				Dec 31	Profit and Loss	40	—
		80	—			80	—
19—3				19—2			
Dec 31	Balance	120	—	Jan 1	Balance	80	—
				Dec 31	Profit and Loss	40	—
		120	—			120	—
				19—2			
				Jan 1	Balance	120	—

BALANCE SHEET
AS AT 31 DECEMBER 19—3
(EXTRACT)

Fixed Assets		
Leasehold Premises at Cost	10 000	
Less Provision for Depreciation	3 750	
		6 250
Motor Van at Cost	5 000	
Less Provision for Depreciation	2 440	
		2 560
Furniture and Fittings at Cost	500	
Less Provision for Depreciation	120	
		380
		9 190

A19.2   T. Shoesmith

(a)   Capital = Assets − Liabilities = £10 579

(b)

T. SHOESMITH
TRADING AND PROFIT AND LOSS ACCOUNT
FOR THE YEAR ENDED 31 DECEMBER 19–1

Stock (1 Jan 19–1)		890	Sales	6 328	
Add Purchases	3 892		Less Returns		
Less Returns Outwards	42	3 850	Inwards	23	6 305
		4 740			
Less Stock (31 Dec 19–1)		750			
Cost of Sales		3 990			
Gross Profit		2 315			
		6 305			6 305
Stationery	50		Gross Profit		2 315
Less Stationery on Hand	10	40			
Advertising	80				
Less Prepaid Advertising	20	60			
Wages	500				
Add Accrued Wages	40	540			
Telephone	60				
Add Accrued Telephone	40	100			
Rates	144				
Less Prepaid Rates	50	94			
Rent	110				
Add Accrued Rent	10	120			
Depreciation:					
Premises	500				
Motor Vehicles	250				
Furniture and Fittings	50	800			
Net Profit		561			
		2 315			2 315

T. SHOESMITH
BALANCE SHEET AS AT
31 DECEMBER 19–1

			Fixed Assets		
Capital	10 579		Premises	10 000	
Add Net Profit	561	11 140	Less Depreciation	500	9 500
			Motor Vehicles	2 500	
			Less Depreciation	250	2 250
			Furniture and		
			Fittings	100	
			Less Depreciation	50	50
					11 800
Current Liabilities			*Current Assets*		
			Stock	750	
Creditors	500		Debtors	300	
Accruals	90		Prepayments	80	
Bank Overdraft	2 000	2 590	Cash in Hand	800	1 930
		13 730			13 730

A19.3   S. Peters

(a)   PROVISION FOR BAD DEBTS ACCOUNT

19–1				19–1				
Dec 31	Balance	187	50	Dec 31	Profit and			
					Loss		187	50
19–2				19–2				
Dec 31	Balance	192	50	Jan 1	Balance		187	50
				Dec 31	Profit and			
					Loss		5	—
		192	50				192	50

19—3 Dec 31	Balance	200	—	19—3 Jan 1 Dec 31	Balance Profit and Loss	192 7	50 50
		200	—			200	—
19—4 Dec 31 Dec 31	Profit and Loss Balance	12 187	50 50	19—4 Jan 1	Balance	200	—
		200	—			200	—
				19—3 Jan 1	Balance	187	50

(b)
S. PETERS
BALANCE SHEET AS AT
31 DECEMBER 19—4 (EXTRACT)

	£	
Current Assets Debtors	7 500	—
Less Provision for Bad Debts (2½%)	187	50
	7 312	50
Less Provision for Discount (1% of 7312.50)	73	12
	7 239	38

Chapter 20

A20.1

Receipts		Date	Particulars	Fol No	Vch No	Payments		Stationery		Fares		Postage		Sundries	
20	–	Feb 1	Cash Book	CBI											
		Feb 1	Bus Fare to Bank		1		20				20				
		Feb 1	Envelopes		2		45		45						
		Feb 2	Window Cleaner		3		85								85
		Feb 3	10 @ 12p Stamps		4	1	20					1	20		
		Feb 4	Ball Pens and Fare to Bank		5	1	88		68		20				
		Feb 6	Stapler and Staples		6	1	90							1	90
						6	48	2	13		40	1	20	2	75
		Feb 6	Balance			13	52								
20	0					20	00								
13	52		Balance												

Receipts £·p	Date	Details	Fo.	Total £·p	Stationery £·p	Travelling £·p	Postage £·p	Office & Sundries £·p
13·60	Feb 8	Balance						
6·40	Feb 8	Cash Book	CBI					
	Feb 8	Bell for Office and Fare	7	2·42		·20		2·22
	Feb 9	Envelopes, Milk, Fare	8	1·40	·80	·20		·40
	Feb 9	Fare to Bank	9	·20		·20		
	Feb 11	10 @ 12p Stamps and Wrapping Paper	10	1·50	·30		1·20	
	Feb 12	Window Cleaner	11	·85				·85
	Feb 12	Taxi to Station	12	1·85		1·85		
				8·22	1·10	2·45	1·20	3·47
	Feb 12	Balance		11·78				
20·00				20·00				
11·78	Feb 15	Balance						
8·22	Feb 15	Cash Book	CBI					

A20.2

Receipts	Date	Cash Book	Payments	Postage	Travel	Cleaning	Stationery	Sundries
20 00	Jan 1	Cash Book						
	Jan 2	Bus Fare to Bank	50		50			
	Jan 3	Window Cleaner	1 20			1 20		
	Jan 4	10 @ 12p Postage Stamps	1 20	1 20				
	Jan 5	Envelopes	75				75	
	Jan 5	Milk	3 20					3 20
	Jan 6	Taxi to Station	3 00		3 00			
			9 85	1 20	3 50	1 20	75	3 20
	Jan 6	Balance	10 15					
20 00			20 00					

Receipts £	Date	Details	Total Payment £	Postage £	Travelling £	Cleaning £	Stationery £	Sundries £
10.15	Jan 8	Balance						
9.85	Jan 8	Cash Book						
	Jan 8	Bus Fare to Bank	0.50		0.50			
	Jan 8	String	0.35					0.35
	Jan 9	Window Cleaner	1.20			1.20		
	Jan 10	Sugar	0.38					0.38
	Jan 10	Fare to Stationers and Pens	3.20		0.20		3.00	
	Jan 11	Envelopes	0.85				0.85	
	Jan 12	10 @ 12p Postage Stamps	1.20	1.20				
	Jan 13	Lunch for Client	3.20					3.20
			10.88	1.20	0.70	1.20	3.85	3.93
	Jan 13	Balance	9.12					
20.00			20.00					
9.12	Jan 15	Balance						

Chapter 21

A21.1 Working capital of Regal Industries is £2270

Ratio $\dfrac{£5870}{£3600}$ = 1.63 times

A21.2 (a) Working capital = £2487

(b) Liquid capital ratio = $\dfrac{1995}{3108}$ = 0.64

A21.3

		Year 1	Year 2
(a)	Gross profit %	30%	27%
(b)	Net profit %	11%	11.75%

A21.4 (a) Leeds net profit % = 15%

(b) Net profit at Leeds = £9300

(c) Gross profit % for Liverpool = 27.5%

Gross profit for Leeds = 30%

Chapter 22

A22.1

BALANCE SHEET
AS AT 4 JANUARY 19–1
C. FIDDLER

Capital	10 000		Assets		
Net Profit (–10)	490		Fixed Assets		
		10 490	Motor Vehicle		3 000
Current Liabilities			Current Assets		
Creditors (+750)		250	Stock (+250)	1250	
			Debtors (–1500)	—	
			Cash (+1500)		
			(– 10)	6490	
					7 740
		10 740			10 740

TABLE A–FREE PAY

Code	Total free pay to date	Code	Total free pay to date	Code	Total free pay to date	Code	Total free pay to date	Code	Total free pay to date	Code	Total free pay to date	Code	Total free pay to date	Code	Total free pay to date
	£		£		£		£		£		£		£		£
0	NIL														
1	0·37	61	11·91	121	23·45	181	34·99	241	46·52	301	58·06	361	69·60	421	81·14
2	0·56	62	12·10	122	23·64	182	35·18	242	46·72	302	58·25	362	69·79	422	81·33
3	0·75	63	12·29	123	23·83	183	35·37	243	46·91	303	58·45	363	69·99	423	81·52
4	0·95	64	12·49	124	24·02	184	35·56	244	47·10	304	58·64	364	70·18	424	81·72
5	1·14	65	12·68	125	24·22	185	35·75	245	47·29	305	58·83	365	70·37	425	81·91
6	1·33	66	12·87	126	24·41	186	35·95	246	47·49	306	59·02	366	70·56	426	82·10
7	1·52	67	13·06	127	24·60	187	36·14	247	47·68	307	59·22	367	70·75	427	82·29
8	1·72	68	13·25	128	24·79	188	36·33	248	47·87	308	59·41	368	70·95	428	82·49
9	1·91	69	13·45	129	24·99	189	36·52	249	48·06	309	59·60	369	71·14	429	82·68
10	2·10	70	13·64	130	25·18	190	36·72	250	48·25	310	59·79	370	71·33	430	82·87
11	2·29	71	13·83	131	25·37	191	36·91	251	48·45	311	59·99	371	71·52	431	83·06
12	2·49	72	14·02	132	25·56	192	37·10	252	48·64	312	60·18	372	71·72	432	83·25
13	2·68	73	14·22	133	25·75	193	37·29	253	48·83	313	60·37	373	71·91	433	83·45
14	2·87	74	14·41	134	25·95	194	37·49	254	49·02	314	60·56	374	72·10	434	83·64
15	3·06	75	14·60	135	26·14	195	37·68	255	49·22	315	60·75	375	72·29	435	83·83
16	3·25	76	14·79	136	26·33	196	37·87	256	49·41	316	60·95	376	72·49	436	84·02
17	3·45	77	14·99	137	26·52	197	38·06	257	49·60	317	61·14	377	72·68	437	84·22
18	3·64	78	15·18	138	26·72	198	38·25	258	49·79	318	61·33	378	72·87	438	84·41
19	3·83	79	15·37	139	26·91	199	38·45	259	49·99	319	61·52	379	73·06	439	84·60
20	4·02	80	15·56	140	27·10	200	38·64	260	50·18	320	61·72	380	73·25	440	84·79
21	4·22	81	15·75	141	27·29	201	38·83	261	50·37	321	61·91	381	73·45	441	84·99
22	4·41	82	15·95	142	27·49	202	39·02	262	50·56	322	62·10	382	73·64	442	85·18
23	4·60	83	16·14	143	27·68	203	39·22	263	50·75	323	62·29	383	73·83	443	85·37
24	4·79	84	16·33	144	27·87	204	39·41	264	50·95	324	62·49	384	74·02	444	85·56
25	4·99	85	16·52	145	28·06	205	39·60	265	51·14	325	62·68	385	74·22	445	85·75
26	5·18	86	16·72	146	28·25	206	39·79	266	51·33	326	62·87	386	74·41	446	85·95
27	5·37	87	16·91	147	28·45	207	39·99	267	51·52	327	63·06	387	74·60	447	86·14
28	5·56	88	17·10	148	28·64	208	40·18	268	51·72	328	63·25	388	74·79	448	86·33
29	5·75	89	17·29	149	28·83	209	40·37	269	51·91	329	63·45	389	74·99	449	86·52
30	5·95	90	17·49	150	29·02	210	40·56	270	52·10	330	63·64	390	75·18	450	86·72
31	6·14	91	17·68	151	29·22	211	40·75	271	52·29	331	63·83	391	75·37	451	86·91
32	6·33	92	17·87	152	29·41	212	40·95	272	52·49	332	64·02	392	75·56	452	87·10
33	6·52	93	18·06	153	29·60	213	41·14	273	52·68	333	64·22	393	75·75	453	87·29
34	6·72	94	18·25	154	29·79	214	41·33	274	52·87	334	64·41	394	75·95	454	87·49
35	6·91	95	18·45	155	29·99	215	41·52	275	53·06	335	64·60	395	76·14	455	87·68
36	7·10	96	18·64	156	30·18	216	41·72	276	53·25	336	64·79	396	76·33	456	87·87
37	7·29	97	18·83	157	30·37	217	41·91	277	53·45	337	64·99	397	76·52	457	88·06
38	7·49	98	19·02	158	30·56	218	42·10	278	53·64	338	65·18	398	76·72	458	88·25
39	7·68	99	19·22	159	30·75	219	42·29	279	53·83	339	65·37	399	76·91	459	88·45
40	7·87	100	19·41	160	30·95	220	42·49	280	54·02	340	65·56	400	77·10	460	88·64
41	8·06	101	19·60	161	31·14	221	42·68	281	54·22	341	65·75	401	77·29	461	88·83
42	8·25	102	19·79	162	31·33	222	42·87	282	54·41	342	65·95	402	77·49	462	89·02
43	8·45	103	19·99	163	31·52	223	43·06	283	54·60	343	66·14	403	77·68	463	89·22
44	8·64	104	20·18	164	31·72	224	43·25	284	54·79	344	66·33	404	77·87	464	89·41
45	8·83	105	20·37	165	31·91	225	43·45	285	54·99	345	66·52	405	78·06	465	89·60
46	9·02	106	20·56	166	32·10	226	43·64	286	55·18	346	66·72	406	78·25	466	89·79
47	9·22	107	20·75	167	32·29	227	43·83	287	55·37	347	66·91	407	78·45	467	89·99
48	9·41	108	20·95	168	32·49	228	44·02	288	55·56	348	67·10	408	78·64	468	90·18
49	9·60	109	21·14	169	32·68	229	44·22	289	55·75	349	67·29	409	78·83	469	90·37
50	9·79	110	21·33	170	32·87	230	44·41	290	55·95	350	67·49	410	79·02	470	90·56
51	9·99	111	21·52	171	33·06	231	44·60	291	56·14	351	67·68	411	79·22	471	90·75
52	10·18	112	21·72	172	33·25	232	44·79	292	56·33	352	67·87	412	79·41	472	90·95
53	10·37	113	21·91	173	33·45	233	44·99	293	56·52	353	68·06	413	79·60	473	91·14
54	10·56	114	22·10	174	33·64	234	45·18	294	56·72	354	68·25	414	79·79	474	91·33
55	10·75	115	22·29	175	33·83	235	45·37	295	56·91	355	68·45	415	79·99	475	91·52
56	10·95	116	22·49	176	34·02	236	45·56	296	57·10	356	68·64	416	80·18	476	91·72
57	11·14	117	22·68	177	34·22	237	45·75	297	57·29	357	68·83	417	80·37	477	91·91
58	11·33	118	22·87	178	34·41	238	45·95	298	57·49	358	69·02	418	80·56	478	92·10
59	11·52	119	23·06	179	34·60	239	46·14	299	57·68	359	69·22	419	80·75	479	92·29
60	11·72	120	23·25	180	34·79	240	46·33	300	57·87	360	69·41	420	80·95	480	92·49

see page 2

WEEK 2
Apr 13 to Apr 19

TABLE A—FREE PAY

Code	Total free pay to date	Code	Total free pay to date	Code	Total free pay to date	Code	Total free pay to date	Code	Total free pay to date	Code	Total free pay to date	Code	Total free pay to date	Code	Total free pay to date
	£		£		£		£		£		£		£		£
0	NIL	61	23·82	121	46·90	181	69·98	241	93·04	301	116·12	361	139·20	421	162·28
1	0·74	62	24·20	122	47·28	182	70·36	242	93·44	302	116·50	362	139·58	422	162·66
2	1·12	63	24·58	123	47·66	183	70·74	243	93·82	303	116·90	363	139·98	423	163·04
3	1·50	64	24·98	124	48·04	184	71·12	244	94·20	304	117·28	364	140·36	424	163·44
4	1·90	65	25·36	125	48·44	185	71·50	245	94·58	305	117·66	365	140·74	425	163·82
5	2·28														
6	2·66	66	25·74	126	48·82	186	71·90	246	94·98	306	118·04	366	141·12	426	164·20
7	3·04	67	26·12	127	49·20	187	72·28	247	95·36	307	118·44	367	141·50	427	164·58
8	3·44	68	26·50	128	49·58	188	72·66	248	95·74	308	118·82	368	141·90	428	164·98
9	3·82	69	26·90	129	49·98	189	73·04	249	96·12	309	119·20	369	142·28	429	165·36
10	4·20	70	27·28	130	50·36	190	73·44	250	96·50	310	119·58	370	142·66	430	165·74
11	4·58	71	27·66	131	50·74	191	73·82	251	96·90	311	119·98	371	143·04	431	166·12
12	4·98	72	28·04	132	51·12	192	74·20	252	97·28	312	120·36	372	143·44	432	166·50
13	5·36	73	28·44	133	51·50	193	74·58	253	97·66	313	120·74	373	143·82	433	166·90
14	5·74	74	28·82	134	51·90	194	74·98	254	98·04	314	121·12	374	144·20	434	167·28
15	6·12	75	29·20	135	52·28	195	75·36	255	98·44	315	121·50	375	144·58	435	167·66
16	6·50	76	29·58	136	52·66	196	75·74	256	98·82	316	121·90	376	144·98	436	168·04
17	6·90	77	29·98	137	53·04	197	76·12	257	99·20	317	122·28	377	145·36	437	168·44
18	7·28	78	30·36	138	53·44	198	76·50	258	99·58	318	122·66	378	145·74	438	168·82
19	7·66	79	30·74	139	53·82	199	76·90	259	99·98	319	123·04	379	146·12	439	169·20
20	8·04	80	31·12	140	54·20	200	77·28	260	100·36	320	123·44	380	146·50	440	169·58
21	8·44	81	31·50	141	54·58	201	77·66	261	100·74	321	123·82	381	146·90	441	169·98
22	8·82	82	31·90	142	54·98	202	78·04	262	101·12	322	124·20	382	147·28	442	170·36
23	9·20	83	32·28	143	55·36	203	78·44	263	101·50	323	124·58	383	147·66	443	170·74
24	9·58	84	32·66	144	55·74	204	78·82	264	101·90	324	124·98	384	148·04	444	171·12
25	9·98	85	33·04	145	56·12	205	79·20	265	102·28	325	125·36	385	148·44	445	171·50
26	10·36	86	33·44	146	56·50	206	79·58	266	102·66	326	125·74	386	148·82	446	171·90
27	10·74	87	33·82	147	56·90	207	79·98	267	103·04	327	126·12	387	149·20	447	172·28
28	11·12	88	34·20	148	57·28	208	80·36	268	103·44	328	126·50	388	149·58	448	172·66
29	11·50	89	34·58	149	57·66	209	80·74	269	103·82	329	126·90	389	149·98	449	173·04
30	11·90	90	34·98	150	58·04	210	81·12	270	104·20	330	127·28	390	150·36	450	173·44
31	12·28	91	35·36	151	58·44	211	81·50	271	104·58	331	127·66	391	150·74	451	173·82
32	12·66	92	35·74	152	58·82	212	81·90	272	104·98	332	128·04	392	151·12	452	174·20
33	13·04	93	36·12	153	59·20	213	82·28	273	105·36	333	128·44	393	151·50	453	174·58
34	13·44	94	36·50	154	59·58	214	82·66	274	105·74	334	128·82	394	151·90	454	174·98
35	13·82	95	36·90	155	59·98	215	83·04	275	106·12	335	129·20	395	152·28	455	175·36
36	14·20	96	37·28	156	60·36	216	83·44	276	106·50	336	129·58	396	152·66	456	175·74
37	14·58	97	37·66	157	60·74	217	83·82	277	106·90	337	129·98	397	153·04	457	176·12
38	14·98	98	38·04	158	61·12	218	84·20	278	107·28	338	130·36	398	153·44	458	176·50
39	15·36	99	38·44	159	61·50	219	84·58	279	107·66	339	130·74	399	153·82	459	176·90
40	15·74	100	38·82	160	61·90	220	84·98	280	108·04	340	131·12	400	154·20	460	177·28
41	16·12	101	39·20	161	62·28	221	85·36	281	108·44	341	131·50	401	154·58	461	177·66
42	16·50	102	39·58	162	62·66	222	85·74	282	108·82	342	131·90	402	154·98	462	178·04
43	16·90	103	39·98	163	63·04	223	86·12	283	109·20	343	132·28	403	155·36	463	178·44
44	17·28	104	40·36	164	63·44	224	86·50	284	109·58	344	132·66	404	155·74	464	178·82
45	17·66	105	40·74	165	63·82	225	86·90	285	109·98	345	133·04	405	156·12	465	179·20
46	18·04	106	41·12	166	64·20	226	87·28	286	110·36	346	133·44	406	156·50	466	179·58
47	18·44	107	41·50	167	64·58	227	87·66	287	110·74	347	133·82	407	156·90	467	179·98
48	18·82	108	41·90	168	64·98	228	88·04	288	111·12	348	134·20	408	157·28	468	180·36
49	19·20	109	42·28	169	65·36	229	88·44	289	111·50	349	134·58	409	157·66	469	180·74
50	19·58	110	42·66	170	65·74	230	88·82	290	111·90	350	134·98	410	158·04	470	181·12
51	19·98	111	43·04	171	66·12	231	89·20	291	112·28	351	135·36	411	158·44	471	181·50
52	20·36	112	43·44	172	66·50	232	89·58	292	112·66	352	135·74	412	158·82	472	181·90
53	20·74	113	43·82	173	66·90	233	89·98	293	113·04	353	136·12	413	159·20	473	182·28
54	21·12	114	44·20	174	67·28	234	90·36	294	113·44	354	136·50	414	159·58	474	182·66
55	21·50	115	44·58	175	67·66	235	90·74	295	113·82	355	136·90	415	159·98	475	183·04
56	21·90	116	44·98	176	68·04	236	91·12	296	114·20	356	137·28	416	160·36	476	183·44
57	22·28	117	45·36	177	68·44	237	91·50	297	114·58	357	137·66	417	160·74	477	183·82
58	22·66	118	45·74	178	68·82	238	91·90	298	114·98	358	138·04	418	161·12	478	184·20
59	23·04	119	46·12	179	69·20	239	92·28	299	115·36	359	138·44	419	161·50	479	184·58
60	23·44	120	46·50	180	69·58	240	92·66	300	115·74	360	138·82	420	161·90	480	184·98

see page 2

TABLE A–FREE PAY

WEEK 3
Apr 20 to Apr 26

Code	Total free pay to date	Code	Total free pay to date	Code	Total free pay to date	Code	Total free pay to date	Code	Total free pay to date	Code	Total free pay to date	Code	Total free pay to date	Code	Total free pay to date
	£		£		£		£		£		£		£		£
0	NIL														
1	1·11	61	35·73	121	70·35	181	104·97	241	139·56	301	174·18	361	208·80	421	243·42
2	1·68	62	36·30	122	70·92	182	105·54	242	140·16	302	174·75	362	209·37	422	243·99
3	2·25	63	36·87	123	71·49	183	106·11	243	140·73	303	175·35	363	209·97	423	244·56
4	2·85	64	37·47	124	72·06	184	106·68	244	141·30	304	175·92	364	210·54	424	245·16
5	3·42	65	38·04	125	72·66	185	107·25	245	141·87	305	176·49	365	211·11	425	245·73
6	3·99	66	38·61	126	73·23	186	107·85	246	142·47	306	177·06	366	211·68	426	246·30
7	4·56	67	39·18	127	73·80	187	108·42	247	143·04	307	177·66	367	212·25	427	246·87
8	5·16	68	39·75	128	74·37	188	108·99	248	143·61	308	178·23	368	212·85	428	247·47
9	5·73	69	40·35	129	74·97	189	109·56	249	144·18	309	178·80	369	213·42	429	248·04
10	6·30	70	40·92	130	75·54	190	110·16	250	144·75	310	179·37	370	213·99	430	248·61
11	6·87	71	41·49	131	76·11	191	110·73	251	145·35	311	179·97	371	214·56	431	249·18
12	7·47	72	42·06	132	76·68	192	111·30	252	145·92	312	180·54	372	215·16	432	249·75
13	8·04	73	42·66	133	77·25	193	111·87	253	146·49	313	181·11	373	215·73	433	250·35
14	8·61	74	43·23	134	77·85	194	112·47	254	147·06	314	181·68	374	216·30	434	250·92
15	9·18	75	43·80	135	78·42	195	113·04	255	147·66	315	182·25	375	216·87	435	251·49
16	9·75	76	44·37	136	78·99	196	113·64	256	148·23	316	182·85	376	217·47	436	252·06
17	10·35	77	44·97	137	79·56	197	114·18	257	148·80	317	183·42	377	218·04	437	252·66
18	10·92	78	45·54	138	80·16	198	114·75	258	149·37	318	183·99	378	218·61	438	253·23
19	11·49	79	46·11	139	80·73	199	115·35	259	149·97	319	184·56	379	219·18	439	253·80
20	12·06	80	46·68	140	81·30	200	115·92	260	150·54	320	185·16	380	219·75	440	254·37
21	12·66	81	47·25	141	81·87	201	116·49	261	151·11	321	185·73	381	220·35	441	254·97
22	13·23	82	47·85	142	82·47	202	117·06	262	151·68	322	186·30	382	220·92	442	255·54
23	13·80	83	48·42	143	83·04	203	117·66	263	152·25	323	186·87	383	221·49	443	256·11
24	14·37	84	48·99	144	83·61	204	118·23	264	152·85	324	187·47	384	222·06	444	256·68
25	14·97	85	49·56	145	84·18	205	118·80	265	153·42	325	188·04	385	222·66	445	257·25
26	15·54	86	50·16	146	84·75	206	119·37	266	153·99	326	188·61	386	223·23	446	257·85
27	16·11	87	50·73	147	85·35	207	119·97	267	154·56	327	189·18	387	223·80	447	258·42
28	16·68	88	51·30	148	85·92	208	120·54	268	155·16	328	189·75	388	224·37	448	258·99
29	17·25	89	51·87	149	86·49	209	121·11	269	155·73	329	190·35	389	224·97	449	259·56
30	17·85	90	52·47	150	87·06	210	121·68	270	156·30	330	190·92	390	225·54	450	260·16
31	18·42	91	53·04	151	87·66	211	122·25	271	156·87	331	191·49	391	226·11	451	260·73
32	18·99	92	53·61	152	88·23	212	122·85	272	157·47	332	192·06	392	226·68	452	261·30
33	19·56	93	54·18	153	88·80	213	123·42	273	158·04	333	192·66	393	227·25	453	261·87
34	20·16	94	54·75	154	89·37	214	123·99	274	158·61	334	193·23	394	227·85	454	262·47
35	20·73	95	55·35	155	89·97	215	124·56	275	159·18	335	193·80	395	228·42	455	263·04
36	21·30	96	55·92	156	90·54	216	125·16	276	159·75	336	194·37	396	228·99	456	263·61
37	21·87	97	56·49	157	91·11	217	125·73	277	160·35	337	194·97	397	229·56	457	264·18
38	22·47	98	57·06	158	91·68	218	126·30	278	160·92	338	195·54	398	230·16	458	264·75
39	23·04	99	57·66	159	92·25	219	126·87	279	161·49	339	196·11	399	230·73	459	265·35
40	23·61	100	58·23	160	92·85	220	127·47	280	162·06	340	196·68	400	231·30	460	265·92
41	24·18	101	58·80	161	93·42	221	128·04	281	162·66	341	197·25	401	231·87	461	266·49
42	24·75	102	59·37	162	93·99	222	128·61	282	163·23	342	197·85	402	232·47	462	267·06
43	25·35	103	59·97	163	94·56	223	129·18	283	163·80	343	198·42	403	233·04	463	267·66
44	25·92	104	60·54	164	95·16	224	129·75	284	164·37	344	198·99	404	233·61	464	268·23
45	26·49	105	61·11	165	95·73	225	130·35	285	164·97	345	199·56	405	234·18	465	268·80
46	27·06	106	61·68	166	96·30	226	130·92	286	165·54	346	200·16	406	234·75	466	269·37
47	27·66	107	62·25	167	96·87	227	131·49	287	166·11	347	200·73	407	235·35	467	269·97
48	28·23	108	62·85	168	97·47	228	132·06	288	166·68	348	201·30	408	235·92	468	270·54
49	28·80	109	63·42	169	98·04	229	132·66	289	167·25	349	201·87	409	236·49	469	271·11
50	29·37	110	63·99	170	98·61	230	133·23	290	167·85	350	202·47	410	237·06	470	271·68
51	29·97	111	64·56	171	99·18	231	133·80	291	168·42	351	203·04	411	237·66	471	272·25
52	30·54	112	65·16	172	99·75	232	134·37	292	168·99	352	203·61	412	238·23	472	272·85
53	31·11	113	65·73	173	100·35	233	134·97	293	169·56	353	204·18	413	238·80	473	273·42
54	31·68	114	66·30	174	100·92	234	135·54	294	170·16	354	204·75	414	239·37	474	273·99
55	32·25	115	66·87	175	101·49	235	136·11	295	170·73	355	205·35	415	239·97	475	274·56
56	32·85	116	67·47	176	102·06	236	136·68	296	171·30	356	205·92	416	240·54	476	275·16
57	33·42	117	68·04	177	102·66	237	137·25	297	171·87	357	206·49	417	241·11	477	275·73
58	33·99	118	68·61	178	103·23	238	137·85	298	172·47	358	207·06	418	241·68	478	276·30
59	34·56	119	69·18	179	103·80	239	138·42	299	173·04	359	207·66	419	242·25	479	276·87
60	35·16	120	69·75	180	104·37	240	138·99	300	173·61	360	208·23	420	242·85	480	277·47

see page 2

WEEK 4
Apr 27 to May 3

TABLE A–FREE PAY

Code	Total free pay to date	Code	Total free pay to date	Code	Total free pay to date	Code	Total free pay to date	Code	Total free pay to date	Code	Total free pay to date	Code	Total free pay to date	Code	Total free pay to date
	£		£		£		£		£		£		£		£
0	**NIL**														
1	1·48	61	47·64	121	93·80	181	139·96	241	186·08	301	232·24	361	278·40	421	324·56
2	2·24	62	48·40	122	94·56	182	140·72	242	186·88	302	233·00	362	279·16	422	325·32
3	3·00	63	49·16	123	95·32	183	141·48	243	187·64	303	233·80	363	279·96	423	326·08
4	3·80	64	49·96	124	96·08	184	142·24	244	188·40	304	234·56	364	280·72	424	326·88
5	4·56	65	50·72	125	96·88	185	143·00	245	189·16	305	235·32	365	281·48	425	327·64
6	5·32	66	51·48	126	97·64	186	143·80	246	189·96	306	236·08	366	282·24	426	328·40
7	6·08	67	52·24	127	98·40	187	144·56	247	190·72	307	236·88	367	283·00	427	329·16
8	6·88	68	53·00	128	99·16	188	145·32	248	191·48	308	237·64	368	283·80	428	329·96
9	7·64	69	53·80	129	99·96	189	146·08	249	192·24	309	238·40	369	284·56	429	330·72
10	8·40	70	54·56	130	100·72	190	146·88	250	193·00	310	239·16	370	285·32	430	331·48
11	9·16	71	55·32	131	101·48	191	147·64	251	193·80	311	239·96	371	286·08	431	332·24
12	9·96	72	56·08	132	102·24	192	148·40	252	194·56	312	240·72	372	286·88	432	333·00
13	10·72	73	56·88	133	103·00	193	149·16	253	195·32	313	241·48	373	287·64	433	333·80
14	11·48	74	57·64	134	103·80	194	149·96	254	196·08	314	242·24	374	288·40	434	334·56
15	12·24	75	58·40	135	104·56	195	150·72	255	196·88	315	243·00	375	289·16	435	335·32
16	13·00	76	59·16	136	105·32	196	151·48	256	197·64	316	243·80	376	289·96	436	336·08
17	13·80	77	59·96	137	106·08	197	152·24	257	198·40	317	244·56	377	290·72	437	336·88
18	14·56	78	60·72	138	106·88	198	153·00	258	199·16	318	245·32	378	291·48	438	337·64
19	15·32	79	61·48	139	107·64	199	153·80	259	199·96	319	246·08	379	292·24	439	338·40
20	16·08	80	62·24	140	108·40	200	154·56	260	200·72	320	246·88	380	293·00	440	339·16
21	16·88	81	63·00	141	109·16	201	155·32	261	201·48	321	247·64	381	293·80	441	339·96
22	17·64	82	63·80	142	109·96	202	156·08	262	202·24	322	248·40	382	294·56	442	340·72
23	18·40	83	64·56	143	110·72	203	156·88	263	203·00	323	249·16	383	295·32	443	341·48
24	19·16	84	65·32	144	111·48	204	157·64	264	203·80	324	249·96	384	296·08	444	342·24
25	19·96	85	66·08	145	112·24	205	158·40	265	204·56	325	250·72	385	296·88	445	343·00
26	20·72	86	66·88	146	113·00	206	159·16	266	205·32	326	251·48	386	297·64	446	343·80
27	21·48	87	67·64	147	113·80	207	159·96	267	206·08	327	252·24	387	298·40	447	344·56
28	22·24	88	68·40	148	114·56	208	160·72	268	206·88	328	253·00	388	299·16	448	345·32
29	23·00	89	69·16	149	115·32	209	161·48	269	207·64	329	253·80	389	299·96	449	346·08
30	23·80	90	69·96	150	116·08	210	162·24	270	208·40	330	254·56	390	300·72	450	346·88
31	24·56	91	70·72	151	116·88	211	163·00	271	209·16	331	255·32	391	301·48	451	347·64
32	25·32	92	71·48	152	117·64	212	163·80	272	209·96	332	256·08	392	302·24	452	348·40
33	26·08	93	72·24	153	118·40	213	164·56	273	210·72	333	256·88	393	303·00	453	349·16
34	26·88	94	73·00	154	119·16	214	165·32	274	211·48	334	257·64	394	303·80	454	349·96
35	27·64	95	73·80	155	119·96	215	166·08	275	212·24	335	258·40	395	304·56	455	350·72
36	28·40	96	74·56	156	120·72	216	166·88	276	213·00	336	259·16	396	305·32	456	351·48
37	29·16	97	75·32	157	121·48	217	167·64	277	213·80	337	259·96	397	306·08	457	352·24
38	29·96	98	76·08	158	122·24	218	168·40	278	214·56	338	260·72	398	306·88	458	353·00
39	30·72	99	76·88	159	123·00	219	169·16	279	215·32	339	261·48	399	307·64	459	353·80
40	31·48	100	77·64	160	123·80	220	169·96	280	216·08	340	262·24	400	308·40	460	354·56
41	32·24	101	78·40	161	124·56	221	170·72	281	216·88	341	263·00	401	309·16	461	355·32
42	33·00	102	79·16	162	125·32	222	171·48	282	217·64	342	263·80	402	309·96	462	356·08
43	33·80	103	79·96	163	126·08	223	172·24	283	218·40	343	264·56	403	310·72	463	356·88
44	34·56	104	80·72	164	126·88	224	173·00	284	219·16	344	265·32	404	311·48	464	357·64
45	35·32	105	81·48	165	127·64	225	173·80	285	219·96	345	266·08	405	312·24	465	358·40
46	36·08	106	82·24	166	128·40	226	174·56	286	220·72	346	266·88	406	313·00	466	359·16
47	36·88	107	83·00	167	129·16	227	175·32	287	221·48	347	267·64	407	313·80	467	359·96
48	37·64	108	83·80	168	129·96	228	176·08	288	222·24	348	268·40	408	314·56	468	360·72
49	38·40	109	84·56	169	130·72	229	176·88	289	223·00	349	269·16	409	315·32	469	361·48
50	39·16	110	85·32	170	131·48	230	177·64	290	223·80	350	269·96	410	316·08	470	362·24
51	39·96	111	86·08	171	132·24	231	178·40	291	224·56	351	270·72	411	316·88	471	363·00
52	40·72	112	86·88	172	133·00	232	179·16	292	225·32	352	271·48	412	317·64	472	363·80
53	41·48	113	87·64	173	133·80	233	179·96	293	226·08	353	272·24	413	318·40	473	364·56
54	42·24	114	88·40	174	134·56	234	180·72	294	226·88	354	273·00	414	319·16	474	365·32
55	43·00	115	89·16	175	135·32	235	181·48	295	227·64	355	273·80	415	319·96	475	366·08
56	43·80	116	89·96	176	136·08	236	182·24	296	228·40	356	274·56	416	320·72	476	366·88
57	44·56	117	90·72	177	136·88	237	183·00	297	229·16	357	275·32	417	321·48	477	367·64
58	45·32	118	91·48	178	137·64	238	183·80	298	229·96	358	276·08	418	322·24	478	368·40
59	46·08	119	92·24	179	138·40	239	184·56	299	230·72	359	276·88	419	323·00	479	369·16
60	46·88	120	93·00	180	139·16	240	185·32	300	231·48	360	277·64	420	323·80	480	369·96

see page 2

TABLE B

LIMITATIONS ON USE

Week No.	Pay at Weekly rates If total taxable pay to date does not exceed	Total tax due to date
	(Col. 1) £	(Col. 2) £
1	297	
2	593	
3	889	
4	1185	
5	1481	
6	1777	
7	2074	
8	2370	
9	2666	
10	2962	
11	3258	
12	3554	
13	3850	
14	4147	
15	4443	
16	4739	
17	5035	
18	5331	
19	5627	
20	5924	
21	6220	
22	6516	
23	6812	TAX DUE AS SHOWN IN TABLE B
24	7108	If the total taxable pay exceeds the
25	7404	figure in Col. 1 refer to Table C
26	7700	as appropriate
27	7997	
28	8293	
29	8589	
30	8885	
31	9181	
32	9477	
33	9774	
34	10070	
35	10366	
36	10662	
37	10958	
38	11254	
39	11550	
40	11847	
41	12143	
42	12439	
43	12735	
44	13031	
45	13327	
46	13624	
47	13920	
48	14216	
49	14512	
50	14808	
51	15104	
52	15400	

Month No.	Pay at Monthly rates If total taxable pay to date does not exceed	Total tax due to date
	(Col. 1) £	(Col. 2) £
1	1284	
2	2567	
3	3850	
4	5134	TAX DUE AS SHOWN IN TABLE B
5	6417	If the total taxable pay exceeds the
6	7700	figure in Col. 1 refer to Table C
7	8984	as appropriate
8	10267	
9	11550	
10	12834	
11	14117	
12	15400	

TABLE B

TAX DUE ON TAXABLE PAY FROM £1 TO £360

Total TAXABLE PAY to date	Total TAX DUE to date	Total TAXABLE PAY to date	Total TAX DUE to date	Total TAXABLE PAY to date	Total TAX DUE to date	Total TAXABLE PAY to date	Total TAX DUE to date	Total TAXABLE PAY to date	Total TAX DUE to date	Total TAXABLE PAY to date	Total TAX DUE to date
£	£	£	£	£	£	£	£	£	£	£	£
1	0.30	61	18.30	121	36.30	181	54.30	241	72.30	301	90.30
2	0.60	62	18.60	122	36.60	182	54.60	242	72.60	302	90.60
3	0.90	63	18.90	123	36.90	183	54.90	243	72.90	303	90.90
4	1.20	64	19.20	124	37.20	184	55.20	244	73.20	304	91.20
5	1.50	65	19.50	125	37.50	185	55.50	245	73.50	305	91.50
6	1.80	66	19.80	126	37.80	186	55.80	246	73.80	306	91.80
7	2.10	67	20.10	127	38.10	187	56.10	247	74.10	307	92.10
8	2.40	68	20.40	128	38.40	188	56.40	248	74.40	308	92.40
9	2.70	69	20.70	129	38.70	189	56.70	249	74.70	309	92.70
10	3.00	70	21.00	130	39.00	190	57.00	250	75.00	310	93.00
11	3.30	71	21.30	131	39.30	191	57.30	251	75.30	311	93.30
12	3.60	72	21.60	132	39.60	192	57.60	252	75.60	312	93.60
13	3.90	73	21.90	133	39.90	193	57.90	253	75.90	313	93.90
14	4.20	74	22.20	134	40.20	194	58.20	254	76.20	314	94.20
15	4.50	75	22.50	135	40.50	195	58.50	255	76.50	315	94.50
16	4.80	76	22.80	136	40.80	196	58.80	256	76.80	316	94.80
17	5.10	77	23.10	137	41.10	197	59.10	257	77.10	317	95.10
18	5.40	78	23.40	138	41.40	198	59.40	258	77.40	318	95.40
19	5.70	79	23.70	139	41.70	199	59.70	259	77.70	319	95.70
20	6.00	80	24.00	140	42.00	200	60.00	260	78.00	320	96.00
21	6.30	81	24.30	141	42.30	201	60.30	261	78.30	321	96.30
22	6.60	82	24.60	142	42.60	202	60.60	262	78.60	322	96.60
23	6.90	83	24.90	143	42.90	203	60.90	263	78.90	323	96.90
24	7.20	84	25.20	144	43.20	204	61.20	264	79.20	324	97.20
25	7.50	85	25.50	145	43.50	205	61.50	265	79.50	325	97.50
26	7.80	86	25.80	146	43.80	206	61.80	266	79.80	326	97.80
27	8.10	87	26.10	147	44.10	207	62.10	267	80.10	327	98.10
28	8.40	88	26.40	148	44.40	208	62.40	268	80.40	328	98.40
29	8.70	89	26.70	149	44.70	209	62.70	269	80.70	329	98.70
30	9.00	90	27.00	150	45.00	210	63.00	270	81.00	330	99.00
31	9.30	91	27.30	151	45.30	211	63.30	271	81.30	331	99.30
32	9.60	92	27.60	152	45.60	212	63.60	272	81.60	332	99.60
33	9.90	93	27.90	153	45.90	213	63.90	273	81.90	333	99.90
34	10.20	94	28.20	154	46.20	214	64.20	274	82.20	334	100.20
35	10.50	95	28.50	155	46.50	215	64.50	275	82.50	335	100.50
36	10.80	96	28.80	156	46.80	216	64.80	276	82.80	336	100.80
37	11.10	97	29.10	157	47.10	217	65.10	277	83.10	337	101.10
38	11.40	98	29.40	158	47.40	218	65.40	278	83.40	338	101.40
39	11.70	99	29.70	159	47.70	219	65.70	279	83.70	339	101.70
40	12.00	100	30.00	160	48.00	220	66.00	280	84.00	340	102.00
41	12.30	101	30.30	161	48.30	221	66.30	281	84.30	341	102.30
42	12.60	102	30.60	162	48.60	222	66.60	282	84.60	342	102.60
43	12.90	103	30.90	163	48.90	223	66.90	283	84.90	343	102.90
44	13.20	104	31.20	164	49.20	224	67.20	284	85.20	344	103.20
45	13.50	105	31.50	165	49.50	225	67.50	285	85.50	345	103.50
46	13.80	106	31.80	166	49.80	226	67.80	286	85.80	346	103.80
47	14.10	107	32.10	167	50.10	227	68.10	287	86.10	347	104.10
48	14.40	108	32.40	168	50.40	228	68.40	288	86.40	348	104.40
49	14.70	109	32.70	169	50.70	229	68.70	289	86.70	349	104.70
50	15.00	110	33.00	170	51.00	230	69.00	290	87.00	350	105.00
51	15.30	111	33.30	171	51.30	231	69.30	291	87.30	351	105.30
52	15.60	112	33.60	172	51.60	232	69.60	292	87.60	352	105.60
53	15.90	113	33.90	173	51.90	233	69.90	293	87.90	353	105.90
54	16.20	114	34.20	174	52.20	234	70.20	294	88.20	354	106.20
55	16.50	115	34.50	175	52.50	235	70.50	295	88.50	355	106.50
56	16.80	116	34.80	176	52.80	236	70.80	296	88.80	356	106.80
57	17.10	117	35.10	177	53.10	237	71.10	297	89.10	357	107.10
58	17.40	118	35.40	178	53.40	238	71.40	298	89.40	358	107.40
59	17.70	119	35.70	179	53.70	239	71.70	299	89.70	359	107.70
60	18.00	120	36.00	180	54.00	240	72.00	300	90.00	360	108.00

TABLE B

TAX DUE ON TAXABLE PAY FROM £361 TO £720

Total TAXABLE PAY to date	Total TAX DUE to date	Total TAXABLE PAY to date	Total TAX DUE to date	Total TAXABLE PAY to date	Total TAX DUE to date	Total TAXABLE PAY to date	Total TAX DUE to date	Total TAXABLE PAY to date	Total TAX DUE to date	Total TAXABLE PAY to date	Total TAX DUE to date
£	£	£	£	£	£	£	£	£	£	£	£
361	108.30	421	126.30	481	144.30	541	162.30	601	180.30	661	198.30
362	108.60	422	126.60	482	144.60	542	162.60	602	180.60	662	198.60
363	108.90	423	126.90	483	144.90	543	162.90	603	180.90	663	198.90
364	109.20	424	127.20	484	145.20	544	163.20	604	181.20	664	199.20
365	109.50	425	127.50	485	145.50	545	163.50	605	181.50	665	199.50
366	109.80	426	127.80	486	145.80	546	163.80	606	181.80	666	199.80
367	110.10	427	128.10	487	146.10	547	164.10	607	182.10	667	200.10
368	110.40	428	128.40	488	146.40	548	164.40	608	182.40	668	200.40
369	110.70	429	128.70	489	146.70	549	164.70	609	182.70	669	200.70
370	111.00	430	129.00	490	147.00	550	165.00	610	183.00	670	201.00
371	111.30	431	129.30	491	147.30	551	165.30	611	183.30	671	201.30
372	111.60	432	129.60	492	147.60	552	165.60	612	183.60	672	201.60
373	111.90	433	129.90	493	147.90	553	165.90	613	183.90	673	201.90
374	112.20	434	130.20	494	148.20	554	166.20	614	184.20	674	202.20
375	112.50	435	130.50	495	148.50	555	166.50	615	184.50	675	202.50
376	112.80	436	130.80	496	148.80	556	166.80	616	184.80	676	202.80
377	113.10	437	131.10	497	149.10	557	167.10	617	185.10	677	203.10
378	113.40	438	131.40	498	149.40	558	167.40	618	185.40	678	203.40
379	113.70	439	131.70	499	149.70	559	167.70	619	185.70	679	203.70
380	114.00	440	132.00	500	150.00	560	168.00	620	186.00	680	204.00
381	114.30	441	132.30	501	150.30	561	168.30	621	186.30	681	204.30
382	114.60	442	132.60	502	150.60	562	168.60	622	186.60	682	204.60
383	114.90	443	132.90	503	150.90	563	168.90	623	186.90	683	204.90
384	115.20	444	133.20	504	151.20	564	169.20	624	187.20	684	205.20
385	115.50	445	133.50	505	151.50	565	169.50	625	187.50	685	205.50
386	115.80	446	133.80	506	151.80	566	169.80	626	187.80	686	205.80
387	116.10	447	134.10	507	152.10	567	170.10	627	188.10	687	206.10
388	116.40	448	134.40	508	152.40	568	170.40	628	188.40	688	206.40
389	116.70	449	134.70	509	152.70	569	170.70	629	188.70	689	206.70
390	117.00	450	135.00	510	153.00	570	171.00	630	189.00	690	207.00
391	117.30	451	135.30	511	153.30	571	171.30	631	189.30	691	207.30
392	117.60	452	135.60	512	153.60	572	171.60	632	189.60	692	207.60
393	117.90	453	135.90	513	153.90	573	171.90	633	189.90	693	207.90
394	118.20	454	136.20	514	154.20	574	172.20	634	190.20	694	208.20
395	118.50	455	136.50	515	154.50	575	172.50	635	190.50	695	208.50
396	118.80	456	136.80	516	154.80	576	172.80	636	190.80	696	208.80
397	119.10	457	137.10	517	155.10	577	173.10	637	191.10	697	209.10
398	119.40	458	137.40	518	155.40	578	173.40	638	191.40	698	209.40
399	119.70	459	137.70	519	155.70	579	173.70	639	191.70	699	209.70
400	120.00	460	138.00	520	156.00	580	174.00	640	192.00	700	210.00
401	120.30	461	138.30	521	156.30	581	174.30	641	192.30	701	210.30
402	120.60	462	138.60	522	156.60	582	174.60	642	192.60	702	210.60
403	120.90	463	138.90	523	156.90	583	174.90	643	192.90	703	210.90
404	121.20	464	139.20	524	157.20	584	175.20	644	193.20	704	211.20
405	121.50	465	139.50	525	157.50	585	175.50	645	193.50	705	211.50
406	121.80	466	139.80	526	157.80	586	175.80	646	193.80	706	211.80
407	122.10	467	140.10	527	158.10	587	176.10	647	194.10	707	212.10
408	122.40	468	140.40	528	158.40	588	176.40	648	194.40	708	212.40
409	122.70	469	140.70	529	158.70	589	176.70	649	194.70	709	212.70
410	123.00	470	141.00	530	159.00	590	177.00	650	195.00	710	213.00
411	123.30	471	141.30	531	159.30	591	177.30	651	195.30	711	213.30
412	123.60	472	141.60	532	159.60	592	177.60	652	195.60	712	213.60
413	123.90	473	141.90	533	159.90	593	177.90	653	195.90	713	213.90
414	124.20	474	142.20	534	160.20	594	178.20	654	196.20	714	214.20
415	124.50	475	142.50	535	160.50	595	178.50	655	196.50	715	214.50
416	124.80	476	142.80	536	160.80	596	178.80	656	196.80	716	214.80
417	125.10	477	143.10	537	161.10	597	179.10	657	197.10	717	215.10
418	125.40	478	143.40	538	161.40	598	179.40	658	197.40	718	215.40
419	125.70	479	143.70	539	161.70	599	179.70	659	197.70	719	215.70
420	126.00	480	144.00	540	162.00	600	180.00	660	198.00	720	216.00

TABLE B

TAX DUE ON TAXABLE PAY FROM £721 TO £1080

Total TAXABLE PAY to date	Total TAX DUE to date	Total TAXABLE PAY to date	Total TAX DUE to date	Total TAXABLE PAY to date	Total TAX DUE to date	Total TAXABLE PAY to date	Total TAX DUE to date	Total TAXABLE PAY to date	Total TAX DUE to date	Total TAXABLE PAY to date	Total TAX DUE to date
£	£	£	£	£	£	£	£	£	£	£	£
721	216.30	781	234.30	841	252.30	901	270.30	961	288.30	1021	306.30
722	216.60	782	234.60	842	252.60	902	270.60	962	288.60	1022	306.60
723	216.90	783	234.90	843	252.90	903	270.90	963	288.90	1023	306.90
724	217.20	784	235.20	844	253.20	904	271.20	964	289.20	1024	307.20
725	217.50	785	235.50	845	253.50	905	271.50	965	289.50	1025	307.50
726	217.80	786	235.80	846	253.80	906	271.80	966	289.80	1026	307.80
727	218.10	787	236.10	847	254.10	907	272.10	967	290.10	1027	308.10
728	218.40	788	236.40	848	254.40	908	272.40	968	290.40	1028	308.40
729	218.70	789	236.70	849	254.70	909	272.70	969	290.70	1029	308.70
730	219.00	790	237.00	850	255.00	910	273.00	970	291.00	1030	309.00
731	219.30	791	237.30	851	255.30	911	273.30	971	291.30	1031	309.30
732	219.60	792	237.60	852	255.60	912	273.60	972	291.60	1032	309.60
733	219.90	793	237.90	853	255.90	913	273.90	973	291.90	1033	309.90
734	220.20	794	238.20	854	256.20	914	274.20	974	292.20	1034	310.20
735	220.50	795	238.50	855	256.50	915	274.50	975	292.50	1035	310.50
736	220.80	796	238.80	856	256.80	916	274.80	976	292.80	1036	310.80
737	221.10	797	239.10	857	257.10	917	275.10	977	293.10	1037	311.10
738	221.40	798	239.40	858	257.40	918	275.40	978	293.40	1038	311.40
739	221.70	799	239.70	859	257.70	919	275.70	979	293.70	1039	311.70
740	222.00	800	240.00	860	258.00	920	276.00	980	294.00	1040	312.00
741	222.30	801	240.30	861	258.30	921	276.30	981	294.30	1041	312.30
742	222.60	802	240.60	862	258.60	922	276.60	982	294.60	1042	312.60
743	222.90	803	240.90	863	258.90	923	276.90	983	294.90	1043	312.90
744	223.20	804	241.20	864	259.20	924	277.20	984	295.20	1044	313.20
745	223.50	805	241.50	865	259.50	925	277.50	985	295.50	1045	313.50
746	223.80	806	241.80	866	259.80	926	277.80	986	295.80	1046	313.80
747	224.10	807	242.10	867	260.10	927	278.10	987	296.10	1047	314.10
748	224.40	808	242.40	868	260.40	928	278.40	988	296.40	1048	314.40
749	224.70	809	242.70	869	260.70	929	278.70	989	296.70	1049	314.70
750	225.00	810	243.00	870	261.00	930	279.00	990	297.00	1050	315.00
751	225.30	811	243.30	871	261.30	931	279.30	991	297.30	1051	315.30
752	225.60	812	243.60	872	261.60	932	279.60	992	297.60	1052	315.60
753	225.90	813	243.90	873	261.90	933	279.90	993	297.90	1053	315.90
754	226.20	814	244.20	874	262.20	934	280.20	994	298.20	1054	316.20
755	226.50	815	244.50	875	262.50	935	280.50	995	298.50	1055	316.50
756	226.80	816	244.80	876	262.80	936	280.80	996	298.80	1056	316.80
757	227.10	817	245.10	877	263.10	937	281.10	997	299.10	1057	317.10
758	227.40	818	245.40	878	263.40	938	281.40	998	299.40	1058	317.40
759	227.70	819	245.70	879	263.70	939	281.70	999	299.70	1059	317.70
760	228.00	820	246.00	880	264.00	940	282.00	1000	300.00	1060	318.00
761	228.30	821	246.30	881	264.30	941	282.30	1001	300.30	1061	318.30
762	228.60	822	246.60	882	264.60	942	282.60	1002	300.60	1062	318.60
763	228.90	823	246.90	883	264.90	943	282.90	1003	300.90	1063	318.90
764	229.20	824	247.20	884	265.20	944	283.20	1004	301.20	1064	319.20
765	229.50	825	247.50	885	265.50	945	283.50	1005	301.50	1065	319.50
766	229.80	826	247.80	886	265.80	946	283.80	1006	301.80	1066	319.80
767	230.10	827	248.10	887	266.10	947	284.10	1007	302.10	1067	320.10
768	230.40	828	248.40	888	266.40	948	284.40	1008	302.40	1068	320.40
769	230.70	829	248.70	889	266.70	949	284.70	1009	302.70	1069	320.70
770	231.00	830	249.00	890	267.00	950	285.00	1010	303.00	1070	321.00
771	231.30	831	249.30	891	267.30	951	285.30	1011	303.30	1071	321.30
772	231.60	832	249.60	892	267.60	952	285.60	1012	303.60	1072	321.60
773	231.90	833	249.90	893	267.90	953	285.90	1013	303.90	1073	321.90
774	232.20	834	250.20	894	268.20	954	286.20	1014	304.20	1074	322.20
775	232.50	835	250.50	895	268.50	955	286.50	1015	304.50	1075	322.50
776	232.80	836	250.80	896	268.80	956	286.80	1016	304.80	1076	322.80
777	233.10	837	251.10	897	269.10	957	287.10	1017	305.10	1077	323.10
778	233.40	838	251.40	898	269.40	958	287.40	1018	305.40	1078	323.40
779	233.70	839	251.70	899	269.70	959	287.70	1019	305.70	1079	323.70
780	234.00	840	252.00	900	270.00	960	288.00	1020	306.00	1080	324.00

<table>
<tr><td rowspan="2">

NOT-CONTRACTED-OUT
STANDARD-RATE CONTRIBUTIONS
</td></tr>
</table>

NOT-CONTRACTED-OUT
STANDARD-RATE CONTRIBUTIONS

WEEKLY TABLE

A

Before using this table please
enter "A" in the space provided
on the deductions working sheet
(P11 New)/pay record
(see Instructions)

FOR USE FROM 6 APRIL 1984 TO 5 APRIL 1985

For employees who are over age 16 and under
pension age (65 men, 60 women).
But *excluding* those married women and widows
who are liable to pay contributions at the
Reduced Rate—see Table B.
(For employees over pension age or for whom
form RD 950 is held use Table C in this volume.)

If the exact gross pay figure is not shown in the table, use the next smaller figure shown.

Gross pay	Total of employee's and employer's contributions payable	Employee's contribution payable	Employer's contribution*	Gross pay	Total of employee's and employer's contributions payable	Employee's contribution payable	Employer's contribution*
£	£	£	£	£	£	£	£
34·00	6·95	3·06	3·89	58·50	12·02	5·29	6·73
34·01	7·00	3·08	3·92	59·00	12·11	5·33	6·78
34·50	7·11	3·13	3·98	59·50	12·22	5·38	6·84
35·00	7·21	3·17	4·04	60·00	12·32	5·42	6·90
35·50	7·31	3·22	4·09	60·50	12·43	5·47	6·96
36·00	7·41	3·26	4·15	61·00	12·52	5·51	7·01
36·50	7·52	3·31	4·21	61·50	12·63	5·56	7·07
37·00	7·62	3·35	4·27	62·00	12·73	5·60	7·13
37·50	7·72	3·40	4·32	62·50	12·83	5·65	7·18
38·00	7·82	3·44	4·38	63·00	12·93	5·69	7·24
38·50	7·93	3·49	4·44	63·50	13·04	5·74	7·30
39·00	8·02	3·53	4·49	64·00	13·14	5·78	7·36
39·50	8·13	3·58	4·55	64·50	13·24	5·83	7·41
40·00	8·23	3·62	4·61	65·00	13·34	5·87	7·47
40·50	8·34	3·67	4·67	65·50	13·45	5·92	7·53
41·00	8·43	3·71	4·72	66·00	13·55	5·96	7·59
41·50	8·54	3·76	4·78	66·50	13·65	6·01	7·64
42·00	8·64	3·80	4·84	67·00	13·75	6·05	7·70
42·50	8·74	3·85	4·89	67·50	13·86	6·10	7·76
43·00	8·84	3·89	4·95	68·00	13·95	6·14	7·81
43·50	8·95	3·94	5·01	68·50	14·06	6·19	7·87
44·00	9·05	3·98	5·07	69·00	14·16	6·23	7·93
44·50	9·15	4·03	5·12	69·50	14·27	6·28	7·99
45·00	9·25	4·07	5·18	70·00	14·36	6·32	8·04
45·50	9·36	4·12	5·24	70·50	14·47	6·37	8·10
46·00	9·46	4·16	5·30	71·00	14·57	6·41	8·16
46·50	9·56	4·21	5·35	71·50	14·68	6·46	8·22
47·00	9·66	4·25	5·41	72·00	14·77	6·50	8·27
47·50	9·77	4·30	5·47	72·50	14·88	6·55	8·33
48·00	9·86	4·34	5·52	73·00	14·98	6·59	8·39
48·50	9·97	4·39	5·58	73·50	15·08	6·64	8·44
49·00	10·07	4·43	5·64	74·00	15·18	6·68	8·50
49·50	10·18	4·48	5·70	74·50	15·29	6·73	8·56
50·00	10·27	4·52	5·75	75·00	15·39	6·77	8·62
50·50	10·38	4·57	5·81	75·50	15·49	6·82	8·67
51·00	10·48	4·61	5·87	76·00	15·59	6·86	8·73
51·50	10·59	4·66	5·93	76·50	15·70	6·91	8·79
52·00	10·68	4·70	5·98	77·00	15·80	6·95	8·85
52·50	10·79	4·75	6·04	77·50	15·90	7·00	8·90
53·00	10·89	4·79	6·10	78·00	16·00	7·04	8·96
53·50	10·99	4·84	6·15	78·50	16·11	7·09	9·02
54·00	11·09	4·88	6·21	79·00	16·20	7·13	9·07
54·50	11·20	4·93	6·27	79·50	16·31	7·18	9·13
55·00	11·30	4·97	6·33	80·00	16·41	7·22	9·19
55·50	11·40	5·02	6·38	80·50	16·52	7·27	9·25
56·00	11·50	5·06	6·44	81·00	16·61	7·31	9·30
56·50	11·61	5·11	6·50	81·50	16·72	7·36	9·36
57·00	11·71	5·15	6·56	82·00	16·82	7·40	9·42
57·50	11·81	5·20	6·61	82·50	16·92	7·45	9·47
58·00	11·91	5·24	6·67	83·00	17·02	7·49	9·53

* For information only. DO NOT ENTER ON DEDUCTIONS WORKING SHEET (P11 NEW).

Weekly Table A continued
FOR USE FROM 6 APRIL 1984 TO 5 APRIL 1985

Gross pay	Total of employee's and employer's contributions payable	Employee's contribution payable	Employer's contribution*
£	£	£	£
83.50	17.13	7.54	9.59
84.00	17.23	7.58	9.65
84.50	17.33	7.63	9.70
85.00	17.43	7.67	9.76
85.50	17.54	7.72	9.82
86.00	17.64	7.76	9.88
86.50	17.74	7.81	9.93
87.00	17.84	7.85	9.99
87.50	17.95	7.90	10.05
88.00	18.04	7.94	10.10
88.50	18.15	7.99	10.16
89.00	18.25	8.03	10.22
89.50	18.36	8.08	10.28
90.00	18.45	8.12	10.33
90.50	18.56	8.17	10.39
91.00	18.66	8.21	10.45
91.50	18.77	8.26	10.51
92.00	18.86	8.30	10.56
92.50	18.97	8.35	10.62
93.00	19.07	8.39	10.68
93.50	19.17	8.44	10.73
94.00	19.27	8.48	10.79
94.50	19.38	8.53	10.85
95.00	19.48	8.57	10.91
95.50	19.58	8.62	10.96
96.00	19.68	8.66	11.02
96.50	19.79	8.71	11.08
97.00	19.89	8.75	11.14
97.50	19.99	8.80	11.19
98.00	20.09	8.84	11.25
98.50	20.20	8.89	11.31
99.00	20.29	8.93	11.36
99.50	20.40	8.98	11.42
100.00	20.50	9.02	11.48
100.50	20.61	9.07	11.54
101.00	20.70	9.11	11.59
101.50	20.81	9.16	11.65
102.00	20.91	9.20	11.71
102.50	21.01	9.25	11.76
103.00	21.11	9.29	11.82
103.50	21.22	9.34	11.88
104.00	21.32	9.38	11.94
104.50	21.42	9.43	11.99
105.00	21.52	9.47	12.05
105.50	21.63	9.52	12.11
106.00	21.73	9.56	12.17
106.50	21.83	9.61	12.22
107.00	21.93	9.65	12.28
107.50	22.04	9.70	12.34
108.00	22.13	9.74	12.39
108.50	22.24	9.79	12.45
109.00	22.34	9.83	12.51
109.50	22.45	9.88	12.57
110.00	22.54	9.92	12.62
110.50	22.65	9.97	12.68
111.00	22.75	10.01	12.74
111.50	22.86	10.06	12.80
112.00	22.95	10.10	12.85
112.50	23.06	10.15	12.91
113.00	23.16	10.19	12.97
113.50	23.26	10.24	13.02
114.00	23.36	10.28	13.08
114.50	23.47	10.33	13.14
115.00	23.57	10.37	13.20
115.50	23.67	10.42	13.25
116.00	23.77	10.46	13.31
116.50	23.88	10.51	13.37
117.00	23.98	10.55	13.43
117.50	24.08	10.60	13.48
118.00	24.18	10.64	13.54
118.50	24.29	10.69	13.60
119.00	24.38	10.73	13.65
119.50	24.49	10.78	13.71
120.00	24.59	10.82	13.77
120.50	24.70	10.87	13.83
121.00	24.79	10.91	13.88
121.50	24.90	10.96	13.94
122.00	25.00	11.00	14.00
122.50	25.10	11.05	14.05
123.00	25.20	11.09	14.11
123.50	25.31	11.14	14.17
124.00	25.41	11.18	14.23
124.50	25.51	11.23	14.28
125.00	25.61	11.27	14.34
125.50	25.72	11.32	14.40
126.00	25.82	11.36	14.46
126.50	25.92	11.41	14.51
127.00	26.02	11.45	14.57
127.50	26.13	11.50	14.63
128.00	26.22	11.54	14.68
128.50	26.33	11.59	14.74
129.00	26.43	11.63	14.80
129.50	26.54	11.68	14.86
130.00	26.63	11.72	14.91
130.50	26.74	11.77	14.97
131.00	26.84	11.81	15.03
131.50	26.95	11.86	15.09
132.00	27.04	11.90	15.14
132.50	27.15	11.95	15.20
133.00	27.25	11.99	15.26
133.50	27.35	12.04	15.31
134.00	27.45	12.08	15.37
134.50	27.56	12.13	15.43
135.00	27.66	12.17	15.49
135.50	27.76	12.22	15.54
136.00	27.86	12.26	15.60
136.50	27.97	12.31	15.66
137.00	28.07	12.35	15.72
137.50	28.17	12.40	15.77
138.00	28.27	12.44	15.83
138.50	28.38	12.49	15.89
139.00	28.47	12.53	15.94
139.50	28.58	12.58	16.00
140.00	28.68	12.62	16.06
140.50	28.79	12.67	16.12
141.00	28.88	12.71	16.17
141.50	28.99	12.76	16.23
142.00	29.09	12.80	16.29
142.50	29.19	12.85	16.34
143.00	29.29	12.89	16.40

* For information only. DO NOT ENTER ON DEDUCTIONS WORKING SHEET (P11 NEW)

Weekly Table A continued
FOR USE FROM 6 APRIL 1984 TO 5 APRIL 1985

Gross pay	Total of employee's and employer's contributions payable	Employee's contribution payable	Employer's contribution*
£	£	£	£
143·50	29·40	12·94	16·46
144·00	29·50	12·98	16·52
144·50	29·60	13·03	16·57
145·00	29·70	13·07	16·63
145·50	29·81	13·12	16·69
146·00	29·91	13·16	16·75
146·50	30·01	13·21	16·80
147·00	30·11	13·25	16·86
147·50	30·22	13·30	16·92
148·00	30·31	13·34	16·97
148·50	30·42	13·39	17·03
149·00	30·52	13·43	17·09
149·50	30·63	13·48	17·15
150·00	30·72	13·52	17·20
150·50	30·83	13·57	17·26
151·00	30·93	13·61	17·32
151·50	31·04	13·66	17·38
152·00	31·13	13·70	17·43
152·50	31·24	13·75	17·49
153·00	31·34	13·79	17·55
153·50	31·44	13·84	17·60
154·00	31·54	13·88	17·66
154·50	31·65	13·93	17·72
155·00	31·75	13·97	17·78
155·50	31·85	14·02	17·83
156·00	31·95	14·06	17·89
156·50	32·06	14·11	17·95
157·00	32·16	14·15	18·01
157·50	32·26	14·20	18·06
158·00	32·36	14·24	18·12
158·50	32·47	14·29	18·18
159·00	32·56	14·33	18·23
159·50	32·67	14·38	18·29
160·00	32·77	14·42	18·35
160·50	32·88	14·47	18·41
161·00	32·97	14·51	18·46
161·50	33·08	14·56	18·52
162·00	33·18	14·60	18·58
162·50	33·28	14·65	18·63
163·00	33·38	14·69	18·69
163·50	33·49	14·74	18·75
164·00	33·59	14·78	18·81
164·50	33·69	14·83	18·86
165·00	33·79	14·87	18·92
165·50	33·90	14·92	18·98
166·00	34·00	14·96	19·04
166·50	34·10	15·01	19·09
167·00	34·20	15·05	19·15
167·50	34·31	15·10	19·21
168·00	34·40	15·14	19·26
168·50	34·51	15·19	19·32
169·00	34·61	15·23	19·38
169·50	34·72	15·28	19·44
170·00	34·81	15·32	19·49
170·50	34·92	15·37	19·55
171·00	35·02	15·41	19·61
171·50	35·13	15·46	19·67
172·00	35·22	15·50	19·72
172·50	35·33	15·55	19·78
173·00	35·43	15·59	19·84
173·50	35·53	15·64	19·89
174·00	35·63	15·68	19·95
174·50	35·74	15·73	20·01
175·00	35·84	15·77	20·07
175·50	35·94	15·82	20·12
176·00	36·04	15·86	20·18
176·50	36·15	15·91	20·24
177·00	36·25	15·95	20·30
177·50	36·35	16·00	20·35
178·00	36·45	16·04	20·41
178·50	36·56	16·09	20·47
179·00	36·65	16·13	20·52
179·50	36·76	16·18	20·58
180·00	36·86	16·22	20·64
180·50	36·97	16·27	20·70
181·00	37·06	16·31	20·75
181·50	37·17	16·36	20·81
182·00	37·27	16·40	20·87
182·50	37·37	16·45	20·92
183·00	37·47	16·49	20·98
183·50	37·58	16·54	21·04
184·00	37·68	16·58	21·10
184·50	37·78	16·63	21·15
185·00	37·88	16·67	21·21
185·50	37·99	16·72	21·27
186·00	38·09	16·76	21·33
186·50	38·19	16·81	21·38
187·00	38·29	16·85	21·44
187·50	38·40	16·90	21·50
188·00	38·49	16·94	21·55
188·50	38·60	16·99	21·61
189·00	38·70	17·03	21·67
189·50	38·81	17·08	21·73
190·00	38·90	17·12	21·78
190·50	39·01	17·17	21·84
191·00	39·11	17·21	21·90
191·50	39·22	17·26	21·96
192·00	39·31	17·30	22·01
192·50	39·42	17·35	22·07
193·00	39·52	17·39	22·13
193·50	39·62	17·44	22·18
194·00	39·72	17·48	22·24
194·50	39·83	17·53	22·30
195·00	39·93	17·57	22·36
195·50	40·03	17·62	22·41
196·00	40·13	17·66	22·47
196·50	40·24	17·71	22·53
197·00	40·34	17·75	22·59
197·50	40·44	17·80	22·64
198·00	40·54	17·84	22·70
198·50	40·65	17·89	22·76
199·00	40·74	17·93	22·81
199·50	40·85	17·98	22·87
200·00	40·95	18·02	22·93
200·50	41·06	18·07	22·99
201·00	41·15	18·11	23·04
201·50	41·26	18·16	23·10
202·00	41·36	18·20	23·16
202·50	41·46	18·25	23·21
203·00	41·56	18·29	23·27

* For information only. DO NOT ENTER ON DEDUCTIONS WORKING SHEET (P11 NEW).

Weekly Table A continued

FOR USE FROM 6 APRIL 1984 TO 5 APRIL 1985

Gross pay	Total of employee's and employer's contributions payable	Employee's contribution payable	Employer's contribution*
£	£	£	£
203.50	41.67	18.34	23.33
204.00	41.77	18.38	23.39
204.50	41.87	18.43	23.44
205.00	41.97	18.47	23.50
205.50	42.08	18.52	23.56
206.00	42.18	18.56	23.62
206.50	42.28	18.61	23.67
207.00	42.38	18.65	23.73
207.50	42.49	18.70	23.79
208.00	42.58	18.74	23.84
208.50	42.69	18.79	23.90
209.00	42.79	18.83	23.96
209.50	42.90	18.88	24.02
210.00	42.99	18.92	24.07
210.50	43.10	18.97	24.13
211.00	43.20	19.01	24.19
211.50	43.31	19.06	24.25
212.00	43.40	19.10	24.30
212.50	43.51	19.15	24.36
213.00	43.61	19.19	24.42
213.50	43.71	19.24	24.47
214.00	43.81	19.28	24.53
214.50	43.92	19.33	24.59
215.00	44.02	19.37	24.65
215.50	44.12	19.42	24.70
216.00	44.22	19.46	24.76
216.50	44.33	19.51	24.82
217.00	44.43	19.55	24.88
217.50	44.53	19.60	24.93
218.00	44.63	19.64	24.99
218.50	44.74	19.69	25.05
219.00	44.83	19.73	25.10
219.50	44.94	19.78	25.16
220.00	45.04	19.82	25.22
220.50	45.15	19.87	25.28
221.00	45.24	19.91	25.33
221.50	45.35	19.96	25.39
222.00	45.45	20.00	25.45
222.50	45.55	20.05	25.50
223.00	45.65	20.09	25.56
223.50	45.76	20.14	25.62
224.00	45.86	20.18	25.68
224.50	45.96	20.23	25.73
225.00	46.06	20.27	25.79
225.50	46.17	20.32	25.85
226.00	46.27	20.36	25.91
226.50	46.37	20.41	25.96
227.00	46.47	20.45	26.02
227.50	46.58	20.50	26.08
228.00	46.67	20.54	26.13
228.50	46.78	20.59	26.19
229.00	46.88	20.63	26.25
229.50	46.99	20.68	26.31
230.00	47.08	20.72	26.36
230.50	47.19	20.77	26.42
231.00	47.29	20.81	26.48
231.50	47.40	20.86	26.54
232.00	47.49	20.90	26.59
232.50	47.60	20.95	26.65
233.00	47.70	20.99	26.71

Gross pay	Total of employee's and employer's contributions payable	Employee's contribution payable	Employer's contribution*
£	£	£	£
233.50	47.80	21.04	26.76
234.00	47.90	21.08	26.82
234.50	48.01	21.13	26.88
235.00	48.11	21.17	26.94
235.50	48.21	21.22	26.99
236.00	48.31	21.26	27.05
236.50	48.42	21.31	27.11
237.00	48.52	21.35	27.17
237.50	48.62	21.40	27.22
238.00	48.72	21.44	27.28
238.50	48.83	21.49	27.34
239.00	48.92	21.53	27.39
239.50	49.03	21.58	27.45
240.00	49.13	21.62	27.51
240.50	49.24	21.67	27.57
241.00	49.33	21.71	27.62
241.50	49.44	21.76	27.68
242.00	49.54	21.80	27.74
242.50	49.64	21.85	27.79
243.00	49.74	21.89	27.85
243.50	49.85	21.94	27.91
244.00	49.95	21.98	27.97
244.50	50.05	22.03	28.02
245.00	50.15	22.07	28.08
245.50	50.26	22.12	28.14
246.00	50.36	22.16	28.20
246.50	50.46	22.21	28.25
247.00	50.56	22.25	28.31
247.50	50.67	22.30	28.37
248.00	50.76	22.34	28.42
248.50	50.87	22.39	28.48
249.00	50.97	22.43	28.54
249.50	51.08	22.48	28.60
250.00 or more	51.12	22.50	28.62

* For information only. DO NOT ENTER ON DEDUCTIONS WORKING SHEET (P11 NEW).

```
NOT-CONTRACTED-OUT
STANDARD-RATE CONTRIBUTIONS
                    MONTHLY TABLE
 A    Before using this table please
      enter "A" in the space provided
      on the deductions working sheet
      (P11 New)/pay record
      (see Instructions)
```

FOR USE FROM 6 APRIL 1984 TO 5 APRIL 1985

For employees who are over age 16 and und
pension age (65 men, 60 women).
But *excluding* those married women and wido
who are liable to pay contributions at
Reduced Rate—see Table B.
(For employees over pension age or for whe
form RD 950 is held use Table C in this volume

If the exact gross pay figure is not shown in the table, use the next smaller figure shown.

Gross pay	Total of employee's and employer's contributions payable	Employee's contribution payable	Employer's contribution*	Gross pay	Total of employee's and employer's contributions payable	Employee's contribution payable	Employer contributio
£	£	£	£	£	£	£	£
147·33	30·13	13·26	16·87	245·00	50·31	22·14	28·17
147·34	30·31	13·34	16·97	247·00	50·72	22·32	28·40
149·00	30·67	13·50	17·17	249·00	51·12	22·50	28·62
151·00	31·08	13·68	17·40	251·00	51·53	22·68	28·85
153·00	31·49	13·86	17·63	253·00	51·94	22·86	29·08
155·00	31·90	14·04	17·86	255·00	52·35	23·04	29·31
157·00	32·31	14·22	18·09	257·00	52·76	23·22	29·54
159·00	32·72	14·40	18·32	259·00	53·17	23·40	29·77
161·00	33·13	14·58	18·55	261·00	53·58	23·58	30·00
163·00	33·54	14·76	18·78	263·00	53·99	23·76	30·23
165·00	33·95	14·94	19·01	265·00	54·40	23·94	30·46
167·00	34·36	15·12	19·24	267·00	54·81	24·12	30·69
169·00	34·76	15·30	19·46	269·00	55·21	24·30	30·91
171·00	35·17	15·48	19·69	271·00	55·62	24·48	31·14
173·00	35·58	15·66	19·92	273·00	56·03	24·66	31·37
175·00	35·99	15·84	20·15	275·00	56·44	24·84	31·60
177·00	36·40	16·02	20·38	277·00	56·85	25·02	31·83
179·00	36·81	16·20	20·61	279·00	57·26	25·20	32·06
181·00	37·22	16·38	20·84	281·00	57·67	25·38	32·29
183·00	37·63	16·56	21·07	283·00	58·08	25·56	32·52
185·00	38·04	16·74	21·30	285·00	58·49	25·74	32·75
187·00	38·45	16·92	21·53	287·00	58·90	25·92	32·98
189·00	38·85	17·10	21·75	289·00	59·30	26·10	33·20
191·00	39·26	17·28	21·98	291·00	59·71	26·28	33·43
193·00	39·67	17·46	22·21	293·00	60·12	26·46	33·66
195·00	40·08	17·64	22·44	295·00	60·53	26·64	33·89
197·00	40·49	17·82	22·67	297·00	60·94	26·82	34·12
199·00	40·90	18·00	22·90	299·00	61·35	27·00	34·35
201·00	41·31	18·18	23·13	301·00	61·76	27·18	34·58
203·00	41·72	18·36	23·36	303·00	62·17	27·36	34·81
205·00	42·13	18·54	23·59	305·00	62·58	27·54	35·04
207·00	42·54	18·72	23·82	307·00	62·99	27·72	35·27
209·00	42·94	18·90	24·04	309·00	63·39	27·90	35·49
211·00	43·35	19·08	24·27	311·00	63·80	28·08	35·72
213·00	43·76	19·26	24·50	313·00	64·21	28·26	35·95
215·00	44·17	19·44	24·73	315·00	64·62	28·44	36·18
217·00	44·58	19·62	24·96	317·00	65·03	28·62	36·41
219·00	44·99	19·80	25·19	319·00	65·44	28·80	36·64
221·00	45·40	19·98	25·42	321·00	65·85	28·98	36·87
223·00	45·81	20·16	25·65	323·00	66·26	29·16	37·10
225·00	46·22	20·34	25·88	325·00	66·67	29·34	37·33
227·00	46·63	20·52	26·11	327·00	67·08	29·52	37·56
229·00	47·03	20·70	26·33	329·00	67·48	29·70	37·78
231·00	47·44	20·88	26·56	331·00	67·89	29·88	38·01
233·00	47·85	21·06	26·79	333·00	68·30	30·06	38·24
235·00	48·26	21·24	27·02	335·00	68·71	30·24	38·47
237·00	48·67	21·42	27·25	337·00	69·12	30·42	38·70
239·00	49·08	21·60	27·48	339·00	69·53	30·60	38·93
241·00	49·49	21·78	27·71	341·00	69·94	30·78	39·16
243·00	49·90	21·96	27·94	343·00	70·35	30·96	39·39

* For information only. DO NOT ENTER ON DEDUCTIONS WORKING SHEET (P11 NEW).

Index